A DREAM OF THE TATTERED MAN

A DREAM OF THE TATTERED MAN

Stories from Georgia's Death Row

RANDOLPH LONEY

WILLIAM B. EERDMANS PUBLISHING COMPANY
GRAND RAPIDS, MICHIGAN / CAMBRIDGE, U.K.

© 2001 Wm. B. Eerdmans Publishing Co.
255 Jefferson Ave. S.E., Grand Rapids, Michigan 49503 /
P.O. Box 163, Cambridge CB3 9PU U.K.

Printed in the United States of America

05 04 03 02 01   5 4 3 2 1

Library of Congress Cataloging-in-Publication Data

A dream of the tattered man: stories from Georgia's death row /
Randolph Loney.
p.   cm.
Includes bibliographical references.
ISBN 0-8028-4280-1 (cloth: alk. paper)
1. Church work with prisoners — Georgia.
2. Death row inmates — Georgia.
3. Capital punishment — Religious aspects — Christianity — Meditations.
I. Title.

BV4340.L6 2001
261.8'09758 — dc21

00-052146

www.eerdmans.com

Contents

Acknowledgments

M any people have helped to make this book possible.
I am indebted to the men on death row and their families, who have shared their lives with me.

I am grateful to the members of the Glad River Congregation, who have from the beginning encouraged my trips to death row, listened carefully to my Sunday-morning reflections on my visits there, and challenged me continually to see the deep theological significance of the time that human beings spend together.

I am thankful for a number of extraordinary teachers who have, over the years, set me to thinking about issues that I raise in this book. John Jacobson at Eckerd College, Harvey Cox at Harvard Divinity School, and Rayburn Moore at the University of Georgia encouraged me to explore the relationship between faith and culture, a theme that lies at the heart of this work. Judy Harden and Beth Culler at Goddard College helped me to think through, and write about, my friendships with the condemned men as I explored the consequences of child abuse and neglect for adult behavior. I began to write this book during a period of off-campus study in Goddard's graduate program in psychology.

I am indebted to many people, in addition to Judy Harden and Beth Culler, who have offered support and suggestions after having read all or significant portions of this work as it has emerged through several stages of writing: Michael Bishop, Steve Bright, Will Campbell, Ruth Friedman, Lise Greene, Tanya Greene, Gene Guerrero, Joe Hendricks,

George Kendall, Pat Koester, Miriam Kurman, Renner Loney, Charlotta Norby, Laura-Hill Patton, Lewis Sinclair, Mary Sinclair, Palmer Singleton, Gretchen Stork, and Robert Wootton.

Several other persons offered important help in my research: Steve Bayliss, Jack Boger, Chris Cox, Murphy Davis, Richard Dieter, Tom Dunn, Angie Elleman, Jeff Ertel, Millard Farmer, Deborah Fins, John Hanusz, Ellie Hopkins, Brian McAdams, Mike Mears, Patsy Morris (who died in 1997), Jeffrey Pokorak, Michael Radelet, Mary Shellman, Clive Stafford Smith, Tamara Theiss, Ed Weir, Mary Ruth Weir, and Beth Wells.

In addition, Mary Sinclair has traveled near and far and often to help me secure documents and obtain information to which I refer. Her friendship has meant a great deal not only to me but to many others as well, especially the prisoners on Georgia's death row. For two decades she has been the prisoners' indefatigable champion.

I have been inspired and educated by the work of the attorneys and investigators from the law offices that have handled so many of the appeals, and a few of the trials, of Georgia's death-row prisoners: Team Defense, the Southern Center for Human Rights, the Georgia Resource Center, the Multi-County Public Defender Office, the Federal Defender Program, and the NAACP Legal Defense Fund. I have been uplifted and enlightened by the women and men at the Open Door Community and New Hope House who care for persons at the margins of our culture. It was Murphy Davis of the Open Door Community who accompanied me on my first visit to death row and on whose counsel I still rely.

I owe a special debt of gratitude to the following people: Steve Bright, Joe Hendricks, George Kendall, Laura-Hill Patton, Lewis Sinclair, Mary Sinclair, Palmer Singleton, and Gretchen Stork have always been at the other end of the phone the many, many times when I needed them.

I count myself fortunate to have worked with Mary Hietbrink, my editor at Eerdmans, who has taught me a lot about good writing. Her kindness, expert advice, and belief in this book have played a very large role in helping me to see it through to publication. Any stylistic problems result from my own hardheadedness; any errors in content are my own responsibility.

Finally, I want to thank my wife, Renner, without whose love and support I never could have written these pages. She has never had to ask why I make my trips to death row.

Foreword

One January day a little group sat around a stone fireplace in a remote cabin in a Southern wilderness. The cabin is just off the Little Lazar Creek and a few miles from the place where Franklin Roosevelt spent many hours and days trying to conquer a power called poliomyelitis that had left him unable to walk.

One who sat with us, the author of this volume, was about to battle a power and principality on a journey he was called to walk. It was a journey to be with those held captive. He had read and believed the words of Isaiah and Jesus about proclaiming release to prisoners. He had sung the Psalm of David:

> Let the sighing of the prisoner come before thee:
> according to the greatness of thy power preserve thou
> those that are appointed to die. . . .

Those so appointed were his flock; the place called "death row" the tabernacle in which he would witness to the truth and power of the Gospel.

We who had gathered were bold to say, "We are Church. In witness to the Word, we call ourselves the Glad River Congregation. And we are here on a holy mission: to ordain Randolph Loney, to set him apart as a minister of Jesus Christ."

Some would have considered us a motley crew, sitting there in that Georgia cabin. And in a sense, although we were physician, college professor, farmer, carpenter, high-school teacher, nurse, writer, and unemployed, we were a motley crew. We were not dressed in Sunday finery; no steeple towered over us; no melodious pipes called; no offering was lifted. We were Southern Baptists, United Methodists, Presbyterians, Episcopalians, and no certain declension. At the core of the group were a few folk from Mercer University, where Randy was teaching; they had been meeting together, praying together, singing together for years. The antecedents of us all had once been small and random. My mind drifted back to my own people: the Anabaptists of Europe. They once gathered in similar fashion.

Our preacher that day was Murphy Davis, a Presbyterian of unusual gifts, grit, training, and determination. She had been called, along with her husband and daughter, to help feed and shelter the homeless in Atlanta, and to minister to prisoners awaiting death at the hands of the State. She sat in a ladder-back chair and preached mightily. She talked of grace, of reconciliation, mercy, and forgiveness. And she talked of spitting in the Devil's eye. Others prayed, sang, testified, picked guitar.

I recalled the first time I met Randy Loney. He was teaching literature in a liberal arts college in Louisiana. He had invited me to meet with his classes, read and discuss writing. His wife taught German in a nearby high school. As an honorarium they gave me a lovely painting of a country church-house done by a local artist. They were a modest couple, not given to talking of their accomplishments. From others I learned that he had a Doctor of Philosophy degree from the University of Georgia, had studied abroad, and was considered by his peers to be one of the most brilliant young scholars and teachers in his field. She had a family pedigree of colonial rank. I left their city knowing there was something different, something special, about this couple.

Now we were ordaining Randolph Loney to the Gospel ministry on a cold January day in a wilderness cabin beside the Little Lazar Creek.

◄ ►

That was over fifteen years ago. Since then Randy has gone out as we intended. With the biblical mandate of neither cloak nor script. Without stipend he goes to death row, where he visits, listens, hopes, or just sits. Outside the cell he waits with the families and loved ones of those appointed to die. His is not a message of believing this or that creed, affiliating with this or that denomination. His mission is to *be with*. And when the state has done all that it can do to its captives, he and his colleagues bury them.

Just as Franklin Roosevelt turned to the warm waters of Meriwether County to gain strength to continue the journey, so does Randy Loney turn to his motley crew, his ordaining council, for sustenance in his own journey. Randy turns especially to the little band of mostly Mercer University community members who continue to gather together, week after week, as the Glad River Congregation. They help sustain him as he contends with the powers and principalities that would bring death to his imprisoned friends, many of whom have made that cursed walk.

This book has to do with the ordinand's journey. But its focus is not on what Randy Loney has done. He is still too humble a man for that. You will read of the impact made on him by the condemned, who come fully into our view. And you will learn of their often terrifying childhood odysseys that had such disastrous consequences. Beyond that, you will catch a glimpse of the fallen condition that enslaves us all. Also, there for eyes that will see and ears that will hear is a witness to the grace that overcomes our own fallenness as well as that of our sisters and brothers on what we call death row.

This is an important book. Important because it is painfully apparent that our nation's heart, from the Oval Office to the offices of local prosecuting attorneys, has been hardened toward captives everywhere. In the pages that follow there is firm evidence that our Lord's inaugural proclamation to release the captives and let the oppressed go free is still a viable alternative to the nonsense that death at the hand of the State will put an end to killings among the citizenry.

This is an important book because it is rooted in the radical Gospel. It is about what the Reverend Murphy Davis talked about at Randy's uncommon ordination. Grace. Forgiveness. Reconciliation.

And spitting in the Devil's eye.

WILL D. CAMPBELL

Preface

L egal executions: by hanging, firing squad, electrocution, poison
gas, lethal injection. Since the colonial period, they have claimed
more than 18,000 lives in our country. In the name of justice. Sometimes we have put to death persons who were children at the time of the
crimes for which they were prosecuted; numerous states still allow the
execution of juvenile offenders. At other times we have taken the lives
of people with mental retardation or mental illnesses; many states still
permit this ritual. Most of the time we have executed individuals who
were unable to retain their own trial attorneys and who, typically, had
to make do with the modest or downright questionable interventions
of court-appointed attorneys or public defenders. Sometimes at the
moment of execution, the condemned have not died instantly and have
had to endure prolonged suffering. On a number of occasions we have
executed the innocent: by one count several years ago, at least twenty-
three such people have lost their lives since the turn of the twentieth
century.

Executions have found a home where they have been culturally and
politically popular. From 1930 — when the U.S. Justice Department began keeping track of state executions — to 1967 — after which time,

---

NOTE: Various key phrases here and throughout the book are discussed in the
Notes section.

court challenges led to a temporary cessation of executions — well over half of the country's legal killings took place in southern states. During this period, Georgia led the nation with 366. As of November 1999, the trend of large numbers of executions in the South continues: 473 (195 in Texas alone) out of a nationwide total of 589 since the U.S. Supreme Court, in *Gregg v. Georgia* in 1976, allowed the carnage to proceed again.

In states with death-penalty statutes, local lead prosecutors are almost always the persons who decide whether or not to seek capital punishment in a particular case. Almost inevitably, such decisions are shaped by political motives because these officials are, with few exceptions, elected. Consequently, in areas where the death penalty is popular, the elected prosecutors seek it despite the lack of solid proof that it deters crime. They seek the ultimate form of punishment despite its enormous financial cost — much more than that of a life sentence, for example. And they try their cases before judges who are, for the most part, also elected officials, responsive to their constituents' desire for sentences of death. Throughout the ordeal of trial and appeals — and beyond — the sufferings of murder victims' families continue.

As we have carried out capital punishment, racial bias has played an important part in our actions. For example, from 1930 to 1967, two-thirds of the people executed in the South were African American — a number disproportionate "to any differences in the incidence of relevant crimes by blacks and whites," as Amnesty International has reported. A recent study of Philadelphia makes clear that a similar kind of disproportionality remains in some areas of the country: a black defendant who committed murder in that city was almost four times more likely to get a death sentence than a non-black who committed a similar murder. Since *Gregg v. Georgia,* 44 percent of those individuals executed in the United States have come from minority groups; 35 percent have been black.

Especially suggestive of the way race affects our use of capital punishment today is the fact that, since 1976, over 80 percent of the slain victims of all those persons we have executed have been white, even though only half of the victims of murder in our country are white. Thus, it should come as no surprise to learn what Georgetown University legal scholar David Cole has recently pointed out: "Virtually every study of race and the death penalty has concluded that, all other things being equal, defendants who kill white victims are much more likely to receive the death penalty than those who kill black victims." Needless to say, a white person is only rarely executed for killing a minority man or woman. It hasn't happened once, for instance, since 1976 in Georgia, where the battle flag of the old Confederacy has been incorporated into the state flag and thus can still be seen in most of our courtrooms, and where, according to a study of over two thousand of the state's murder cases from the 1970s, a defendant charged with murdering a white person then was 4.3 times more likely to get a sentence of death than someone charged with killing a black person.

In capital trials in a state such as Georgia, both prosecutor and judge are typically white, and men and women of color too often have limited and sometimes no participation on the juries that decide matters of life and death. Overall, in the thirty-eight states in the United States that permit the death penalty, nearly 98 percent of the lead prosecutors — the driving force behind capital punishment in our legal system — are white.

As a report by Atlanta's Southern Center for Human Rights reminded us not long ago, we still carry out capital punishment in a highly arbitrary fashion years after the U.S. Supreme Court held in *Furman v. Georgia* (1972) that such a practice constituted cruel and unusual punishment. According to the Center, the "death penalty is imposed, on average, in only 250 of the approximately 20,000 homicides that occur each year in the United States. Death sentences are imposed in cases which are similar to thousands of cases in which death is not imposed." Echoing the wisdom of U.S. Court of Appeals Judge Gerald W. Heaney, who summed up three decades of experience on the court in a 1997 opinion, the report notes that the "sentence a defendant receives still depends on the quality of the defense lawyer, the location of the crime, the race of the victim, and the political aspirations of the prosecutor rather than on how bad the crime was or how incorrigible the accused." The report concludes with this statement: "There remains today, as Justice White observed in 1972, 'no meaningful basis for distinguishing the few cases in which [the death penalty] is imposed from the many cases in which it is not.'"

And so we proceed, year after year, with our brand of justice, maintaining through our executions our allegiance to a culture of death. Primarily a matter of the states, which currently hold some 3,600 death-row prisoners, the death penalty is sought in these jurisdictions almost exclusively in murder cases. (Some states also have death-penalty laws on the books for other crimes, such as the rape of a child under twelve.) Capital punishment also plays a role in two other jurisdictions in the United States. Our military permits death sentences for offenses such as murder and espionage; currently it has eight individuals on its death row. The federal government can seek capital punishment for those guilty of some sixty different crimes, including kidnapping that ends in death and drug-dealing on a large scale; there are twenty-one persons on its death row. Today, in our adherence to the death penalty, we part company with Canada and Western Europe. We resist the worldwide trend to outlaw executions. We keep company with countries such as Iran, Iraq, and China.

So enamored are we with this kind of punishment that we seem determined to have even more of it. For this will surely be the result of our latest tinkering with the litigation of capital cases. We have, for example, speeded up the appeals process. And we have taken this measure to shorten the time between trial and execution despite the fact that, since 1973, eighty-four persons who had been sentenced to die were later found to be innocent and were released from death row after they had served, on average, seven-and-a-half years from the time of their convictions. In addition to speeding up appeals and taking other steps to limit the judiciary's ability to review and reverse death sentences, we have also in recent years closed down or slashed the funding of death-penalty resource centers, law offices staffed by publicly financed attorneys who have offered indigent death-row prisoners cost-effective and skilled post-conviction representation.

In the final analysis, our pursuit of capital punishment diminishes the value of all of our lives, as U.S. Supreme Court Justice Harry Blackmun saw at the end of his career, after having affirmed many death sentences over the years. In a 1994 opinion, he wrote the following:

> Perhaps one day this Court will develop procedural rules or verbal formulas that actually will provide consistency, fairness, and reliability in a capital-sentencing scheme. I am not optimistic that such a day will come. I am more optimistic, though, that this Court eventually will conclude that the effort to eliminate arbitrariness while preserving fairness "in the infliction of [death] is so plainly doomed to failure that it — and the death penalty —

must be abandoned altogether." *Godfrey v. Georgia,* 446 U.S. 420, 442 (1980) (Marshall, J., concurring in the judgment). I may not live to see that day, but I have faith that eventually it will arrive. The path the Court has chosen lessens us all. I dissent.

◖   ◗

In early 1985 I began to make trips to the Georgia Diagnostic and Classification Prison near Jackson that houses the men on Georgia's death row — journeys that soon became, for the most part, weekly. In any given year I have visited individually up to sixteen different condemned prisoners there, spending about an hour with each man every three or four weeks, except during times of crisis, when my visits have been longer and more frequent. My time with the men has affected me deeply and has led me to write these pages, which are a record of my own dissent from capital punishment.

The first chapter of this book is a series of introductory reflections concerning the tragedy of the death penalty, my role as a visitor on death row, and what I hope to achieve through my writing. Accounts of the lives of two executed men I knew figure prominently in the chapter. In the following two chapters, I consider in some detail two questions about my visits: Why have I continued, week after week, to visit the men I have met on death row? And what voices from my intellectual and spiritual heritage, influencing my understanding of both Word and world, have shaped my discourse with the prisoners and their families? In answering these questions, I refer not only to men who have been executed. I also write of one man who died of natural causes while he was on death row, and from time to time I mention (without using their names) other men who are currently under the sentence of death or who have been released from death row into the general prison population. In the next five chapters, I focus on six men, the impact they have had on me, and my relationship to them. Each of the six perished at the executioner's hand. Though I have known other condemned men longer and in some cases even better, I was especially moved by my visits with these six persons, perhaps for the very reason that our short time together testifies to the richness of even the briefest of human encounters. In a summary chapter, I try to say what the executed men I knew have meant to me as I reflect on another kind of encounter: my memories of these men at times when my faith has been challenged by the horror of their deaths. Finally, in a postscript, I attempt a meditation in a different mode, concerning a man I knew long and well: it is a letter I addressed to him but actually wrote for myself shortly after he had died in Georgia's electric chair. The letter was an effort to try to come to terms with both his death and his life.

By frequently focusing on how the condemned have reacted to their approaching executions, I show them struggling at the very boundary of life and death. In depicting this struggle, I hope that I indicate something of the dynamic of their very souls: the painful confrontation with their own inner darkness, the process of grieving, the opening to beauty, the giving and receiving of the gift of love. Insofar as I am able to explain my witness to the men in such situations, perhaps some of the deepest currents of my own life also become apparent.

❦   ❧

Many of the basic facts about the prisoners' lives, including the essential and "sensitive" details about their childhoods, have already been made known before various courts and in final pleas for clemency. Often the news media have reported such details to the general public. What I offer here is my own perspective on the men. At its best, my knowledge of them has come, I hope, from that most revealing and thus most holy of places, where I and Thou meet. Ultimately, such knowledge is founded on my belief in the infinite worth of the men as human beings.

1

Introduction: A Distant Spring

When I was a small child, afraid to enter our dark house alone one evening, my father assured me, "There's no darkness deep enough to swallow you whole." After that, I often thought of those words in difficult times. Never in my thirty-nine years had events challenged my father's maxim — part faith, perhaps, part folklore — as much as they did on a June night in 1986. I remember lying awake alone in a motel room then, listening to the traffic roll along Interstate 75, and waiting for Jerome Bowden's execution, which was set for ten o'clock the next morning. Before driving to the Days Inn in Forsyth, Georgia, about twenty minutes from the prison that houses the state's electric chair, I had paid the condemned man a final visit. Waiting at the motel for a death to occur that I was seemingly powerless to stop, I did not know at the time that I would spend other nights similar to this one.

One memory of that night in June — years ago now — remains especially vivid to me: leafing through notes I had made about Jerome's life. Among my very first attempts to write about the men on Georgia's death row, they were notes, I had hoped, that might help his appeals attorney educate the public about Jerome and assist her in a plea for clemency on his behalf before the state's Board of Pardons and Paroles. But that night it was clear that the plea to have his death sentence commuted to life in prison had failed. Jerome was to die in a few hours. I read through notes like these:

He couldn't make a skateboard like other children his age. He would get frustrated and angry, just as he later did, as an adult, when he tried to read a book. His family knew from the beginning that he was no ordinary child. To them he was odd, not capable of fitting in. His mother, Mrs. Josephine Mims, wanted to get psychological assistance for Jerome, but the family was too poor to afford such help.

Jerome was delivered by a midwife in a small frame house in a black neighborhood in Columbus, Georgia, in July of 1952. His father was not Mrs. Mims' husband, who had abandoned her, but a man named Bowden, whom Jerome was never to know. Four other half brothers and his half sister Josie had already left home, so Jerome lived with his mother and his half sister Shirley. The three of them moved from one ramshackle house to another, occasionally staying with Josie and her family when Mrs. Mims couldn't afford to rent a place of her own.

Doing housework for white families, Jerome's mother supported herself and her two children as well as she could. Their diet consisted primarily of commodities provided by local relief agencies: powdered milk and eggs, rice, lard, and Spam. Because the houses in which they lived had no electricity or running water, Shirley and Jerome would chop wood for the cooking stove and the fireplace. The children's chores also included bringing water home in cans and jars and going to a nearby filling station to buy kerosene for the lamps they used at night. There was little or no money to help treat the asthma attacks that Jerome frequently experienced as a young child. Though his family was once able to take him to the hospital, most of the time they simply sat up with him, sometimes all night.

Since their mother worked away from home when they were very young, both Shirley and Jerome often went without adult supervision. Occasionally a neighbor would look in on the children when the little family was living alone. In a segregated school, Jerome had been placed in special education classes, but he was often absent. The classes did little more than "warehouse" him. He was evaluated at age fourteen by a clinical psychologist and diagnosed as "very definitely retarded": the teenager's full-scale IQ was 59, well under the traditional upper limit of mental retardation, which is 70. The psychologist concluded that Jerome had "little or no insight into his situation."

As Jerome grew older, he committed petty thefts, often giving the money away. He sometimes spent time in a local juvenile home, and he eventually dropped out of school. Known in his neighborhood as someone who liked to play with small children, he was a "follower," easily influenced by others, as is so often the case with persons with mental retardation. He held odd jobs — once he was a carpenter's helper, carrying buckets of nails and pieces of lumber — but he would get discouraged and quit. He would do things that seemed strange to his family but not to him. Once, for example, when attempting to cut his sister's grass with a power mower, he filled it with water after it had run out of gas. In 1972 he began serving time in prison for burglary. Released after three years, he took up his routine of odd jobs again.

One day in October of 1976, Kathryn Stryker, a white woman, was found murdered at her home in Columbus. She had been beaten with a pellet gun and stabbed; her invalid mother had also been beaten but survived (only to die of a heart attack at a nursing home several weeks later). Valuables had been taken. The twenty-four-year-old Jerome and a sixteen-year-old friend — who, like Jerome, was black — were arrested for the crimes. Having heard that the police were looking for him, Jerome had gone up to a police car and asked if the officers wanted him.

I do not know how many times I read through Jerome's biography that night. It was a way of counting away the hours until dawn. All the while, I was hoping perhaps that one time, magically, the story would have a different ending. It did not.

At Jerome's trial, his court-appointed attorneys had not been able to do much for him, even though there had been some question about his involvement in Ms. Stryker's death and the other crimes. There had been no physical evidence incriminating him. In fact, evidence had been located at the house of his co-defendant: police had found the pellet gun used in the murder and jewelry taken from Ms. Stryker. Still, the co-defendant had ended up receiving a life sentence and had later been sent to a state prison hospital for the mentally ill. But Jerome, who had denied at trial that he had been at the Stryker home at the time of the crimes, had been able to produce no alibi witnesses. Working against him, too, had been the fact that his co-defendant had implicated him in the case. A written confession that Jerome had purportedly dictated to authorities had also been damaging to him — although the document contains oddly elevated language. He had testified that he had originally professed his innocence to the police; he had signed the confession handed to him by law officers only because he had been told that by doing so he could avoid the death penalty. Finally, an all-white jury, which had never heard expert testimony concerning Jerome's mental retardation, had decided that he should die for the murder of Ms. Stryker, an act they saw as aggravated by robbery and burglary. After a decade, the ultimate wisdom of the appeals courts was that the jury's verdict of death should stand.

I had learned that Jerome's fate was finally sealed about mid-afternoon of the day of my last visit with him, the day before his execution. I had received a phone call then from his sister Shirley. She had hardly been able to get her words out: "They gonna kill him, Randy." Georgia's Board of Pardons and Paroles, which had stayed Jerome's execution so that a psychologist it had chosen could test his intelligence, had lifted its stay. The results of the psychologist's test — IQ scores of 71 (verbal), 62 (nonverbal), and 65 (full-scale) — had not been low enough for a majority of the Board, composed of four whites and one black, political appointees of the governor. "I done my very best," Jerome told me when I last saw him.

Just a few days earlier, the captain of the guards in charge of death row had brought the news of the stay to Jerome and me. Elated, I had given Jerome a hug, and in doing so I had knocked over our chairs in the cramped attorney's visiting room where we had been talking. For a while after receiving the good news, I had even begun to laugh a little when I recalled the comic stories I had heard about Jerome in prison. There had been the time when he had been disciplined for supposedly having drawn up an elaborate escape plan. As it had turned out, the plan had been a chart about the coming Kingdom, based on the book of Revelation. A fellow prisoner had made the chart for him. Then there had been the meeting between Jerome and a rabbi who had been visiting the prison. Jerome had praised the man of the cloth for his great faith in Jesus. But once the Pardons and Paroles Board had lifted its stay, such stories seemed far from humorous; they were cruel reminders of a fate that had led Jerome toward his execution.

Some three hours after Shirley's call, I was driving along Georgia's Route 36 toward the prison to visit Jerome. On this evening before his death, it was hot and steamy, even for Georgia in late June. When I crossed the Flint River, as I had so often that spring, knowing that with each crossing time was running out for a man who had become my friend in the last sixteen months of his life, mist had begun to slip lightly over the bright green island in the water, just to the west of the bridge. The river's springtime beauty, which I had occasionally glimpsed before, seemed distant, perhaps lost forever, blocked by the specter of the looming execution.

When I reached the prison, all was quiet outside, in marked contrast to the bustle during normal visiting hours. Inside, only an occasional employee could be seen. When the guards brought Jerome to the main visiting room, two of them stayed inside with us, just out of hearing range. Jerome had been crying a lot, and his eyes were red. He was wearing a baggy new "execution" uniform. His belt had been taken from him for "safety" reasons — so that he could not hang himself. On his feet were a pair of cheap, prison-issue slippers. His regular shoes, with laces, had also been taken away — again for "safety" reasons. He was hardly the affable, gregarious Jerome I had come to know. Without uttering a word, he sat down on a small ledge that runs the length of the room. He placed his hands between his knees and held his head down.

After several minutes, he began to speak in short bursts: "I'm gonna die, aren't I? Why they doin' this? I thought. . . ." Then he was silent again for a while — and despondent, as if he expected no reply. His cries, even to God, had gone unanswered for too long, I thought. Something terrible was about to happen to him, the full dimensions of which and the reasons for which were beyond him. He was greatly bewildered — even more so than he normally was concerning the long ordeal of his trial, appeals, and imprisonment. Eventually he raised his head and got down off the ledge.

He moved to a chair beside me and slowly began telling me about people who had loved him. It was the kind of thing he liked to talk about. He mentioned his sister Shirley, who had stuck by him during the most difficult of times, finding a way to get from Columbus to Jackson to visit him as often as she could. He talked for a long time about her. Then he went on to speak of persons who had befriended him in prison. There was Father Wise, a Catholic priest who had made Jerome, a Baptist, feel like "family." There was a fellow death-row prisoner from Columbus, William Boyd Tucker, who had helped Jerome write letters. And there was the captain of the guards, who had treated him well, Jerome felt. Becoming animated in his conversation, he relaxed a bit and propped his feet on a nearby stool. He was smiling. The old Jerome I had come to know was returning to form.

After about an hour, one of the guards told us that it was time to go. And so my "Brother" Jerome — as he signed his occasional letters to me — and I took leave of each other after embracing. For a moment I stood near the door of the visiting room and looked at him as he was escorted down a long hallway; eager, as always, to be liked, he was waving energetically to someone in the distance. The old Jerome was indeed back.

I carried that last image of him with me as a few of us stood in vigil outside the prison at ten o'clock the next morning. A young Catholic priest held his palms upward to the sky and asked for God's enduring care for the man who was being taken from our midst. Inside the prison, Jerome was saying a few last words from the death chamber. Among them were these: "I would like to thank the people of this institution."

◄ ►

Although I have felt deeply sad about Jerome's death, it has also become a source of hope for me over the years. Responding to his tragedy, in 1988 the Georgia legislature barred future juries from giving death sentences to persons with mental retardation. And in 1989 the Georgia Supreme Court protected those individuals with mental retardation who had received death sentences before 1988 by ruling that the execution of such persons was cruel and unusual and thus in violation of the state's constitution. These actions proved that it is possible for the citizens of Georgia to grapple with their wrongs and seek to change old and deep-seated habits.

Still, much remains to be done. Acting in the spirit of our new understanding that people with mental retardation should not be sentenced to death has been difficult. Tom Stevens, who possibly had some degree of mental retardation, was executed in 1993, and less than a year later William Hance, whose intellectual functioning was arguably significantly impaired, was also executed. Moreover, the executions of those persons without mental retardation have continued apace. All told, sixteen of our state's condemned men have been put to death since Jerome's electrocution, as have over five hundred other prisoners across the country. Now, over 130 men and one woman — who make up a small fraction of the total number of persons on death rows nationwide — await their executions in Georgia.

The persistent carrying out of executions is an issue that touches us all. The condemned have died in our names. We have called for their deaths.

As long as we speak these words of death, we will tell only a perverse winter's tale of the frozen spirit. We will wait for a spring that will remain forever distant. There will be no genuine vitality in our national life: we will give mere lip service to building true community. So important is this issue of capital punishment. For the mark of real community is always revealed by a people's embracing the "least" of those in their midst. And if we look closely enough, we will see that among the "least" of those in our presence have been the persons we have executed.

◀ ▶

Our brutality against the powerless reaches far into our national past — and far into my family's past as well.

I see him standing at the edge of a dark red field, which the light slowly fills on a March morning in the 1850s. Though I have no way of knowing for sure, I always picture him as resembling my maternal grandfather: he has a long, narrow face, slightly protruding ears, and eyes that do not seem quite focused. The man is thinking of spring planting. He is my great-great-grandfather, Wiley Stanton Edmundson, and he envisions what will be happening soon: he sees slaves bending to the earth. They are his, and they are planting his crops: cotton, beans, corn. It is his earth, some thirty miles from the family farm where I now live. He is enmeshed in a culture of death-in-life, sustained at the expense of black slaves and poor whites whose lives have little value in human terms.

Wiley Stanton's legacy — manifest over the years in his descendants' predilection for both court-mandated sentences of death and mob-instigated lynchings in defense of a way of life — has now come to my generation. He stood at the edge of his fields year after year. But he never saw the spring in all its fullness. Neither, I fear, can any of us who are his heirs, unless we renounce his legacy. So profoundly affected are we, I believe, by our practice of executions — by our pursuit of power at the expense of the weak.

❧ ❧

At odds with a frightening portion of my own history, I have made my way to the men on Georgia's death row. Ordained by a small church in the Anabaptist tradition, I have come as a pastor to the condemned men — so my visits are officially registered in the annals of the Georgia Diagnostic and Classification Prison near Jackson. Frequently, I have been simply a bewildered seeker of light long after the night has fallen. Moved by what Henry James once called the "strange irregular rhythm of life," the men and I have spent time at the imagination's edge, sometimes searching together for insight into the meaning and value of the human experience.

I have made my visits as a person with theological training and as someone whose curiosity over the years has led him to explore the psychological dimensions of our existence. Yet increasingly I have seen myself as someone not bound by the roles of a clerical or therapeutic visitor. I hope I have become, most importantly, simply a friend to the men under the sentence of death. I hope that our relationship has been what Jürgen Moltmann has suggested that friendship should be: "unpretentious" and "personal," something quite apart from one's "office" or "title."

As their friend, I was invited by the men to join them in their struggle for dignity, meaning, and love — and for freedom from the chains of an oppressive judicial system. As a friend, I hope I carry on their struggle in these pages. For only in this struggle — against the cold and dark and death of winter — will the spring be born.

❧ ❧

I have no illusions about the small part that I have played in the struggle for life.

I know what heroism and moral courage are; I have been privileged to witness these things. From time to time I have seen them in the prisoners I have visited. I have also seen such virtues in the women and men working for the loosely knit group of law offices that have tried to keep the machinery of death from claiming the prisoners' lives, for none of the condemned men could afford legal representation to exercise their right of appeal in the courts. These attorneys and investigators have worked long hours for years, often operating with small, inadequate budgets and fighting against almost impossible odds. Many of these individuals have devoted their lives to the cause of justice, to the handling of the appeals of persons who otherwise would have had no voice. I have performed no such bold or courageous deeds.

I do talk to my church, a most sympathetic audience, about the struggles of the condemned men. Sometimes I have spoken to individual legislators — once, to a gathering of them in committee — trying to convince them that we as a people would be better off without executions. And now and then I have tried to provide solace to the relatives of murder victims. But it is primarily as a weekly visitor of death-row prisoners and sometime guest of their families that I have played my small part in responding to the state's practice of the death penalty.

Why have I not done more? Perhaps out of fear of challenging the powers and principalities intent on using death as a means to solve our problems; perhaps out of a reluctance to work as hard as necessary; perhaps out of a distrust of my own abilities. For whatever reason, I have played no important role in stemming the tide of capital punishment or in bringing about reconciliation between the families of murder victims on the one hand, and condemned prisoners and their loved ones on the other.

I have been a frail witness to the process of murder by the state as it has responded to murder by individuals. In a time when the fear of crime and violence clouds our vision, I have seen us reach again and again for one of the old terrors of history, capital punishment. Despite its frailty, perhaps my witness can help us see that there is no hope in terror. Perhaps my words can help us understand that the new life of community and the spirit that we as a people so desperately need remains as distant in our time as it was in my great-great-grandfather's day, one hundred fifty years ago.

9

◄ ►

In writing these pages, and thus reaffirming an act that I began with my notes about Jerome Bowden, I have had no assurance that my meditations would mean much to anyone. I have thought at times that my reflections might, at most, consist of little more than a personal message in a bottle flung into a vast ocean. During such moments I have asked myself, Why continue writing? One answer that has kept me going has arisen from my relationship to Jim Messer, who was executed in Georgia in the summer of 1988.

My memories of Jim are still colored in part by emotions that I began to experience shortly after I started visiting him: sadness, frustration, even despair. These kinds of feelings shaped much of Jim's life and invariably affected our relationship, too. They are feelings that we both had one day a few months before he was executed.

On that day, Jim ended up telling me, in effect, the story of his life, some of the details of which I had heard before. His body went almost limp as he spoke: "I've felt low, depressed, all my life. Mostly, it's been a waste." Emphasizing his points occasionally with pale white hands stained from the tobacco he used to roll his own cigarettes, he explained that he had always wanted a father but had never really had one. For some reason this was a "hurt" he never could manage to get over, he said, though he felt now that his mother, aunt, and grandmother — who had had enough problems of their own, just making ends meet — had done their best in raising him.

As Jim continued to talk, this is what I heard: His father, an alcoholic, never showed much interest in him. In fact, the man often beat Jim and his mother. One time he struck his young son after he had cried, refusing to drink his father's beer. His father left the family before Jim started school. When his grandfather occasionally assumed the role of father, Jim was very grateful. Unfortunately, this relationship with a surrogate father ended tragically when the grandfather, himself depressed, committed suicide. Jim was nine at the time.

As Jim grew older, his listlessness, hopelessness, and longing for a loving father who was never to appear only increased. After failing the eighth grade, he quit school and began to move from one low-paying job to another. At the age of twenty, he married and began a stint in the Army, which ended after two years when he became disillusioned with military life. Discharged from the service, he still had difficulty summoning enough drive or energy to keep himself employed in one place for long, even though his family had grown to include two children, whom he loved and wanted to help support. In February of 1979, just before his twenty-fifth birthday, he murdered his eight-year-old niece. After he had picked her up from school one day, he began sexually molesting her. When she protested, he eventually beat her and stabbed her repeatedly. He was tried for the crime and received a death sentence.

According to Jim, all of the frustration of his inner life came rushing outward during the murder of his niece, an event he viewed as beyond his control. He explained that at the time of the killing, he had been an observer, almost like someone watching a horrible scene on TV. He had felt "helpless." He said that talking about the murder was hard for him, very hard, and the difficulty showed in his clipped, halting speech and the tortured expression on his face, signs of shame over his failures in life.

Jim did not speak in this vein often, and I seldom encouraged him to do so because of what would almost inevitably occur. Recalling one painful scene would bring up another, and another, and still another, until he would become hopelessly lost in depression, and his fragile faith would be threatened. He seemed to be helped the most by our talking about the things that reminded him of the small joys in his life before his arrest. He had been a baseball fan since his boyhood days, so we mulled over the victories and losses of the Atlanta Braves. He had loved working on cars from the time he had been a teenager, so we puzzled over ways to keep my '63 Falcon running. But even in our lighter moments, I often felt myself caught, trapped, in his underlying depression.

I carried Jim's depression within me during the summer of 1988, when my wife, Renner, and I spent ten weeks in Germany. Our plan for the trip suited us both. She, a teacher of German, would participate in a seminar at the Goethe Institute in the old university city of Göttingen. I would brush up on my German at the Institute and attend lectures in theology at the university where Karl Barth began his teaching career. When Renner and I left in early June, I knew that there was a possibility that Jim could be executed later in the summer. But I took the chance. I had been through six executions in the past two years. I needed a break. The continued confrontation with death had left me increasingly weary.

But "getting away" was not so easy. Whenever I thought of Jim during the first few weeks of our trip, I focused on his overwhelming sadness and helplessness. I tended to lose sight of things that I had assumed from the beginning of our visits, and that he had confirmed from time to time: he had gifts to give, life to live.

Near the middle of our stay in Göttingen, I received a telegram from Mary Sinclair, who for years had done research on capital punishment and had visited death-row prisoners for the Southern Center for Human Rights in Atlanta. She had news about Jim: he had an execution date in late July, only a couple of weeks away. During these weeks I repeatedly confronted the meaning of my relationships to the men on death row, one of whom — Jim — I felt I had abandoned. But Jim himself was not often at the center of my thoughts. His depression had made his person too difficult for me to contemplate for long. Mostly I focused on my own tortured conscience — or, worse, my ego.

On the evening of the execution, I called Jim's mother about an hour after he had died. I do not remember what I said. I tried to express my sorrow for her, I am sure. No doubt I could not avoid also expressing something of my frustration at not having been with her and Jim during the last days of his life. Whatever I said, I could not have been much help. As I talked, Jim's inner darkness slowly became almost palpable to me.

After the call, long past midnight in Germany, Jim's despair continued with me as I wandered through empty streets over to the university. I went as far as the Platz der Göttinger Sieben, a memorial to seven university professors (including the Grimm brothers) who had protested against injustices of the government in their day and had lost their professorships as a consequence. The memorial was set amid a maze of university buildings that had been hurriedly constructed in a postmodern style; they were cold and anonymous. The professors' protest seemed small and meaningless, overwhelmed by the products of a civilization whose secularity and impoverished soul were embodied in the ugliness of its architecture.

As I stood there at the memorial site, I thought about what Judge Frank Johnson of the 11th Circuit U.S. Court of Appeals had pointed out three years earlier in regard to Jim's case. The court had turned down Jim's appeal, but, summarizing the performance of Jim's trial attorney, the judge had noted in his dissenting opinion that there had been "a complete breakdown of the adversarial process." At the trial's sentencing phase, for example, when the jury was to decide between life in prison or the death penalty for Jim, the lawyer had ignored substantial mitigating evidence, hinting finally that a death sentence was appropriate. Reflecting on the judge's opinion, I was reminded of the sad fate in the courts faced by those in our society such as Jim who were not wealthy or powerful. And I remembered that Jim had been better off than most other death-row prisoners, for he had been able to scrape together enough money to hire his own lawyer, marginal as he was. As I contemplated these things and then thought of the Göttinger Sieben, whose voices seemed stilled forever, my sense of the futility of taking moral stands against the powers and principalities grew. For a time, Jim's despair became my own.

When I returned to Georgia, the desperation that Jim carried within him still haunted me whenever I thought of him. Then something important happened when I paid a visit to his mother and her sister, who had never married and had lived with Jim's mother for years. The visit did not completely dispel my sad feelings about Jim, but it did help me to begin to see him differently than I had in Göttingen. As the three of us ate together in the tiny, poorly lit house in the white mill district where Jim had grown up, I saw that the chicken and biscuits from Colonel Sanders, the huge bowl of black-eyed peas, the Coke in extra-large glasses filled with ice, the fresh strawberry cake, and the homemade table decorations of plastic flowers — all of the things before me — were ultimately expressions of gratitude for the life of someone whom the sisters loved deeply and who had, in his own way, come to love them deeply, too. As they spoke of their occasional visits with Jim, who had always wanted to be reassured that their car was in good enough condition for them to make the trips to the prison safely, and as they turned over in their hands a stack of letters they had received from him over the years, my hosts were responding in joy to small but enduring acts of love he had shown them. To them, he was not just someone hopelessly trapped by depression. This experience affected me powerfully. When his mother, aunt, and I left for his burial plot, I took with me an image of him as a person not completely bound by the forces of darkness. I did not try to put him out of mind, as I had for a time in Göttingen.

I held on to my brightening image of him even as I stood by his gravesite and looked out over the cemetery, a large, rolling expanse of grass and marble markers, bounded by a busy U.S. highway, a strip of car dealerships and fast-food restaurants, and an industrial complex. Driving toward home that evening, I continued to hold on to this image of Jim. On my truck's radio I heard George Bush campaigning for the presidency. He was uttering his oft-quoted words about wanting a "kinder and gentler America," and I felt a deep sadness as I wondered when such a time would begin. But I also felt the dimensions of a love that reached through and beyond the sadness. It was a love that Jim and his mother and aunt had shown to one other.

I recognized more signs of Jim's love when I heard a story about him that a friend in his cellblock told me later that fall. The story goes this way: For years, the friend, a tough ex-Marine, had exercised daily to strengthen himself physically and to break the monotony of life on the "row." Some time before he died, Jim — who was not much of an athlete because of back problems caused by a car accident he had been involved in as a teenager — began recording his friend's exercise routine: situps, perhaps, or leg lifts, and rounds that the man jogged in the cellblock and on the yard. All the while, the friend apparently never knew what Jim was doing. Just before he was executed, Jim put the lists together and placed them in a paper sack containing a few belongings that he wanted the man to have. I do not think there was much else in the sack — maybe a few photos and other small pieces of memorabilia. In the weeks after Jim's death, the lists became something special in the ex-Marine's eyes. And they have also become special to me. For both Jim's friend and I know that Jim showed his capacity for life beyond despair — his capacity for love — in these small acts.

Since the fall of 1988, as I have thought about how profoundly Jim's mother, his aunt, and his friend affected my view of his life, I have been deeply moved by the power of their testimony. They helped me reclaim knowledge of the whole person that Jim Messer was. I see clearly now — as I grasped occasionally when I was with him — the gifts he gave me even as he was courageously struggling against depression: for example, his careful explanations of the strengths and weaknesses of the Braves and his detailed instructions about how to start my old car on a cold morning. Alongside the darkness he faced, such gifts of love loom large in my memory.

Having learned so much from the testimony of the three persons who knew Jim well, I tell myself now that it may be that I can also offer important testimony concerning the inner lives of the condemned men about whom I write. I know now the difference an engaged witness can make.

I realize that there is much about the men's lives that I have missed, but there is, I trust, much that I have seen, and I hope that I have learned to see more and more over the years. Thus, when I write, I may indeed be performing an act of greater significance than simply casting a message in a bottle into a hopelessly vast sea. It may be that my words will lead to a deeper understanding of those we have consigned to death. Perhaps in some small way, these words may help those who read them to reject capital punishment — to choose life instead of death and thereby begin to experience a spring tide of the spirit for which we all long. Guided by such a spirit, we might start to foster healing in the families of murder victims, the men and women who have killed, and their families. We might help them all in their struggle for peace by leading them toward reconciliation.

2

The Ties

It has happened at odd moments over the years. Having driven for a time through an early morning drizzle toward death row, I have rounded a sweeping curve of Georgia's Route 36 to find the rain suddenly gone and the sun resting like a bright red ball on the highway, burning away the last traces of fog from the lowland and the sleep from my eyes, and I have asked the question. Or sitting in the area outside the visiting room of the prison, I have waited and waited for the prisoner I am to spend time with to be brought from the cellblock; I have watched the steady stream of guards that signals the two o'clock shift-change move noisily through the yellow trap gate toward the prison's interior, where the men I visit live, and sometimes die, and the question has risen within me, filling my consciousness. Or I have been sitting with one of the condemned men in the visiting room, and neither of us has spoken a single word for several minutes. Except for the occasional passing of a guard in front of the metal bars that form the door of the room, it has been almost quiet. Like a traveler resting briefly on a journey in a harsh land, I have allowed my mind free play, and I have thought of my relationships with the men on death row. Lost in such reflection, I have felt the question seize my mind: Why have I come their way again and again? As I have wrestled with this question, one answer has grown to have special importance to me: increasingly, I have seen my visits as responses to certain ties — based on common experiences — that have bound the men and me together. They have been ties that have helped make friendship possible.

16

At first, many of the ties were hard for me to discern. Where were the points of contact between the men's childhoods — filled with the terror of abuse and neglect — and my own? In their early years, the only journey so many of the men knew was, in a sense, a journey through wilderness. They scarcely heard a word of genuine promise spoken or glimpsed any fulfillment.

At the beginning of my visits, it would have been very difficult for me to say that I could really identify with a childhood like that of Tom Stevens, for instance, who was executed in June of 1993 for his role in a 1977 murder.

I remember Tom one day shortly before his death: A small white man, he speaks with gratitude about the expressions of love of a brother and half sister who in the last few months have helped him face his past. Then he painfully and slowly moves through the events of his life, frequently staring into space as he talks. Interviews of his family conducted by an investigator working on his plea for clemency have helped him put this story together as well as he can. He has also had to contend with the view of a licensed psychologist, whose opinion Tom's appeals attorney has sought and who has recently evaluated Tom. Though it conflicts with some evidence from previous testing, the psychologist's evaluation indicates that his client is a person with mental retardation.

During previous visits, I have wondered if Tom was ever held, lovingly, as a child, and if he ever found moments of acceptance in his family when he was growing up. Listening to him on this visit, I know for sure that in his childhood he saw few of the signs of promise and fulfillment embodied in such things as holding and acceptance. The story he tells is one of childhood trauma, a story that does not point directly to — but does not exclude — mental retardation. Though the words he uses are simple, and I must often ask for clarification, the picture he gradually paints is vivid.

As he speaks, this is what I see: His mother, married at fourteen, pregnant with Tom's half brother at fifteen, recoils one day in horror because of the beatings her husband gives her. Having had enough of her drunken tormentor, she ties him up, beats him with an iron skillet until he is black and blue, and then throws him out of the house, never to take him back again. Instead, she moves on to find another poor, alcoholic husband, this time Tom's father. One day when she is pregnant with Tom, she stumbles and falls down the basement steps. For him, there is wilderness even in the womb, it seems. I see his mother's face contorted by the depression that plagues her entire married life and that is exacerbated by a series of miscarriages. I see my friend in anguish, at age three, his soul tormented in a way he cannot fully comprehend, as he begins to struggle with the fact that his mother is dying, an ordeal that lasts five long years. After a time, she is so ill that she cannot even recognize Tom.

The story goes on. After the death of Tom's mother when he is eight, he is reared, in turn, by two other family members as his father retreats further and further into alcoholism. Tom does not find acceptance. The first family member, another alcoholic, has a habit of locking him in the basement so that she can drink undisturbed and not have to watch out for him. The second relative possesses a fundamentalist faith that might seem humorous if it did not lead to such disastrous consequences. For instance, she calls her preacher one day and asks him to rush over and exorcise a demon in the refrigerator. The trouble is, she apparently thinks the demons are in Tom, too. And so she begins to carry out exorcisms of a sort on her own. One such time occurs when she discovers urine and feces on a pair of her shoes and thinks that Tom is responsible for the misdeed. Although he denies it, she seizes him by the hair and drags him into her closet. There she takes my friend's face and smears it with the feces on her shoes. Perhaps Tom also begins to think he is demon-possessed, for he sometimes awakens and screams in the night. No one holds him.

Exorcisms, after a fashion, become part of his life for years in the wilderness. But the nightly baths of garlic and vinegar, followed by an enema, given by his fundamentalist caregiver, fail to purify him. And the beatings his father inflicts upon him, once with a car fanbelt when the man's own belt breaks after repeated lashings, never really straighten the boy out. Tom retreats within himself and, alone, begins to "huff" lighter fluid. Homeless at sixteen, he is eventually put in a state home for boys. He later works as an itinerant laborer and then joins the Army.

By the time he is twenty, he is already taking large doses of drugs and has been drinking heavily for years. At that age he experiences terrifying effects of his childhood, which is still alive as a tormenting and dehumanizing presence within him: he takes part in the robbery and abduction of moonlighting cab driver Roger Honeycutt. Tom sodomizes the man, who is white, and later watches as a young white accomplice, Chris Burger, drives the cab, with Honeycutt locked in the trunk, into a pond. Honeycutt dies in the trunk. It is a murder that neither Tom nor his seventeen-year-old partner, also a soldier, plans . . . on an evening that ends impulsively in tragedy after both have consumed large quantities of alcohol. The tragedy shakes Tom with remorse from his first sober moment. For his part in the killing, Chris Burger is given the death penalty. With the State arguing that the idea of the murder originated with Tom, he also receives a death sentence — in part because of the assertion of another soldier, who rode in the cab with Tom and Chris for a time after the robbery and sodomy, and who testifies that Tom suggested in the taxi that Roger Honeycutt should be killed. Years later, as Tom's execution date looms, the soldier recants a key part of his testimony and says in a sworn affidavit that Tom did not talk at all about killing the victim: the former prosecution witness reveals that he succumbed to police pressure and testified falsely, fearing that if he did not he too would be charged in the murder.

Tom's story, in which the consequences of his childhood live on far beyond his earliest years, ends a couple of days after the visit during which he has told me so many of the details of his life. In the last hours before he is executed, I accompany a young woman who has befriended him into the visiting room to tell him that his appeals are, in effect, over. The first thing he does when he finds out what has happened is to allow himself to be held by the woman, almost as a child is held by its mother, who cradles its head with her hand. As I stand there, watching Tom and the woman embracing and talking softly to one another, I think to myself, "At least at the end of his days, when his long sojourn in the wilderness is nearly over, he receives something of the nurture and acceptance that were denied him so often in his boyhood." I also think of the occasional theological discussions Tom and I have had, and I ask myself, "Does he finally hear the word of promise of a God he has sought so long — a word that the horrors of his youth have made so difficult for him to grasp?"

19

Meditating on the stories of the men's childhoods, such as that of Tom Stevens, has led me to explore my own early years and, eventually, the resulting twists and turns of my entire life and the course of my deepest feelings. I have moved down dark corridors that might have been closed to me forever, and sometimes I have experienced again the light of joy I had forgotten. I value much more deeply the garments of love knit up for me by those who cared for me. But I also see where the garments were worn thin. In sum, I have discovered that the childhoods of the men on death row and, in turn, much of their lives are not as alien as they seemed at first. Indeed, I have come to feel deeply certain ties with the men.

◄ ►

For example, I have come to see that I, too, experienced something of the childhood loneliness that men such as Tom Stevens suffered. Listening to the condemned prisoners' stories, I began to see scenes like the following: I am facing my mother one day as she and I stand in the narrow hallway of a house my family lived in when I was five. Her arms are heavy with clothes that she has spent hours ironing. As she towers over me, I am filled with the incomprehensible sadness that draws and darkens her face. And I flee the hallway, run away from a woman who has struggled valiantly each day to make a place of love for me in the world, but who has never recovered from the loss of her father when she was eight. She suffered through crushing poverty in the Great Depression and, after she married, was often faced with raising two children alone, while my father, first a traveling salesman and then a soldier, moved about the state and later the world, trying to provide for our family. I burst from the house and churn through neighborhood streets. Once again I seek my place of safety between piles of lumber and sawdust on the seemingly endless grounds of a construction company not far away. And I sit there, alone, smelling the freshly cut wood and waiting for whatever signs a child recognizes that tell it to pick up the thread of its life again with someone it must love to survive.

I have not known what almost all of the men I have visited have experienced: consistent neglect or unrelenting abuse or both. I have not known the depth and breadth of the loneliness that can freeze the soul, but I have felt its penetrating cold. I have tasted its poison. Over the

20

years my memories of this experience of loneliness from my childhood have drawn me time and again to the men on death row; I have felt a tie of great power.

◀ ▶

I have also been drawn to the men for another reason.

As a boy, I would lie awake in my bed on summer nights and slowly turn the dial of my Silvertone radio in search of the Cardinals or White Sox or Tigers. Finding a game, I moved effortlessly through what one student of baseball called with precision "the green fields of the mind." With ease, I could drift back toward the center field wall, my glove finally dipping into the seats to make a catch to stop a rally in the top of the ninth. I felt the cadences of the announcer's voice echo within me through the night, long after the game was over, when the lights of the cheering stadium became the light of my dreams. And, in the early morning hours in my backyard in Florida, I treasured those — to a boy's mind — unparalleled moments of our nation's history, our voyages toward the stars. My heart raced when, in the distance, a rocket's small orange flame arched out over the Atlantic, became a trail of white smoke, and finally disappeared, as if blown away by the sun.

In these and many other ways, my life has been profoundly shaped by our popular culture, which has plied me with its subtle sweetnesses and tense melodramas. Though only occasionally offering badly needed moments of ultimate depth in a largely one-dimensional, secular world, this culture has often been powerfully alluring nonetheless. To a degree that surprised me at first, the men I have gone to see on death row have also been shaped by many of the raptures of the popular culture. Our experiences have not always been the same, of course, for these things are shaped by the circumstance of time and by such forces as race and geography and class. A blue note of John Coltrane touches one person; the fierce whine of a high-powered automobile engine exhilarates another. But many of our experiences have had the same point of origin: our popular culture, fed by diverse currents that have mixed and mingled. Knowing this at some level, the condemned men and I have been joined together.

Most of the time, the experiences that the men and I have had with the popular culture have not been major themes of our meetings.

Typically, such experiences have found expression at the edges of our conversations, in the form of occasional questions or comments, words that have served to frame our time together: Had I picked up a late baseball score from a game on the West Coast the night before? Had I caught a new country song on the radio? Did I see the move one basketball player put on another in a championship game a few nights earlier? What did I think of an outfit that a young woman, a visitor of one of the men, wore in the visiting room a week ago?

From time to time, however, the men's fascination with events in the popular culture has played a greater role in our visits. I remember, for instance, one man's elaborate description of the first junior-league football game in which he, a second-string lineman, had finally played. His excitement had been almost overwhelming as he had waited for the kickoff. Eventually the ball had sailed high through the night sky toward — of all people — him. As the man described the event to me, he gazed upward and threw his arms into the air as if he was still waiting nervously to catch a ball that had not yet descended. Of course, the ball had descended, but it had landed at his feet rather than in his arms. And he had never been able to put his hands firmly on the leather, which a nearby teammate had finally rescued from "the enemy." Though the incident had been a small one, it loomed large in the storyteller's memory and imagination. For a few brief seconds he was able to forget the difficulties of his childhood and his life on death row and remember a time that, at least in retrospect, was genuinely humorous for him. He was actually smiling for the first time in months.

I recall another man's rendition of an experience that was shaped by the popular culture: a junior-high football game in which he had participated and which his older brother had watched from the stands. When his time to play had come, his brother had yelled out at him to tackle fiercely an older and stronger player on the opposing team, someone whose runs with the ball had been menacing. Taking his brother's advice, my friend had charged headlong into the opposing player, only to be knocked down with a thud. Returning to his teammates, my friend had then heard his brother's voice telling him how great he had done and how he must do the same thing again. And he had followed his brother's advice a second time — with the same result. As he told me about the incident, the storyteller laughed easily at his boyhood ardor. But there was more to the episode, he felt, than an occasion for laughter: his brother had shown that he believed in him. This had become clear to him only in retrospect, a couple of years after that game — after the brother had been killed in Viet Nam. Though the loss of his brother's love had devastated my friend and sent him into a depression that continued as we spoke, remembering the many manifestations of that love put him in contact with some of the most precious moments of his own life. Among those moments were ones formed in the context of our popular culture — at the junior-high stadium, for instance. Because I too had been shaped by this culture, my moments as a listener to the prisoner's football story were all that more poignant.

◀ ▶

Yet another important tie that I have come to feel with most of the condemned men results from our lifelong knowledge of the harsh reality faced by those at the economic margins of our society. I spent my years as a boy and a teenager with many persons like the great majority of those on death row: individuals who were raised in poverty or at the boundaries of it and who were thus subject to stresses unknown to those reared in wealth and power. Coming of age in the 1950s, I was like most of those in the lower middle class who grew up in a time before the cresting of the great wave of prosperity that swept over the country after the Second World War. In some respects there were no great barriers of class between us and the truly poor, and friendships between persons of the two classes were not difficult to form. None of us had many of the material possessions that would later separate children and teenagers. Consequently, when I have listened to many of the men on death row tell the stories of their youth, I have seen the faces and heard the voices of people I knew years ago and to whom I am still bound by deep feelings. Frequently they were faces that carried taut expressions in which one could glimpse a constricted spirit. Typically they were weary, anxious voices; their words would often trail off into nothingness or, sometimes, clumsily form the substance of a threat.

These persons out of my past were expendable, on the edge of a culture in which I lived only somewhat closer to the life-giving center, to safety. When I think of such individuals, I remember one teenager I knew who took up long-distance running. He loped through often yet-to-be-developed marginal land or the grassy strips between power poles that Florida entrepreneurs could not turn into profits. Sometimes he made his way through subdivision streets. Often he pushed his thin, hardly robust body to exhaustion, finding some faint nods of recognition that were necessary to sustain him. Neither especially talented in school nor particularly gifted as a runner, he grew up in a largely rural area — adjacent to the city in which I lived — where one often found rusting, wrecked cars and carelessly tended farming plots. It seems to me that he surged through the Florida heat with some dim hope that if he ran far enough or fast enough, he might escape what was already becoming an oppressive fate.

A couple of years after graduation from high school, I heard that the young man had lost his life while on patrol in a land whose fierce heat and lush vegetation resembled that of his central Florida home. Immediately after I learned the sad news, I thought of him running, his forearms bent awkwardly high toward his body, his face twisted and pained. I could hear his frightened voice one day while he was resting, mumbling a few sentences about what he hoped to accomplish as an athlete. And his plight grew in my mind. He remains for me a vivid example of what our poor must endure as they face the economic, political, and social forces of this nation. Now and then, when I am talking with one of the men on death row and our conversation turns to his teenage years, the young long-distance runner I knew still comes to mind, furiously trying to outrun his past.

☜ ☞

As I have become aware of the ties that have linked me to the prisoners on death row, I have realized that an important reason why I have come again and again to the condemned men is because the dark specter of failure that has haunted their lives has appeared to me too and has shaken me deeply.

Recently one of the men told me about the pride his family felt when one of his distant cousins completed Marine Corps basic training. Then he added, "None of the rest of us ever amounted to much." This man speaks for almost all of his fellow death-row prisoners, including those who have died. Often moving from job to job, from one tiny, unkempt house or apartment or trailer to another, sometimes from one beleaguered woman to another, the men typically struggled daily with the undertow of their failed lives. Frequently they used alcohol or other drugs to try to still the pain of their lack of success.

The condemned men learned the consequences of life in a society that is (to use Gershen Kaufman's expression) "shame-based," founded on three often conflicting "scripts": the quests for success, for independence and self-sufficiency, and for popularity and conformity. Time and again, we cannot meet these goals and are inevitably exposed to the gaze of others and ourselves; we feel shame. As the men have known firsthand, this happens especially to those persons whose lives are weakened by stresses like poverty and racism. From childhood on, such persons are easily frustrated in their efforts to achieve adequate self-esteem and thus feel themselves lacking, flawed. Consequently, they frequently form their very identities around this perhaps most painful of emotions: shame. As I have watched the demeanor of the men I have visited on death row, I have seen some of the effects of the penetrating gaze of a culture of shame: the hung head, the inability to make consistent eye contact, the silence, the absence of spontaneous movement.

As I have thought about the men's shame, I have also gradually come to grips with my own moments of failure, of shame. I have thought a lot, for example, about a time when I was an army of one on seemingly interminable parade, moving evening after evening across the disciplinary area at the Air Force Academy in Colorado Springs. A seventeen-year-old cadet in basic training who carried with him the high hopes of his family, I resisted the regimen of military life. I moved when I should have been still, grimaced when I should have held my face in stoic submission, and was subject to countless other lapses. Thus, I "marched off" demerits after supper each day. Held between my thumb and first finger, my heavy M-1 rifle, suspended a foot above the ground, was at my side. With my eyes set straight ahead, often toward the impenetrable Rocky Mountains in the distance, I tried to beat time and memory into the concrete with each step. I sought to escape what I felt: failure, disgrace. Finally, after six or seven weeks, I resigned. When I was mustering out, one officer told me that by leaving I was throwing my life away.

On my visiting days at the prison, when my mind occasionally wanders to the difficult, windswept hours on those cold summer evenings over thirty-five years ago now, I "return" to the visiting room and realize that the shame of the man I am with has been even more numbing than the length of rifle was in my hand. The tie I feel then with my friend is profound. I realize that I have not felt personally the uttermost depths of shame's destructiveness, but I know that I have experienced something of the pull of its dark power.

◖   ◗

There have been still other ties that have bound me to the condemned men, helped me to understand their plight, and fostered our friendships. For example, I have come to see that, like the death-row prisoners, I am a creature subject to rage.

Born of impotence, it is a feeling that so many of the men I have visited have experienced throughout their lives, beginning with their mistreatment as children. It is an emotion that led many of them to murder. It is a feeling that they must still have at times, for each man is trapped, confined to his cage, where he awaits the moment of his death, the date of which he will know some two weeks ahead of time and the reality of which he is reminded of each morning when he awakens and realizes, once more, where he is.

The following scene illustrates well my own susceptibility to rage: The man who enters the death-row visiting room carries multiple psychiatric diagnoses. Overcome with fear and loneliness, he grasps my hand tightly, as if he does not want to let go. As he sits down beside me, I wonder when he last bathed or brushed his teeth or shaved. His smell seems to fill the room. Countless times he has tried to commit suicide by slashing his wrists and arms — places, he has told me, where he was beaten severely as a child. After his last suicide attempt, prison officials have put him in solitary confinement — as they have done before on similar occasions. The light in his isolation cell is always on, he explains. He has tried, unsuccessfully, to sleep. His glasses have been taken from him, so he can barely see me; he squints through eyes surrounded by dried, caked mucus. I ask him about the psychotropic medication he has been given. (Any real psychotherapy is out of the question.) Is he still getting it? He cannot remember; he is too disoriented. I think about one of his several personalities, who says that my friend must kill himself to "get to the mountaintop," where, presumably, he will feel safe for the first time in his life. This suicidal part of him is ravaging what is left of his mind and spirit. I begin to shake with rage as I

26

look into the prisoner's hollow eyes. He wants to die, he says, and he re-
peats himself again and again. What can I do? After a few minutes, I
leave so that I can call his attorney, who perhaps can bring about some
change in the man's present living conditions, I tell myself.

I learned a day after this scene that the attorney had tried, in vain, to
reach the proper officials. Nevertheless, the prisoner was brought back
to his regular cell, allowed to shower, brush his teeth, reclaim his
glasses, sleep. Why? Perhaps because the prison officials knew that
someone had seen him in such bad shape, and they did not want the
spectacle to be repeated again. Most likely, however, it was because the
"suicide watch" had simply ended after a prescribed length of time.
Probably I was able to do nothing to help my friend.

Nor can I do much — if anything — now or in the future, it seems, to
cause his intense suffering to abate. In my gloomiest moments I think
that his best prospects are these: to be taken off death row because
some judge somewhere will realize the extent of the man's profound
mental illness, then to be medicated to the point of stupor and thrown
into the gulag of the state prison system. Each time I think of his fate,
rage builds inside me.

Reflecting on my own rage, I have been able to imagine how this
feeling can lead people who have been consistently abused or neglected
to commit terrifying acts of violence. Knowing the fierce power of this
emotion, which might have led me to violence if I had not experienced
love from so many people over the years, I have felt a deep kinship with
the men on death row.

Yet another kind of kinship has also played an important role in my deciding to return to death row, week after week: I have felt at one with
the desperation the men have known.

I have shared this mood with them during our visits. I have sat with
them as they have sent their cries out into the cosmos, toward some
sanctuary of the gods. I have listened with the men when they have
heard nothing in response but the echo of their own desperate voices,
and then silence. I have tried to be with them at times when they have
searched in vain for sources of life in a world that has spoken to them
so often of death.

Lost in vast, empty spaces, the men have inevitably experienced the outcome of the modern secular worldview. The ultimate loneliness implicit in such secularism has only exacerbated the terror of the men's imprisonment on death row and the horror of the fate so many of the prisoners have experienced since they were children. The brutality of these prisoners' lives — typically shaken time and again by disappointments that have threatened the most basic of spiritual forces, the capacity for trust — has hardly helped the men to challenge a view of existence that obstructs the evidence of a creation ultimately drawn together by love.

My own experience of the absence of the sacred — and the presence of despair — began long before I met the prisoners on death row. In my case, the silence of God began in the time of my youth in a culture whose secularism was, it seems, even more pronounced than that encountered by most of the condemned men. For so many of them grew up in the traditional cultures of the South, a region somewhat less affected than others by the modern experience. I spent many of my important early years in a world that was, despite its many allurements, ultimately unsatisfactory to the needs of the spirit. It was a world symbolized by the neatly drawn streets and small treeless lawns of the postwar Florida suburbs, sprawled on the edges of towns obsessed with growing wealthy from tourism.

In such a suburban culture, the celebrations of the sacred — to cite but one example from traditional religious life — had lost their intimate connection to the divine. In this regard, I remember one Christmas Eve when I was in high school. Near the end of that evening, I stood in readiness with three other teenagers under a street lamp and watched as a basketball arced above a goal mounted on a post at curbside. Then I hurtled through a thick mist to rebound, dribbled toward an imaginary point just far enough from the net to test my skill, pivoted suddenly in the direction of the basket, and shot through the heavy air. Having played for hours, I fell in exhaustion on the wet street. This was how I spent the most holy of nights. I now think of my activity that night as a kind of ode in sweat and motion to an era in the grips of an often unrecognized despair, the dark underside of pleasures cut off from the life of the spirit.

Sensing that there had to be something "more" beyond the expanding plane of asphalt and concrete that increasingly defines our culture,

I went on to search for transcendence. Today, in my moments of despair during this search, which still continues, I feel an especially important tie to the men on death row.

◀ ▶

But, over the years, I could not have sustained my visits to the men of "G-House" — the name given by the prison to their cellblocks, dictated perhaps by some inscrutable algebra of torture — if the only words the prisoners consistently spoke about the human journey were those of desperation. In fact, I have been drawn to the men because most of them have come to the point where they have also given profound expression to a fundamental faith in life and love — affirming their enduring preciousness, sometimes in Christian imagery, sometimes not. Continually battling against such foes as death and shame and loneliness, the men have at significant moments been carried along by this faith, which, considering their lot afforded by history, has sometimes struck me as improbable. It is a faith that I have shared, in my own way.

One example of the faith the men have displayed was clear to me on a morning that I spent in the spring of 1996 with G-House prisoner Leonard Frazier, who, though only fifty-one, had experienced the latest of several strokes just days earlier. My memories of that morning of our visit still rise vividly before me: Leonard and I sit on stools opposite each other. He is trying to tell me something. Because of his strokes, he can speak only a few words, haltingly. Most of the time he prints with a pencil stub in quarter-inch-high letters, on a battered legal pad the guards have allowed him to bring to our visit. He is frustrated at first, unable to get his point across. He transposes letters, then gives up temporarily. After a few moments, he moves his body awkwardly (he has no feeling in many places) into another position, as if that will help, and tries again. This time I understand: he wants to tell me that he is dying. I am aided in my understanding by his physical appearance: he is almost paper-white and looks worse than I have ever seen him. He smiles faintly at my success in comprehending him, and he begins the slow process of trying to explain something else that is on his mind. Minutes pass. The light in the visiting room accents creases in his face that are, no doubt, the result of the hard life he has known since his childhood in a remote mountain hollow in northern Georgia. I wonder, in fear, what I would do if he experiences another stroke and dies in front of me. He is filled with determination and frustration, not the fear of death, as he wrestles with word after word. Finally I acknowledge that I follow him: he wants to see his children and a sister before he dies, persons he has not visited with in years — individuals he has hurt deeply (the scratches on the legal pad seem to say) by the way he has lived his life. After my acknowledgment, the pain of his moral failures — he was convicted years ago of the beating deaths of an elderly white couple — lingers in his silence for several minutes and reveals his long struggle to come to grips with himself. Eventually he smiles again at my comprehension. And as he does so, this becomes clear to me: as has happened on other visits to death row, the space where the prisoner and I meet becomes hallowed. Faith in the value of life and the power of love reigns there; neither death nor shame — including guilt, the shame caused by our moral failures — triumphs. On the morning of our visit, only a few weeks before a heart attack finally claims his life, Leonard is conveyed from moment to moment by such a faith, which becomes a cry of his heart.

It is a faith that I experienced in a different context on a cold January day in 1985. A small group of believers from Mercer University, where I was teaching, gathered together then with a few friends in a cabin outside of Woodland, Georgia, to ordain me, to send me to the men on death row. On that occasion, we called ourselves the Glad River Congregation — in reference to a passage in Psalm 46 that testifies to the joy-bringing waters of the city of God — and the name has stuck to the Mercer group ever since. Throughout its history of some ten years, the little group had tried to remain true to an Anabaptist conception of church. A trace of salt in the life of a university community, it had met together regularly wherever it could, owned no buildings or other assets, had no budget or paid staff. Its only possession was a scandalous conviction: where two or three are gathered together in the name of a redeeming Love that defies the powers of shame and death, the meaning and destiny of all creation are revealed. Strengthened by powerful words from each person in the congregation, I knew that this conviction was my own as I knelt before the church, and, one by one, its members came to place their hands upon me. Late that afternoon, after I had returned home to my farm, I continued to hear deep within me the congregation's cry of faith.

30

And I heard other cries of faith then, too. Whose could they be? As I wandered across winter fields, I had not yet discovered, of course, the many ties that would bind me to men like Leonard Frazier; nor had I learned that the ultimate reach of so many of the condemned men's understandings of the human story would transcend despair. With my question in mind, I walked out to the end of a pasture where a small stand of hardwood trees rose up, bare black sticks held in relief against the sky by the very last remaining light of the day. I stood there for a long time, letting the bitter chill surround my body, allowing the forces within me to speak of the remarkable day's events and perhaps answer my query. Puzzled, I went back to the house. When I look back on that time now, it seems as if somehow I had begun to hear cries of faith which I would recognize later as coming from the men of G-House, cries that would draw me to them week after week and, with other ties, shape a "call" to be with them.

3

Voices

During the years of my visits with prisoners on Georgia's death row, I have seen myself as the guest of the men who spend their days there. Much of the time, I have been the recipient of my hosts' gifts, especially the stories the men have told me that have reflected their many moods. But I have also had opportunities to offer gifts, words of my own.

When I have had these opportunities, I have often been aware that I have not come alone to the men on the "row." Having sounded within me for years, certain voices other than my own have accompanied me. At times they have spoken through me in various ways. Even when I have had an important chance to speak and have been able to say nothing, there have been moments when I have heard one or another of the voices echo within me, in my silence. Whether audible to my hosts or not, the sometimes contradictory voices of my intellectual and spiritual heritage have powerfully influenced the ways I have understood my meetings with the men — and my times with their families as well.

These are some of the voices.

◀ ▶

It is the late 1980s. In the prison's visiting room, I am sitting with a man who has just learned that one of his family members has been jailed on a drug-related charge. She was a person who came to see him for years, the first to attend college in a family whose forbears were once slaves. Sitting at a ninety-degree angle from me, the man takes off his battered glasses, swings them in front of him, and stares into the hard wire mesh that forms part of the wall of our room. I know what he is thinking, though for the longest time he cannot get the words out: he wants to know why his kinswoman has fallen and why his people's hope has been stifled, over and over. After he finally speaks, he turns slowly around toward me, fixing me with his gaze. His withered pulpwooder's hands hang idly at his sides. The strain of his years of waiting to die is written across his face.

I can say nothing, but I hear a voice within me: that of Nietzsche's madman. I have heard his words ringing inside me since my college days. Racing to the marketplace early one morning, the madman shouts, "I seek God! I seek God!" "Whither is God?" he asks. And he begins to answer his own question: *"We have killed him* — you and I. All of us are his murderers." Then more questions come, exploding into the crowd of onlookers:

What did we do when we unchained this earth from its sun? Whither is it moving now? Whither are we moving now? Away from all suns? Are we not plunging continually? . . . Is there any up or down left? Are we not straying as through an infinite nothing? . . . Has it not become colder? Is not night and more night coming on all the while?

Though the prisoner cannot hear Nietzsche's words inside me, I believe he experiences something of their meaning, deeply. The night descends around us. Cold chills the bone. The room shifts and swirls. We feel the silence, the absence of God, fill the room. The man's questions concerning the fate of his kinswoman and that of all of his people go unanswered. He senses nothing beyond himself to embrace him in his pain — as he needs to be embraced.

As I sit with my friend, I focus on another of the madman's questions: How have we killed God? And I think: Max Weber was right. The "fate of our times" is indeed the "disenchantment of the world." Our rage for what he called "rationalisation and intellectualisation" has eclipsed that which enchants, the sacred. No mystery can live in the net of abstractions that we have cast and recast through the universe. This thought comes to me also: Reason has become divorced from the heart and has been pressed into the service of refined and unparalleled techniques of destruction. And I wonder: How could any God live amid such precise acts of brutality as we humans have committed in the twentieth century? Have we finally broken God's heart? The terrifying presence of Auschwitz — another place of state-sponsored murder — becomes almost palpable to me in the visiting room.

I hear more words of Nietzsche's madman within me:

How shall we, the murderers of all murderers, comfort ourselves?
... Who will wipe this blood off us? What water is there for us to clean ourselves? What festivals of atonement, what sacred games shall we have to invent?

Frightened, I simply sit quietly, in a daze. In the visiting room, as minute after minute passes, silence persists.

◀ ▶

On another occasion, late one afternoon in September of 1991, the prisoner before me is awaiting the time of his execution, just days away. Warren McCleskey and I have talked for almost three hours, longer than allowed. The guards have "forgotten us" for a time. Both Warren and I are weary. Still, his brown face remains alert, full of intelligence, as he begins a short monologue. He speaks about the workings of God's will — something about the difference between a perfect will and how this will is realized in a fallen world. Whatever happens is in some way a result of God's intention, he says quietly, but with great earnestness. He reminds me of something he told me earlier, on a day when one court had stopped his seemingly inexorable movement toward execution:

Life's like a wheel of fortune, you see. Something like that idea of old Lady Fortune in the Middle Ages. She sure was fickle. In life we have our ups and downs. This is a big "up" today. My life has been saved. But we can't take things for granted. Who knows what tomorrow will bring? The main thing is to see that God is in control of all the ups and downs. Every little thing. And in the end, it's all for the best. As a Christian, I accept this. That's where my peace comes from. Yeah, I'm happy today. But I can't get too confident.

After he presents these ideas, he pauses, and I reflect silently on the fact that he has been meditating on such matters for more than a decade of imprisonment on death row, trying to come to grips with a terrifying fate. I marvel to myself at the astonishing equanimity of the man — and at other things as well: his using his scant resources to help other prisoners in his cellblock buy stamps, his role as peacemaker on the "row," his value as a trusted friend to so many of those facing sentences of death, both the scared newcomer and the old-timer beginning to crack under years of stress.

I begin to think of some of the details of the harsh reality of his life; they are things that Warren has struggled to face in prison and that we have talked about from time to time during the years we have known one another. I recall his descriptions of his difficult days when he was growing up in the black "skid row" section of Marietta, Georgia, where his mother and stepfather ran a gambling establishment in their home. Domestic violence recurred continually in his presence when he was young. At one point he walked into his house just seconds after his mother had shot and killed her abusive spouse. I think of how Warren sold bootleg whiskey in his early years to help put food on the table and how, later, he led a life of crime — to survive — as a young man. I remember his sharing with me the tremendous feelings of guilt he has experienced because of his involvement with three other men in a 1978 furniture-store robbery during which white Atlanta policeman Frank Schlatt was murdered. He has regretted his involvement deeply, even though — he has maintained all along — he did not shoot the policeman. He has also regretted denying his participation in the robbery at his trial. His words about the crimes have always been compelling to me.

Immersed in my thoughts, I contemplate what happened in the courts to Warren and his three African American co-defendants. He was sentenced to death as the person who had actually done the killing, although there were no eyewitnesses to the shooting, and police never located the murder weapon. Two of the other men received multiple life sentences. A third co-defendant — who testified against Warren, saying that Warren had confessed to him that he was the shooter — was allowed to plead guilty to charges less than murder and received a twenty-year sentence.

I go on to reflect on the landmark 1987 U.S. Supreme Court ruling that (by a one-vote margin) ignored, in effect, the relevance of an exacting statistical analysis and thus rejected Warren's appeals attorneys' argument that capital punishment in Georgia was meted out in a racially biased fashion. It was not enough that his attorneys had shown that in Georgia a defendant charged with killing a white person was 4.3 times more likely to get the death penalty than a defendant charged with killing someone black. To be granted relief from the court on the issue of racism, a petitioner would have to prove that there was bias in his or her particular case — an extraordinarily difficult burden of proof.

At this point in my reflections, I wonder for an instant why Warren is no longer speaking. Then the answer comes to me. His pause means, of course, that he is giving me a chance to reply to his analysis of the divine will. After five years of visiting him, I should understand his ways well enough. I stall for time, not knowing exactly what to say. I look into the distance. A woman and child leave the visiting room across the hall — the room where families visit "diagnostics," new prisoners who are not under the sentence of death and who are being "processed." But before walking very far, the two turn around and watch the man they have apparently been visiting return to his cellblock. The woman takes the little girl's hand and makes a waving motion to the man just before he disappears from view. Then the child hugs the woman's leg as a trap gate in the distance slams shut. The woman picks up the child, and they move toward the prison exit.

As they go, I begin to speak. The voice of Albert Camus echoes within me, influencing the words I utter: "Life. Everything. It's all so much more than I can grasp, so inexplicable." I go on in this vein for a little while, carefully avoiding Camus's term "absurd" to be gentle, for I know that Warren's theological beliefs, adhered to in faith, may help get him through the coming days. Soon I run out of words to say and sink back into myself. I wonder in vain why my friend, whose humanity has moved me so greatly, should be on the verge of such a terrible death, and I hear Camus commenting about the world's "denseness" and "strangeness," its "unreasonable silence," which gives birth to our experience of the absurd. As I grapple with Warren's fate, he sits before me with his legs stretched out in front of him; he looks almost relaxed.

I think he knows that I have traveled with him as far as I can go on this day, and he accepts this with a love and understanding characteristic of him. I simply do not know the things he does. At the most, I can entertain the slim possibility that the hidden God of the Bible, veiled and inscrutable, inhabits the "unreasonable silence" with us.

Moments pass, and I hear more of Camus's words as he speaks of Sisyphus, the "absurd hero": "His scorn of the gods, his hatred of death, and his passion for life won him that unspeakable penalty in which the whole being is exerted toward accomplishing nothing." He was condemned by the deities "to ceaselessly rolling a rock to the top of a mountain, whence the stone would fall back of its own weight." I know that Sisyphus was heroic for Camus because of the lucidity and resoluteness with which the Corinthian king faced his absurd fate, represented by the rock. I also know that the Frenchman patterned his ideal of the radically honest thinker after the mythological figure: such a thinker is someone who faces squarely his or her own absurd plight as a seeker of knowledge in a world that must remain essentially opaque. The philosopher's voice sounds within me as he argues that in "the hour of consciousness" when Sisyphus pauses after the rock has just fallen, "he is superior to his fate. He is stronger than the rock." And Camus must be on the right track, I tell myself: there is something important in the fully conscious, uncompromising encounter with reality. There is value, for example, in maintaining the tension between mind and being, not surrendering to answers about ultimate things when one cannot honestly defend such answers. But on this day, as Warren turns to small talk in the remaining moments of our visit, I do not feel stronger than the rock.

Nor do I on another day, in the last hours of Warren's life, when he takes leave of me and a few other friends and family members. Georgia's Board of Pardons and Paroles has refused to commute his sentence to life in prison, despite learning what two of Warren's former jurors have explained to its members. The two would never have voted for his death years ago had they known what Warren's appeals attorneys had been able to establish after his trial, even though the State had tried to hide the fact: a key trial witness, a county-jail prisoner who had testified that Warren had confessed to him that he had shot Officer Schlatt, had been "planted" by police, it turned out, in a cell next to Warren's and had been offered leniency in exchange for his testimony.

(Both jurors had put little stock in the obviously self-serving testimony of Warren's co-defendant, who had also claimed that Warren had confessed the murder to him.) Camus's voice resounds within me again, and my experience of the absurd overwhelms me, even as Warren places his hands on my shoulders, looks straight into my eyes, and tells me in effect that his faith is stronger than death.

As we part, neither of us knows things that will later make his death seem even more absurd to me. Neither of us can guess that he will have to endure eight long hours after his scheduled time of execution at seven o'clock in the evening. We do not know, in other words, that the courts will issue a number of stays that will delay his death and that he will, in fact, be electrocuted shortly after three o'clock the next morning. As he looks me in the eyes, we do not know what he will have to go through at the end: In the span of less than an hour, he will be strapped into the electric chair, begin his final statement, learn of the last stay, be led from the chair and execution chamber . . . and return in a few minutes to die there, after he has spoken his final words, including this sentence directed to Officer Frank Schlatt's family: "I pray that you would find it in your heart to forgive me for my participation in the crime that caused the loss of your loved one."

➤ ➤

I think of another visit with a death-row prisoner, less than a year-and-a-half later: Larry Lonchar, a white man who was convicted in 1987 for murdering three other white people over a gambling debt. Waiting for a judge to sign an execution order, he has given up his appeals and is resolved to die soon. He has been talking angrily for some minutes about "those lawyers," his appeals attorneys, who cannot be trusted, he feels. They will tell you anything, promise you the moon, he explains, in order to keep you alive, so that they can continue the appeals process, keep up their fight for a principle. They really do not care about the individual prisoner. As he talks, he swings his arms through the air and cuts our common space into fragments. He has spoken and acted this way for the five years that I have known him — years when his depression has been so profound that medication has scarcely helped him, a time when the life of faith has made no sense to him. Looking toward the visiting-room door, he says that if he were to allow his appeals to go forward, the most he could hope for would be to spend the rest of his life in prison. And he knows what that means. Now approaching middle age, he has been in and out of reform schools and prisons since he was thirteen. Early parole is a joke, he exclaims. He is smart enough to know that. The political climate is too mean for that. He is shouting now. He rants that his life has no meaning. Others in the visiting room — a couple of attorneys and their clients — are staring at us. He gets up from his stool, picks up a piece of a candy wrapper left over from last weekend's visits, crushes it into a ball, and flicks it into a nearby plastic trash can. Pacing back and forth along the cinder-block wall in front of me, he becomes quiet.

Finally he sits down again on the stool next to me, but his back is toward me. As has happened before in this man's presence, I begin to hear something that Viktor Frankl said in regard to prisoners in the Nazi death camps: "Woe to him who saw no more sense in his life, no aim, no purpose, and therefore no point in carrying on. He was soon lost." I turn over in my mind the Viennese psychiatrist's powerful argument: Psychologically and spiritually, we can get through the worst of crises if we have some meaning in life to sustain us. Such meaning is unique to each person and calls out to us to be realized. It draws us out from our constricted and painful inner spaces. With Frankl's words inside me, I begin talking to my friend, who still has his back turned to me. I remind him of the letters he frequently writes to his mother, whose health is poor. It has become clear to me that these letters are, for her, a vital sign of his love, though he does not appreciate this fact fully. Eventually I ask him if his acts of love toward this woman — whom he admires for her struggle, with the help of welfare payments, to care for her children after her marriage had failed — could be a source of meaning for him, an important reason to continue to live with dignity.

After several seconds, he turns slightly toward me, acknowledging my question, variations of which I have raised with good effect with other prisoners. Indeed, I have also raised versions of the question with Larry, during a couple of prior visits, but with no success. This time he looks upward and shakes his head back and forth, staring into space. "I just don't want to talk about it all," he says. "It hurts too much." Perhaps he is thinking in part of the chaotic family in which he was raised — a family, as his siblings have made clear, that he saw torn apart by alcohol abuse and racked by outbursts of rage, such as the time his father repeatedly stomped on Larry's mother's bare feet with his boot heels. I think of how, knowing of my interest in childhood trauma, Larry has devotedly scoured two daily newspapers in search of relevant articles for me but has seldom been able to face his own trauma in my presence. I wonder if I should press my question.

After a minute or two, I decide to drop the question. And I ask myself: Should I resume my efforts as an advocate of meaning on another day, stalking this man, bobbing and weaving, almost as if I were a prizefighter looking for a way to break through the barrier he has put up around his pain, his entire inner life? Or should I simply stick to sports, which he likes, and try to help him get his mind off his problems for a few minutes? Is he simply too depressed to entertain the possibility of deep meaning? I am overpowered by these questions on this particular day. Frankl's voice is stilled. But I know I will hear it during other visits with Larry as I face his despair, once again, in the days before his death, which seems to be imminent.

And I do hear the voice again — for years — in my visits with him. After learning that one of his brothers is threatening to commit suicide if the execution is carried out, Larry decides to resume the appeals process just minutes before his scheduled electrocution. But his resolve to live is hardly firm. Beset by a sense of worthlessness that has accompanied him much of his life, he continues to be plagued with hopelessness and confusion and changes his mind several times about his appeals. At one point, desperately searching for meaning just before another date with death, he decides to resume his appeals once again so that he can arrange to donate his organs; when his plan fails, he once more seeks his electrocution. Eventually, in November of 1996, he is executed. When the first burst of electricity fails to kill him, a second finally does the job. In the hours before his death, he tells me that he has found the Lord, and thus meaning in life; in the same breath, he relates that he is still depressed and does not really mind dying.

◀ ▶

It is a day in the early 1990s. I am in the visiting room with a young African American man who is awaiting word from his lawyer about an agreement with a district attorney, an agreement that could save him from execution. The young man is surprisingly composed. I am on edge. So much is at stake in the hours and days ahead.

40

Though the prisoner left school with the equivalent of about a fourth-grade education, he is full of insight. On this day he is asking me questions, but not legal questions. He is eager to learn what I think of a black woman writer I once mentioned to him in passing: Toni Morrison. He knows I am teaching one of her books in a university class. I do not seem to be in the right frame of mind to engage his questions, so he moves to another topic. Capable of that consistent give-and-take upon which the deepest friendships are based, he proceeds to tell me of a theory of the black family that he has come up with. It is a theory he offers in response to a question that he and several others in his cellblock have been wrestling with lately: Why do many family members of prisoners fail, over the years, to give emotional support to their loved ones behind bars? Not having seen any of his relatives in years, he talks slowly and with authority, saying that for now he can speak only about the black family. As he speaks, I reflect on things he once told me: He has grown up, matured, in prison. Here he has become a man, learned much of what is important in life, learned to "act with the mind instead of a knife." I wonder if this man, who over the years has become so important to me, such a friend, will make it, survive death row. He notices that my attention is for some reason diverted, smiles, and begins again. In slave days, members of black families had to learn to turn loose of each other emotionally, he figures, so as not to be destroyed by loss when one of them was sold down the river by the master. What do I think of the theory? he asks. Do many black families today carry on this tradition of "letting go" when their kinfolks end up in jail or prison?

Before I begin to try to answer his questions, I notice the fierceness of concentration about him, which I have come to admire greatly. I tell him he reminds me of a Zen master. He wants to know what that is, and I explain briefly. I talk of things I have learned over the years from reading D. T. Suzuki, the great interpreter of Buddhism to the West — someone whose voice shapes mine for a minute or two. The Zen master teaches that we should cultivate the "no-mind" — detached from, emptied of, the thousand distractions of the grasping ego. In this state of attentiveness, we are capable of receiving the fullness of the present moment. We can listen and respond with spontaneous ease. We can experience real empathy for others. Genuine intersubjectivity occurs. My friend smiles again (this time, at the level of my diction) and asks if I think that the black slave families ever achieved this kind of "detach-

41

ment." I am moved profoundly by his question, his imaginative leap, and my mind suddenly becomes empty of everything but the present moment, just as Suzuki says it is when our experience is the most compelling. My friend is before me, filling my field of vision: an unschooled black man, imprisoned on death row, his life hanging by a thread. I begin to discover him anew. Empty too, he is making discoveries of his own.

⋖ ⋗

I think of yet another encounter in prison — in early 1994 — in which a moment of discovery figures prominently. My "host" and I are reminiscing about Chris Burger, who was executed some months previously. For the first time since Chris's death, we are able to get enough distance to talk over the zany antics of a person we both knew well and whose friendship we valued so much. At one point, the man recalls the time when Chris sensed the tension in the cellblock building up and felt the need for some comic relief. So our friend stripped down to his underwear, donned his bath towel as a cape, held out an open pillowcase for "goodies," and bounded from cell to cell "trick or treating." After repeating and relishing key details of the story, both the storyteller and I are doubled over and in tears from our laughter — at a time when a recent court ruling has placed his life in grave jeopardy.

Suddenly, something both simple and profound occurs to me as I look at the man sitting across from me: the wonder of his existence. I grasp afresh the fact that he does not *have* to be, of course. He is called into being. I realize that each thing that exists is a mysterious presence. The voice of Martin Heidegger is mingled with mine as I try to explain to my friend how it is to be gripped by, astonished by, being. And I think to myself of a time when I was a twenty-year-old student of philosophy, studying at the university in Freiburg, Germany, where Heidegger had once taught. I remember the summer day when I took what I believed to be the sage's way along a narrow, wandering path in the dense forest above the city, where he had lived for years. I turned suddenly into a bright clearing, stood in the full flood of sunlight, and looked out at Freiburg below in the distance, its dark red stone cathedral rising from its center. At that moment, I knew the underlying experience that had motivated the philosopher all his life: he was seized by wonder in the face of being, manifested in the greatest and smallest of things. It is the same kind of experience that I have now, sitting in the prison visiting room — just after I have talked of Chris Burger's antics and felt both laughter and the fear of death pass through me.

After a while, when my visit with Chris's friend is over and I am walking toward my pickup, I think of other days when I have been led to this experience of wonder, with yet other "hosts" on the row. Given sufficient space and light by men facing sentences of death, these experiences are, I realize, among the greatest gifts I have ever received. Indeed, they are gifts of such magnitude that they seem to point at times toward a Giver of all gifts somehow acting through the prisoners sitting immediately before me in the visiting room.

I am with another man — a few years ago. He is the mentally ill death-row prisoner whose stint in "isolation" made me so enraged on an earlier visit. On this day, when the man comes into the visiting room, I sense immediately that things are different. The deep sadness that usually fills his soul has abated somewhat. He begins to talk lucidly of his struggle with the distinct persons who vie within him for recognition. He tells how ashamed he has been of this struggle and how he kept his pain to himself for years, thinking at times that he would break under the pressure of holding the truth inside. And he relates how he finally found the courage to begin to talk about it all to an investigator working with his appeals attorney on his case. Since he has opened up, he explains, things are a little better. After pausing for a while, he goes on to talk about one of his personalities and wonders if this force of death within him, which has driven him to attempt suicide time and again, will finally get its revenge against him for his revelations to the investigator. He is afraid, knowing that his terror-filled struggle is far from over. But he is also proud of his truthfulness, of his courage in facing his demons.

I reflect briefly on the trust he places in me and on the moments when we have been truly present to one other, and I become aware of something that I have often felt in my visits with the men on death row. It is something that Martin Buber proclaimed in writings that I read years ago: A person's humanity does not reside in him or her alone. In-

43

stead, it is a product of relationship and thus emerges when an *I* meets a *Thou;* it comes ultimately from the realm between them. As I tell my friend how moved I am by our time together, I remark how our very lives seem to grow out of the space "between" us, and Buber's voice rises within me. In response, my friend's eyes light up behind his thick glasses, which he pushes back on his nose with his index finger. Grinning widely, he runs his hand across the salt-and-pepper stubble on his face. Apparently his razor has been taken away again — a precaution against suicide. I simply enjoy his warmth and good humor for a few seconds. Then I think: How uncanny it is that two persons can actually *meet* and truly find themselves in the encounter. And I tell myself: There, in the space where *I* meet *Thou,* even the sun was created, and being itself finds its origin.

◀ ▶

It is late 1993, and I am visiting Chris Burger's mother and stepfather at a time when Chris is nearing execution. We are sitting around a dining-room table in their trailer and drinking coffee. After talking for hours, the three of us seem to have nothing else to say. We understand what is about to happen. We have known one another for years and are comfortable with the absence of words. Without asking, Chris's stepfather gives me a biscuit from the batch I know he made fresh earlier in the day. As I slowly eat, a steady rain beats against the trailer roof and fills the depressions in a red clay path outside, which I can see through the window in front of me.

Before I go, my friends ask me if I will "offer up" a prayer — something I have done countless times, on other visits, sitting at this table. I do not start speaking right away, for prayer is a mysterious act, whose uses and reach I scarcely understand; I always struggle for words. As I consider what I might say, I hear Dietrich Bonhoeffer's voice within me, calling out from the time of the Third Reich and restraining any tendency I might have toward traditional religious piety that fails to take seriously our worldly existence:

> I feel a resistance to everything "religious" growing in me. . . . I am not a religious type. But I am constantly thinking of God and of Christ, and genuineness, life, freedom, and mercy mean a lot to

me. Only the religious trappings they wear I find so uncomfortable.

How do we speak of God — without religion . . . ? How do we speak (or perhaps we cannot now even "speak" as we used to) in a "secular" way about "God"? In what way are we "religionless-secular" Christians, in what way are we the ἐκ-κλησία, those who are called forth, not regarding ourselves from a religious point of view as specially favored, but rather as belonging wholly to the world? In that case Christ is no longer an object of religion, but something quite different, really the Lord of the world. But what does that mean? What is the place of worship and prayer in a religionless situation?

It is not the religious act that makes the Christian, but participation in the sufferings of God in the secular life.

Jesus calls us not to a new religion, but to life.

Finally, I speak. The refrigerator to my back whirs lightly while I ask, in effect, simply that we may know that we are loved; it is all I know to say.

After I pray, I wonder how much Bonhoeffer's words have been audible to the man and woman across from me, for I hardly form the words of the Baptist prayers they hear in church each Sunday. Sitting quietly at the table, I realize that much of what I do or say is somehow conditioned by the German theologian's assertions — and questions, which I cannot answer any better than he could when he formulated them, decades ago, in the prison cell in which the Nazis confined him. His search is my own. Though I have felt that he sometimes too eagerly embraced our secular age, I have long sensed the importance of taking it as the starting point for all serious theological inquiry. I have also sensed that his vision of a secular Christianity was much more than a facile accommodation to a fashionable scientism. It was ultimately a vision based on the doctrine of the incarnation: an affirmation that the Word was indeed made flesh in creation, in the world.

For a minute or two, my thoughts about such matters fade away, and I simply listen to the rain, which continues without ceasing. Soon I recall something else that Bonhoeffer said; it was as close as he got to answering his question about how to speak of God in these days: "God is beyond in the midst of our life." Then I ask again and again inside of myself that the man and woman before me, all of us, may be loved and that we may know this. And I think: The experience of this love is the "beyond" in our midst, the presence of the eternal Thou.

With brief good-byes and embraces, I leave my hosts.

It is late on a summer afternoon in 1995, and I am in my small basement office talking on the telephone with the mother of Darrell Devier, a man who was executed two months earlier and whom I knew in the last year of his life. I stare at the large gray table before me that serves as my desk. Its paint is peeling badly in places, especially near the back, at the base of a row of brightly colored, neatly arranged books. It was once the examining table of my wife's grandfather before he gave up his medical practice during the Second World War. I have been alone all day and have spoken to no one, save Darrell's mother.

As is always the case when I call her, she has invited me into the inner circle of her life. A strong woman who has been full of faith, she is telling me once again of a vision she had, years ago, of her son coming down the steps of the county jail in the city where he was tried. Until Darrell's death, she took the vision as God's assurance that her son would one day be free, not only of his sentence of death but also of prison. Now, weeks after Darrell's execution, her heart broken, she faces the possibility that her faith will shatter against the sharp edge of reality. After she speaks, I ask her if her vision might entail a kind of freedom that exceeds her literal interpretation, and I remind her of the frequently symbolic language of Scripture, which often confronts us with the unexpected. She pauses, as if to reflect on my statement; then I hear her begin to weep.

Greatly moved by her sadness, I fumble for a few words. "You love him very much, I know," I say after a while. In her heart she has reached a place where I cannot easily join her. Still, in my awkward way, I am with her, somehow a part of her and her fate. And in the brief time of silence before we say good-bye, I hear the voice of fellow Georgian Alice Walker within me. The writer's words come from her character Shug

Avery in the novel *The Color Purple*: "But one day when I was sitting quiet and feeling like a motherless child, which I was, it come to me: that feeling of being part of everything, not separate at all. I knew that if I cut a tree, my arm would bleed."

Sitting before a chipped and peeling gray table on a hot August afternoon, I begin to feel something of what Shug Avery does — if only with a fraction of the heart's capacity. My sense of kinship with all of creation grows, and I begin to glimpse the range and rightness of her perception. After my friend's mother and I finish our conversation and I hang up the phone, I am caught up in vivid images that move deep within me: time seems to disappear as I think of people and things whose being I have experienced so intensely that I have felt a part of them.

Memories of Darrell's mother flow through me. I recall one day after visitation at the prison. She and I are standing together in the prison parking lot. I am listening to her tell her story, and I feel her struggle profoundly: Years ago, she was beaten savagely by her alcoholic husband, now dead. He was a man whose violence and drunkenness often landed him in jail. He frequently threatened her life, and on at least one occasion he shaved her head while he had her pinned to the floor of the shack in which they were living, as their young son Darrell watched. As she talks, I look into her worn face, which has all the strength of her kin — the poor white women of the Depression-era South — highlighted in Walker Evans' photographs. And there on the steaming asphalt, I feel a part of her: a woman who, after her own battle with alcohol, worked long and tirelessly to support her two sons, found solace in a God who suffered with her, and who year after year drove one wheezing, battered car after another to visit Darrell in prison, until the day he died.

Also within me are images of the mother of the twelve-year-old white girl Darrell murdered. She and I are sitting in her living room on an evening years after her daughter's death. Along with one of Darrell's appeals attorneys, I have come to ask her if she can somehow find the strength, the grace, to request that the state's Board of Pardons and Paroles spare Darrell's life. Such a request might save another mother, and perhaps her, too, the anguish of a lifetime. I sense quickly that she cannot do such a thing. Still, her sorrow is mine — I feel a part of her — as she expresses the devastation of her loss. Once more caught up in her sorrow, I again feel a part of her on another evening, a few days later: she is inside the prison walls, counting away the minutes, awaiting Darrell's execution, which she chooses not to witness, while I stand outside those walls with a small group of persons who do not wish the man who murdered her daughter to die.

Yet other images that move within me are those of Darrell himself. I recall moments during our visits when his rambling but deeply moving accounts of the events of his life make it mine. Once, when he was a small boy, he watched his father, who would often beat him to the floor, cut off the heads of the family's kittens and threaten that his son could be next. At some point, the boy turned to sniffing glue to try to find some refuge from his violent world. He also began to take drugs and drink, eventually dropping out of school after failing the eighth grade. His marriage, when he was seventeen, went sour, as did another later. Struggling to help support two children, he was unable to overcome his past. One day he killed. He raped a young girl and took her life by crushing her skull with rocks. He was twenty-four years old at the time.

His last days come back to me. At that time, his anguish wells up from within him as he reflects on all of these things, as well as others. I am a part of him then, and his pain cuts at me as I listen to him speak of the outcome of a recent neuropsychological evaluation requested by his appeals attorneys: He suffered brain damage as a result of his mother's drinking when she was pregnant with him and as a consequence of his own heavy consumption of drugs and alcohol. Such damage, which has made it difficult for him to control his impulses, was only aggravated by the marijuana he smoked on the day of the murder. In the final hours before his death, his hurt and bewilderment become unbearable for both of us as he wrestles with the question of God. It is a question that he can never quite utter directly, but one that almost consumes him: Where are You?

Other memories, images, that move within me have to do with Darrell's older brother. I feel a part of him, too, as we talk together: at the truck stop across from the prison when he returns from a visit with Darrell, in front of the small-town funeral home while we are waiting for his brother's service to begin, and on the telephone the night after his brother has been buried. At the truck stop, his anxiety unsettles me as he tears at the edges of the paper place-mat in front of him. At the funeral home, the look in his eyes is arresting as he tries to express his love for Darrell, his feelings of overpowering sadness at how his brother's life turned out, and his anger at a system of "justice" that he senses preys upon the weak. One night later, the puzzlement in his voice on the telephone affects me deeply as he tries to understand how he has escaped Darrell's fate. Perhaps his own life took another turn, he muses, because he was a bit older, had a break or two at just the right time. Maybe. He does not know for sure, he says, as his words trail off slowly, leaving only his sorrow — and his love.

The images within me seem to have no end. They include those of yet another death-row prisoner, executed in September of 1987: Wes McCorquodale, something of a legend to Darrell and many others awaiting electrocution, someone whose antics Darrell and I would talk about. I think of one day in the visiting room when Wes — a huge, tattooed ex-biker, a hulking bear of a white man — is relating a story to me with glee. I am a part of him, caught up in his joy, as I listen to him. He tells how on yard call recently a fellow prisoner splashed water on him from a huge puddle, then pranced tauntingly on the other side of it, where he thought he was safe. But the much slower "bear" was not to be outdone. He dove headfirst into the standing water. His "belly flop" drenched his taunter and filled a small crowd of onlookers with delight.

My memory of this episode brings with it other images. I remember an afternoon a few years ago, long after Wes's execution, when I am reading a passage from a letter written to me by one of Wes's friends, who did time with him on death row. The letter writer, who is still imprisoned but is no longer under the sentence of death, describes another occasion when a downpour drenched the exercise yard. I feel especially close to both men — I am a part of them — as I read about a further exploit of the "bear," and its meaning for his fellow prisoners:

> One day while a handful of us were on the yard and playing in the mud, an officer working the guard tower tried to stop our fun. We were laughing and splashing around like fish when the guard in the tower slid his window open and yelled for us to quit playing in the water and to get out of the mud. Well, Wes, being true to his nature, dropped his shorts and "mooned" the officer. The officer had a spasm of anger and called on his radio for other guards to

break up the "disturbance" on the yard. When they arrived, Wes, innocent as a lamb, explained that he didn't really "moon" the guard in the tower. He said that he had only lowered his shorts to remove some sand. We rolled with laughter as once again Wes had given us something no one could take from us.

Still other images, charged with feeling, move through me and fill my soul with more of the stuff of Wes's life. One day in the last months before his death, his enthusiasm becomes my own as he exclaims over the poetry of one of the prisoners in his cellblock: he writes with a chisel in a world of concrete and steel. I am moved deeply by Wes's capacity for friendship as he asks if I, a college teacher, would visit the man and encourage him in his efforts.

I also remember another day, near the very end of Wes's life. It is the last time just the two of us have the chance to talk together alone. We speak for a long time about one of our favorite themes: the simple pleasures of hard work on the land, something we both have experienced. Then, in our last couple of minutes, he tells me that among the witnesses to his execution will be his father — a man who attempted to save Wes's life at trial, trying to explain what had gone wrong, how the breakup of his family had affected Wes deeply when the boy was in his teens. Is it right that his father, who wants to be with him at the end, should see the electrocution? Wes seems to be asking me this question, though not quite directly. I say nothing. Having no idea how one makes such judgments, I must leave him questioning. And as I do, I feel his life intensely; I feel a part of him.

I continue to feel this way in the moments immediately after our visit. Once I leave him and walk toward the prison's last gate, I imagine him in the room by himself, waiting to be brought back to his cell. His large body stooped over, his hands balled into fists and pressed hard against the wire mesh running the length of the room, he is staring at the floor. Nearly thirty-five, he contemplates some of his sad and terrifying past actions: how he lost his life in daily bouts of drunkenness, and how, on a day in 1974 when he was drinking heavily, he took the life of a seventeen-year-old young white woman whose body he mutilated before he killed her. He is just the kind of person to reflect in this way after I have left him; others who know him well have told me so. He is, in other words, just the kind of person to have such a confrontation

50

with his shadow, that part of the personality, as Jung reminded us, that we like to keep hidden from both ourselves and others.

I recall yet another day. Wes has said his final good-byes, and several of us — relatives, friends, and one of his appeals attorneys — have left the prison to go to a motel not far away. With not much more than two hours left in Wes's life, the attorney and I are sitting in the motel dining room. A gifted constitutional lawyer and theological thinker, the man has worked not only for a principle he believes in — the immorality of the death penalty — but also on behalf of a man he has come to care about deeply, even love. The lawyer and I eat and drink together, have little to say. We wait as long as we can: until the time of execution. Then we go to a motel room where we join Wes's family members and a couple of his friends — among them, a friend of mine, Murphy Davis, a pastor who has visited and encouraged Wes for years. We stand there, seven or eight of us, lodged between pieces of motel furniture, as Wes's sister prays that her brother and her father, who is witnessing the death of his son, may somehow find the strength to get through the hour. With words of such power that they reach further than the night that is falling, she also prays for the family of Wes's victim. As I listen to her, I become a part of all who hear her and of all those she prays for, even though I have never met the family of the person Wes killed. I also feel that I am somehow a part of someone else I have never met whose violence horrifies me as much as Wes's: the executioner, who sends the voltage through Wes's muscle and sinew.

Seemingly within the span of a moment, all of these images — beginning with those of Darrell Devier's mother — flow through me. As do others: memories, for example, of my wife's grandfather, who gave us the land I now farm. Images of the nonhuman also come to me: the good land itself, the soft pine wood of the peeling gray table before me, and. . . . As a result of my experience, a powerful truth is reconfirmed: I am a part of all the people and things of the earth. Indeed, nothing in creation stands completely apart from me.

Occasions such as this one have been rare, but when they have come over the years, I have known the rightness of Shug Avery's words. Feeling my imagination stretched to its limits, I have sensed that each least particle of creation is a part of every other thing in a universe whose ultimate purpose is the fulfillment of a Love of infinite grandeur. In my meetings with the men on death row and their families, I have not al-

51

ways acted on the basis of such insight, such revelation. At times, its vividness has faded. I have simply stumbled along then, prey to the divisiveness and bitterness of a vision too small to save. But after a while, I have been guided back toward an inclusiveness of spirit that we can only receive as a gift. Hearing Alice Walker's voice within me, I have known "that if I cut a tree, my arm would bleed."

4

A Dream of the Tattered Man

This was not a part of the dream. We strained under the weight of our burden. There were some ten or twelve of us: family, friends, and one or two others who never knew him. Moving slowly, we took the hill in short, measured steps. His father's hands — strong, boat-maker's hands — changed their grip several times before we turned into the small clearing that made up the burial plot. We passed the graves of the few persons who had found their rest here before him; among them were other executed prisoners, whose stories I did not know. Finally, a recently dug grave lay open before us, the red earth still fresh and damp in the May sunlight. We lowered the coffin into place, where Joe had wanted to be buried, far from his home in Beaufort, South Carolina, far from his family. A few days before his execution, just before signing over to me the care of his body, he had asked me to honor this wish — a job that I had viewed with fear and trembling.

Jubilee Partners, the intentional Christian community whose cemetery we had reached, had worked for years with refugees from around the world. The little community in north Georgia had provided its guests with simple shelter and food, taught them language skills, and served as a stopping-over place on their journey. The community had agreed to make a place for him, too, Joseph Holcombe Mulligan, also a refugee of sorts, at the end of his journey.

Our service did not last long. We shared our love, our grief, our frustration. George Kendall, a young ACLU attorney, spoke of his sadness after losing friend after friend. He had worked almost without ceasing during the last several weeks to save Joe's life and had seen seven other of his clients meet Joe's fate in the past few years. George's words touched us all. We sang of a "balm in Gilead," and we prayed to feel its healing power.

That day at the Jubilee Partners community, I thought of something my wife's uncle, Joe's trial judge, had told me at a family gathering in Columbus, Georgia, some two years earlier. The judge, who had also presided at Jerome Bowden's trial, had just finished giving a talk to the Sunday-school class in the Presbyterian church where he had been a longtime member. In the talk, he had explained that the death penalty serves the important role of restoring "peace and good order" in a community where a grievous wrong has been committed.

Listening to the then-retired judge, a man I admired a lot for his love for his family, I had sensed once again the chasm between him and those who viewed capital punishment as I did — a chasm that reached deeply into my family's history. After he had spoken, I had tried to close this gap. I had tried to explain to him that the death penalty hardly ever applies to the wealthy, that race often plays an important role in its application, that it has taken the lives of innocent persons, and that it calls forth our worst impulses, such as revenge, rather than fostering genuine peace or good order. For all my effort, my words had failed to convince; they had never really reached the heart, the only place where genuine transformation can take place.

As I stood at Jubilee's cemetery and thought of my conversation with the judge, I wondered if I ever would find the right words to articulate my views about the death penalty. I wondered, too, if I would ever find the words to explain my view of Joe Mulligan, a man who had been convicted of a double murder over a decade earlier and who had been executed in Georgia's electric chair on May 15, 1987. I left Jubilee not knowing the answers to my questions.

I continue to look for the words.

◄ ►

I can still hear Joe affirming his innocence. Once he did this near the end of his life, as he and I awaited the outcome of his Pardons and Paroles Board petition, which sought to have his death sentence commuted to life in prison. Having refused to accept a plea bargain for a life sentence before his trial, he had held to his claim of innocence since his arrest. Unlike Joe, his co-defendant in the 1974 murder case had cut a deal with the authorities: arrested months before police had finally located Joe, Timothy Helms at some point had agreed to testify as a witness for the State in exchange for complete immunity from prosecution.

Helms was a twenty-year-old Marine at the time of the killings. He testified that he and Joe had been friends for about a year when Joe offered to pay him a thousand dollars to drive him from Beaufort, South Carolina, to Columbus, Georgia, on Easter weekend of 1974. En route, Joe, who was twenty-two then, supposedly had remarked that he was going to "ice" someone — a comment that Helms said he had not taken seriously. According to Helms, Joe's target that weekend had turned out to be Army captain Patrick Doe, who had been stationed at Fort Benning, a part of the greater Columbus community, and who had been in the process of divorcing Joe's sister. Helms testified that Joe had shot not only Doe but also the captain's girlfriend, Marian Miller. The prosecution's star witness explained that both killings had happened in Doe's car after the three men had picked up Miller on the way to a party. The deaths had occurred in the first hour of Easter Sunday morning.

The motive for the shootings? The State alleged that Joe had planned to gain access to insurance money due to his sister upon Doe's death — if he could kill the captain before the Does' divorce was final. Joe had to kill Marian Miller because she was a witness to his brother-in-law's murder.

Joe — who, like Helms, Doe, and Miller, was African American — told his court-appointed trial attorney — who was white — that he had been in Beaufort at the time of the murders in Columbus. When an expert testified in court that Joe's fingerprint had been found on Doe's car, Joe leaned over to his lawyer and admitted to him something important that he had not disclosed to him earlier: he had been in Columbus only hours before the shootings. But he went on to explain that Doe, Helms, and Miller had driven him to Atlanta before the time of the killings, and from there he had taken a bus to return home. Thus, he continued to maintain his innocence.

When the attorney learned that he had been deceived, he felt, as he put it later, that he was "sunk in the water." His predicament was not brought on by Joe alone, for the lawyer had failed to interview the State's witnesses before trial. Indeed, he had even failed to request the State's witness list — which would have included the name of the fingerprint expert — so he was completely surprised by the man's testimony. In brief, the attorney, who was working on a shoestring budget and thus without co-counsel or investigators or experts, hardly put on the kind of defense a person of wealth would have had.

In the lawyer's judgment, family witnesses he had told the jury he would present to corroborate Joe's alibi had been discredited by the fingerprint evidence. Consequently, he did not call on them at the trial's guilt-innocence phase. This was a mistake, in the view of Joe's Pardons and Paroles Board petition, which argues that the witnesses were not necessarily lying and contends that the attorney still might have used them in a manner consistent with his opening statement: to place Joe in Beaufort on Easter Sunday morning of 1974. Such testimony would have supported — if not completely confirmed — Joe's revised story. At the trial's subsequent penalty phase, for which the defense lawyer had not done any real preparation, he had the job of pleading that Joe be given a life sentence instead of death. But he continued to feel that he could not call the — in his mind, compromised — family members as witnesses. In fact, the attorney presented no witnesses or evidence at all at either phase of the proceedings. By the trial's end, the jury members never heard what Joe claimed to be the true version of events, much less why they should believe it. Nor had they heard from persons — and there were many, as Joe's appeals attorneys documented — who knew Joe and who might have helped humanize him by pointing out, for instance, that he had once rescued another boy in a swimming accident, that he had been a Boy Scout camp leader, and that he had been helpful to the elderly in the community, where he was well-liked.

But the trial lawyer did do some things on Joe's behalf. Most importantly, he challenged Helms's story and argued, if briefly, that Helms might have been much more guilty than he was letting on. For by his own admission, the key witness had been illegally carrying a gun during his stay in Columbus the weekend of the murders, and after the killings he had been concerned with collecting his audio tapes from Doe's car, wiping the captain's car down for fingerprints, disposing of his own bloody shirt, and fleeing the scene of the crimes. The

State's case rested ultimately on the testimony of such a person, Joe's defense attorney pointed out. And against the backdrop of his explanation of the deal that the prosecution had made with Helms, who would go free, Joe's attorney asked the members of the jury to use compassion in their deliberations and spare the life of his client, who was, after all, a "human being."

They did not.

After the trial, the Georgia Supreme Court, which let stand Joe's death sentence for the murder of Marian Miller, directed that he be given a life sentence for killing Captain Doe. Among the court's findings was that there was insufficient evidence to prove that Patrick Doe had been killed for financial gain — the criterion for a death sentence, in the case of the Army officer, in the judge's instructions to the jury.

With Joe's appeals in other courts almost exhausted, his case came before Georgia's Board of Pardons and Paroles in May of 1987. His petition before the Board acknowledged that though he had no criminal record prior to the murders, he had helped both Timothy Helms and Patrick Doe in drug dealing and had, in fact, introduced the two. Armed, he had gone along to Columbus with Helms, where the latter had hoped to work out a problem he had been having with Doe in their drug trade. Joe contended in his petition that Helms and Doe had made a trip to Atlanta shortly before the time of the murders to pick up a kilo of drugs, and that he and Marian Miller had gone with them. Joe asserted that Doe, Miller, and Helms had let him off near an Atlanta bus station before the three had evidently driven back to Columbus, because he had had to get home to make a drug run. From Atlanta, he had taken a bus to Savannah and returned home to nearby Beaufort. Joe asked that the Board allow him to take a lie-detector test to enable him to support his claim of innocence. He was willing to stake everything on such a test. But the Board denied his request. Among the final words — words of rage, perhaps — that he spoke while he was sitting in the electric chair were these: "I'm innocent. You are killing an innocent man. I have told you over and over and over."

And so Joe died. Through the years I have often reflected on these last words. In doing so, I have realized that there are certainly reasons to conclude that he may well have been lying in denying his involvement in the murders of Patrick Doe and Marian Miller. Though his fingerprints could not be recovered from the murder weapon, there is especially troubling circumstantial evidence against him. For example, according to the testimony of an Army officer, Joe had argued with and brandished a gun in front of Captain Doe at Fort Benning several hours before the murders. Moreover, a woman's testimony that she had seen two black men wiping off Patrick Doe's car just after the time of the killings is significant, for who, if not Joe, had been the other man apparently helping Helms get rid of fingerprint evidence? Furthermore, when police located Timothy Helms after the shootings, they found a signed note, in Joe's handwriting, in Helms's car. The date on the note is the day of the slayings — the day, according to Helms's testimony, when he had used his car to drive Joe back to South Carolina after the crimes and when Joe had written the note to a friend before the two fugitives arrived in Beaufort. The existence of the note suggests that Joe had not taken a bus toward home, as he later contended, and points toward his guilt.

Still, I puzzle over what motive Joe might have had to kill Captain Doe. And even on days when the evidence against Joe seems the most compelling, I wonder if there is not some chance, if slight, that he might have been innocent — especially because so much of the case against him rested on the obviously self-serving testimony of Timothy Helms.

In regard to Joe's trial, I have also asked myself this question, which I have not been able to answer: Would a differently composed jury have reached a different conclusion in regard to his sentence and possibly even concerning his guilt? In asking this question, I have felt that his jury faced imposing obstacles in carrying out its tasks impartially. Drawn from a town pervaded for years by a strong military ethos, it had to contend with a double murder case in which the victims were an Army officer and his girlfriend and in which the star witness was an honorably discharged Marine who had been on active duty at the time of the crimes. Furthermore, the jury, composed of all whites, had to decide the fate of an indigent black defendant. It was a jury, as it turned out, that could condemn Joe Mulligan to death and live with a deal that set Timothy Helms free.

◀ ▶

As I have reflected on Joe's fate, I have, of course, also thought a lot about the time that he and I spent together during the last six months of his life, the period when I visited him. I have thought especially of the difficult last days before his death.

One important indication of how difficult those final days were for him is the decision he made then to turn the care of his body over to me, not to his mother and father. He made the decision because he was deeply ashamed at having caused great heartache to "those I love," as he described his family in a letter he wrote to me the day he was executed. He talked with me only occasionally about the shame itself; when he did, he wanted to make sure that I understood why I, not his family, was to be responsible for his burial.

Had Joe's mother and father, working hard to try to support their large family in a society rife with racism, been able to offer him enough nurturing love from the earliest days of his childhood? Could his sense of shame have arisen in part from difficulties, such as neglect, that he faced when he was growing up? I do not know, for he never mentioned problems of his childhood to me.

But in the last days of his life, this much was clear to me: Joe's family cared deeply about him. I heard their love, mixed with their bewilderment and hurt, as they spoke to me and reluctantly agreed to accede to his burial wishes. And Joe cared deeply about the members of his family. Moreover, out of shame, he was committed to an act — empowering me to bury his body far from Beaufort — that he apparently hoped would reduce the burden that he had placed on these persons by his having ended up on death row.

I visited with Joe several times during his final days — the very last time for about five minutes on the day of his execution, after his father, brother, a cousin, and his lawyers had left, just before the guards led him away to make preparations for his death. During those days I saw how much his shame, combined with the trauma of his coming execution, had weakened him. In fact, he often showed signs of things clinically associated with depression, just as one would expect under the circumstances: sadness, an inability to sleep and eat, fatigue.

But I sensed something else underneath layer after layer of his pain: Joe felt that the powers of death would not have the last word about his life. I did not think that his soul was completely rested; there was too much hurt and fear in his eyes for that, especially in our last minutes together. Still, elements of the faith that he had learned as a boy at the Tabernacle Baptist Church in Beaufort remained with him. He spoke simply of God's "care" for him. Such a God would help us "get through" it all, he remarked tersely from time to time as the end drew near.

By the time our last five minutes together arrived, Joe's petition before the Pardons and Paroles Board had been rejected, and he had given up waiting for some miracle to be wrought in the judicial process, though his appeals in the courts were technically not yet exhausted. He made clear that he was resigned to dying. As he sat before me, his struggle with shame continued — something his posture and physical appearance suggested. Stooped over on the stool next to mine, he finally raised his head up enough to look at me but said nothing. His prison uniform, which was too large, was badly wrinkled, as if he had slept in it. And in all probability, he had spent the night in it, but he had not slept, as his tired eyes revealed. He was waiting for me to say something. I was not at all sure what to say to a man who was having his life taken from him for a crime that he had steadfastly denied having committed. I just looked into the distance for a time, and then the words came. They have become for me the most significant testament of faith that I have been able to make over the years as I have sat with condemned men in the final days and hours of their lives. They were words that triumphed over my occasional experiences — which perhaps Joe shared — of the absence of God as the time of death approached.

What I said owed as much to men on death row and certain members of their families as to the passage from the New Testament that I quoted, more or less, to Joe. For in the love of these persons, who for years had contended with the prison and justice systems, I had seen signs of an even more encompassing Love. The love the men and their family members showed one another was demonstrated, for instance, in the small gifts they exchanged. The prisoners, Joe among them, offered up such things as delicate crocheted pieces they had made. The family members, Joe's included, sent items such as cakes and breads that they had baked and cheeses and sausages that they had to scrimp for. The love of both captive and free was also shown in the letters they sent each other and the lingering hugs and handshakes they exchanged in the visiting room. There was no reason to expect this love to exist when faced with so much cinder block and steel, indifference and punishment, but it did. And I saw divine Love keep breaking into view, regardless of our efforts to edge it out of the world.

Thus, in large measure because of the resiliency of love in the lives of condemned prisoners and some members of their often fragmented families, I told Joe the greatest truth I knew, one that I hoped would not cheapen the intensity of his suffering. The words reflected my struggle with Dietrich Bonhoeffer's legacy. They were my own attempt to respond to the reality of the holy — the presence of an eternal "Thou" — in the very midst of our lives: "For I am sure that neither death, nor life, nor angels, nor principalities, nor things present, nor things to come, nor powers, nor height, nor depth, nor anything else in all creation, will be able to separate us from the love of God in Christ Jesus our Lord." To these words I added only the following: "I wouldn't be here, Joe, if I didn't believe this, if I didn't stake my life on this Love. It's given without exception, without precondition." And then I was silent. I did not tell him, as I could have, that I was too perplexed to say more, to affirm anything more specific.

I do not recall that he said much at all in response, other than a brief good-bye as we embraced before leaving the visiting room. But he was not a totally broken man, and the letter that he wrote to me at some point on the day he was executed helps explain why he was not. In this letter, in which he thanked me for trying to help him and his family through the crisis of his execution, he shed light on his sustaining faith by quoting a part of Psalm 31, where we are told that God will strengthen the hearts of those who "hope in the Lord." Acknowledging that he did not always understand "the ways of our Lord," Joe went on to write, "I assume by the time my body is at rest in the ground . . . my soul God will redeem." He added, "I know that God is looking down from heaven and hears my cries." And he ended with the salutation "Yours in Christ." But there was nothing more specific; the faith preached in the Tabernacle Baptist Church was reduced to the essentials in the life of a man passing through the fire. In light of this spare faith, I think that he understood not only the last words that I spoke to him but possibly also my silence, what I did not tell him, after I quoted Scripture.

Something else that I never told Joe about, as well as I can recall, was a dream that I have had over the years — even before the days when I visited him. I probably never spoke to him about it because its meaning was not clear enough to me at the time of our visits. I had no name for the dream then. Now I call it a dream of the tattered man. Call it a revelation, if you will.

At times, before and after Joe's execution, I have gotten up in the night, shaken by the images of the dream. Sometimes, wandering through the darkness in the house I share with my wife, I have moved among familiar pieces of furniture, touching them, relishing their solidity, seeking refuge perhaps in a world less threatening than that of the dream. Standing before our bedroom window, I have sought to calm myself by watching such things as the remains of a spring rain drip silently from the eaves or the scarcely visible figures of our small herd of cows bedded down for the night in a nearby hardwood grove. Once, when the experience of the dream was especially powerful, I walked outside to the edge of our pasture, sat down on the grass, and sought to quiet myself by watching the stars move slowly about a solitary red oak in the middle of the field. But whatever I have done after the dream in the years following Joe's execution, I have thought of him.

In the dream, I am visited by a tattered man, occasionally by two or three at once. Some nights the tattered man is obviously homeless and afraid and seeks help with an outstretched hand. On other nights he is driven by such things as greed and a desire for control over others, and he is prepared to use violence to get what he wants. From time to time he is a person who suffers from timidity in the face of bold, creative projects. Always, some things are the same: his clothes are rumpled and a bit ragged, his hair is tousled, and he is in need of a shave. Often he wears a battered tweed coat, the sleeves of which are a little too short. Frequently he is rather dark-skinned, as if he is perhaps Italian or Turkish, though it is difficult to tell because he always comes in the night. He is no one I actually know.

Who is the tattered man? I have come to see that he represents facets of my personality that I am not proud of or that I am unsure of. He frequently represents forces destructive of love and relationships. But he also embodies creative life within me that is stunted, that I will not allow to be expressed. Perhaps to some degree, he is tattered because of the struggles he and I have when I try to keep him at bay. He seems to be at his shabbiest when I am smug about my life. He is a manifestation of the personality's shadow, which, as Carl Jung detailed, belongs in some fashion to us all and which we can, with courage, face.

Since Joe's death, whenever I have had my dream of the tattered man, my mind has turned to my friend's often disheveled and needy appearance, particularly in those final days and hours of his life. He resembled the figure in the dream — more so than the other condemned men I have known, some of whom have taken pride in trying to look well-groomed as an act of defiance toward those who would take away their lives. How did Joe come to look this way? I think that he was deeply shaken by his own shadow, even if he managed to come to grips with a small portion of it.

In my presence, and at other times alone or maybe in the company of others, he confronted his past, in which he had, for instance, trafficked in drugs and placed himself in a situation that eventually resulted in, he felt, his family's disgrace. Because of such confrontations — which no doubt occurred at times in his dreams — Joe's conscience was surely quickened, something one would hope would occur from grappling with the shadow. Thus I, for one, never felt manipulated by him. He asked little of me: only that I visit him whenever I could and that I take care of his body after he died. But the result of Joe's encounter with his shadow was unlike any other encounter of the kind that I have ever witnessed. He almost allowed this confrontation to consume him. Reminded of elements of his shadow by his inner gaze, he almost succumbed to the belief that these dark presences made up his entire identity. So great was his shame.

I think that his faith played a significant role in keeping him from identifying completely with aspects of his inner darkness. Such faith led him to believe, even in his last and most difficult hours, that he was worthy enough for God to "redeem" his soul, to take a word from his last letter to me. Was he a murderer whose faith allowed him to speak only to God of his crimes, while denying the full scope of his shadow to everyone else in the desperate attempt to spare his family grief and embarrassment and to save his life? He may have been such a man. Alternatively, if he did in fact kill Patrick Doe and Marian Miller, did he perhaps lie to himself, and thus also to God, about the Easter murders because he could not bear the shadow's darkest revelations? Although I cannot rule out this latter possibility, it seems unlikely to me in view of Joe's ability to confront himself. He was not the kind of person simply to turn his back on his shortcomings. In any event, if he did lie to others and even to himself about his guilt, I do believe deeply that his faith

— unpretentious and moving — had a significant place in his life. I think grace reached that far into our world. Limited as his faith may have been in ways that I cannot know, it was of sufficient strength and authenticity to help keep his shadow from totally obscuring the light within him.

By allowing me to witness the pain of his struggles and to see something of how he survived them, Joe gave me a gift: He allowed me the opportunity to gain insight into the power of the confrontation with the shadow and the depth of the Love that complements our inner darkness and denies shame its final triumph. He helped me gain insight into the meaning and ultimate implications of my dream of the tattered man.

What did I give to Joe? In his last letter to me, he said that my own "part throughout this cruel experience was always one of not wanting the system to swallow my faith in our Lord." But what did I do to further my "part" in the whole ordeal? I was never able to offer him some ultimate theological justification of the events that were taking him toward his death. At the end, when I did tell him my brief credo, it was not to try to explain away his suffering. My words were — clearly, I hope — offered to him *in spite of* the tragedy that I was witnessing. Maybe they confirmed his theological intuitions and helped him face his death.

Aside from being a speaker of such words, I had perhaps a more important part to play in the drama of Joe's life of faith. This part did not oblige me to focus on probing his story of his innocence — to try to get him to face the fact that he was a murderer, if indeed he was. I hardly saw myself as his inquisitor. My main concern was to offer a man already stalked by shame whatever support I could to help him get through the time before his execution, which I saw as barbaric, regardless of what he might have done. On a couple of occasions, I did, of course, ask him about the murders to give him a chance to talk about the crimes if he wanted to. When he did speak about the killings, it was only briefly. He would talk about a crucial detail or two: for example, how he had left Patrick Doe, Marian Miller, and Timothy Helms before the murders had occurred. The story of his innocence was set firmly in his mind, and he showed no compelling need to rehearse the tale with me.

But he did show a need to speak of something else, and in this regard I began to play a role that may have been of greater theological importance than any words I uttered. This role in Joe's life emerged one day in the early spring of 1987 — about six weeks before his death — when he started talking about certain events of his youth and early manhood in Beaufort. His recounting of these events was not something that I had tried to get him to do. He just started talking about them, and his words clearly had a momentum of their own. The momentum was so great, in fact, that I sensed quickly that he was performing one of those crucial tasks that, as Viktor Frankl would have understood, life sets before us from time to time. Such tasks offer us powerful meaning. Mostly I did nothing but listen as Joe told his stories during substantial portions of two or three visits.

He began by speaking with increasing passion and relish of such things as sitting outdoors with his grandfather and knitting casting nets, in competition with the older man to see who could work faster. Then Joe continued by telling stories of his voyages in small boats, farther and farther out into the waters off Beaufort. He described how at one point in a voyage, his body would be bent double into the wind as his craft made little forward progress — and how at another point, his boat would glide effortlessly on the onrushing tide. Often he went fishing, sometimes in the company of a friend or, later, a girlfriend. There were times when he simply set out to enjoy the beauty of the ocean by himself; when he did so at night, he was frequently guided by the constellations once the light from the shore became too dim to see. On some voyages he would approach an island or sandbar amid the pounding surf and never know if he would be swamped before reaching shore. Occasionally, in his early teens, he set forth because he was spurred on by a boy's fantasy of chancing on some undiscovered territory. When he was older, there were days when he was propelled by the desire to move beyond the despair he felt after seeing Beaufort's unemployed young black men "shuffling," as he once put it, over the bleached oyster shells of meandering streets.

As story followed story, I listened to Joe talk about something that mattered deeply to him: his intimate contact with the natural world. Speaking with obvious joy, he was regaining knowledge of a place of color, texture, and possibility in which he had been a creative agent. After a decade of imprisonment on death row, he was gaining access to "subjugated knowledges" — to take an expression from Michel Foucault. For a brief time Joe broke through to a realm in which he felt alive. Through his storytelling, he was able to rediscover a vitality that helped him to break out, to some extent, from the isolation of a totalitarian world of shame. I am inclined to say that he could sense, as Jung might put it, that the shadow reveals not only our capacity to hurt others but also our neglected creative possibilities.

And maybe Joe discovered something more. It may not be going too far to say that, through the stories he told, he was able to grasp more fully the creative Love at the heart of all being — including his own life. Living increasingly in the richness of his own subjugated story, perhaps he was able to open up more fully to another rich and often subjugated story that he had first heard as a child: the narrative of the acts of God in the life of a small, ancient Near Eastern nation and in the life of a Nazarene carpenter, a story ultimately of Love in search of even the lowliest of us. In the end, perhaps his storytelling helped stave off his inner destruction by leading him to experience and reflect on this Love more deeply, even its power to embrace him in his failings, to forgive him. If he had lived longer, maybe he would have explored more deeply still the liberating power of such Love.

All in all, by listening to him tell his stories in the final weeks of his life, perhaps I played a part in keeping the system from swallowing Joe's faith in this Love and thus delivering him over to despair.

However I might have helped him, I think it is important to make something clear: because of Joe's ability to "meet" me as a Thou, to care for me, the Love that he opened himself up to in faith moved through him toward me. Thus, it was a Love that nurtured me as well as him.

The time of my visits with him was one of turmoil in my vocational life. I found myself working at two jobs, each quite different from the traditional college teaching profession for which I had prepared myself for years. Increasingly, I was involved in Mercer University's college-degree program for prisoners, and I was experimenting more and more with a sustainable organic agriculture on the farm where I lived. I have forgotten now exactly how much I told Joe of my turmoil. The times when I actually talked about my struggles were few, I am sure; no doubt I communicated a lot about my problems by nuances of my speech and behavior. In response to my difficulties, Joe would joke now and then about how I was trying to teach poetry-writing to "cons," or ask if I had taken up plowing with mules yet, or inquire if I had gotten my manure spreader out of the ditch again. At other times he simply let me talk for a minute or two: about moving down an unmarked road toward a destination I saw only dimly, about my own doubts concerning my ability to hold a "normal" job. Once or twice he reassured me with real warmth. Sometimes he just smiled, as if to say that I would "get it" one day. I do not recall exactly all he said or did in this regard. The point is, whatever he did or said, I felt increasingly that he was *with* me. Far different from the man the State portrayed as an irredeemable killer, he was a companion of great gentleness, somewhere out on that unmarked road.

It was a road where my shadow was, of course, also traveling, often just at the edge of my field of vision. In those days the person I now call the tattered man represented, for one thing, my own stunted capacity to live my life creatively, beyond the expectations of society; he was a casualty of my conventional "wisdom," from which I still suffer. As Joe walked along the road with me, I was able to find the courage to catch a glimpse of the tattered man from time to time. Consequently, I was learning about the meaning of my dream not only because Joe allowed me to witness his struggle with his shadow; I was also learning about the tattered man because of Joe's support of me as I encountered my own shadow. At its depths, that support revealed a Love that embraced us both.

◀ ▶

In the years since those few months when I knew Joe, I have come to understand more and more about the meaning of my dream of the tattered man. Among other things, I have come to understand more clearly the relationship between the dream and the story of incarnated Love that Joe learned as a child in Beaufort, and perhaps relearned in the closing days and hours of his life. I have seen how the dream and the story go together, explicate each other. The shadow, embodied in the dream, reveals by contrast how great the story's transfiguring, redemptive Love must be to triumph and make a broken creature whole. And the Love makes clear the shadow's limits: there will be no eternal rule of the night.

There have been times, however, when the terrifying power that issues from our darkest inner spaces has seemed overwhelming, and I have doubted the efficacy and even the existence of that Love. During the years since Joe's death, such times have occurred when I have contemplated the violence that explodes with regularity in our streets. These moments of doubt have occurred, too, when I have thought of our response to this violence. For our system of justice has taken the lives of many persons in our attempts, as my kinsman the judge might put it, to achieve "peace and good order." My times of doubt have been especially agonizing whenever I have thought of the fact that years after the civil rights movement we could try an African American (Joe Mulligan) for capital murder before an all-white jury in a community (Columbus, Georgia) with a substantial (over 30 percent) black population. My doubts have also been particularly troubling whenever I have thought of the deal that the prosecution in Columbus made with Timothy Helms. By engaging in such deals and seeking the death penalty, those who carry out the work of our justice system set themselves up — eventually, if it did not happen in Joe's case — for the execution of an innocent person. Such a strategy is an affront to the lives of Marian Miller and Patrick Doe and to whatever decency we as a people can claim.

Regardless of my difficult moments of doubt, I keep coming back to this central truth: One day, things will be different; Love will be all in all. The story that Joe learned at the Tabernacle Baptist Church promises this. In the meantime, as I make my trips to death row, I realize that nothing I or anyone else has been able to say has helped to close the gap that separates most of my kinspeople from me and those who share my beliefs about the death penalty. Indeed, the voices of the men sitting inside a pickup truck on the prison grounds and cheering the arrival of Joe's hearse on the night of his execution still go unchallenged for the most part, I fear — and not only among members of my family but across the land. I listened to the men, who were demonstrating in favor of capital punishment that night when I stood not far from them and thought of Joe, bent over into the wind, on one last voyage. Such voices diminished us all then; they continue to do so. They are a sign that we have attained neither peace nor good order. Failing to challenge them furthers the brutal heritage of my slaveholding great-great-grandfather and, after him, those who carried out the lynchings of African Americans.

In the worst of times — as I used to tell Joe — I have been tempted to hate many of my kinspeople, whether we are related by blood or geography. But in my more lucid moments, I realize that to hate such persons would mean to hate myself, so much are we a part of each other, so inextricably are we bound together. In a sense we all cast a single shadow. That is, I believe now, one of the implications of my dream of the tattered man, a gift of Love given to me so that I might grapple with my shortcomings and struggle for a life of compassion, not hate.

5

A Lesson in Grieving

He was supposed to have died on Wednesday, the 27th of May, 1987, just days after Joe Mulligan's execution. Then on Thursday, the 28th. It was on Friday, the 29th, a few minutes after seven o'clock in the evening, after all his appeals had finally been exhausted, that William Boyd Tucker eventually did die, on the first day of the ninth month of the thirty-first year of his life.

Deeply despondent and seeking refuge in drugs and alcohol as a result of the recent tragic death of his father, he had fatally stabbed a newly wed, pregnant woman — who, like Bill, was white — in Columbus, Georgia, in 1977, after he had robbed her and abducted her from a local convenience store. Unable to pay for his own legal representation, he had had to rely on an overworked public defender and his assistant at his trial, which had been held in early 1978. Columbus had been seized by fear then: just three weeks before the trial, the sixth in a series of murders of older white women — "the stocking stranglings" — had taken place in the city. Many, including the county coroner, had thought the "strangler" was black, though no one could be sure. Things had been so bad that an editorial in the local newspaper had called for mobilizing National Guard troops to protect the area's women. This was the climate in which the jury made its decision — without hearing from a mental-health professional who could have examined Bill and carefully described the defendant's distressed state of mind at the time of the killing. The jury gave Bill a death sentence for the murder of nineteen-year-old Kathleen Perry.

As his petition before Georgia's Board of Pardons and Paroles had pointed out, Bill had been greatly remorseful about the murder. Moreover, it had explained that during his years of incarceration, his prison record had been exemplary, he had attained an admirable religious faith, and he had grown to have a close relationship with his family. But the Board, faced with the decision of whether or not to give a life sentence to a white man after the state had electrocuted eight black men in a row, had not been sufficiently moved by the petition. The Board had affirmed Bill's death sentence.

◄ ►

Bill Tucker received visits from his family from nine o'clock in the morning until mid-afternoon during the last week of his life, which began with a long Memorial Day weekend. During his final four days, with his execution imminent, prison officials allowed him no more than three visitors at a time; a larger group was considered a security risk. Thus, during those four days, there were almost always at least six or eight members of Bill's family waiting for their turn to see him. Wanting to be as close to him as possible, they encamped on the grounds of the prison, about fifty yards from its main building's entrance.

Though she was most often visiting with her son, Bill's mother was occasionally waiting with those outside. During his incarceration on death row, she had worked as a waitress, saving what money she could to make trips to see him. Also among those sometimes waiting at the family camp was Bill's stepfather, a retired Army veteran, who had become so close to his stepson that Bill referred to him simply as "Dad," though the two had met only in the prison visiting room. At various times, Bill's brother, sisters, aunts, uncles, and cousins were outside as well; they hoped to spend a few minutes with a person they had, in some cases, not seen for months or longer. They sat on blankets or quilts or in folding chairs — in front of an uncle's RV that served as a kind of headquarters. As they sipped Coke or iced tea or tried to eat the sandwiches they had prepared, they struggled with the fate of their kinsman inside the prison, which was almost out of sight, just up the steep rise and across the hot asphalt parking lot to the north of them. Now and then, one of them would leave quickly to replace another visitor in shuttle fashion.

Quiet ruled those spring mornings and afternoons, except for a time on Thursday, when a siren split the air and guards were everywhere, yelling and loading weapons. Michael Cervi, Bill's friend for years, was making an attempt to stop what seemed almost inevitable. The fellow death-row prisoner had scaled the fence that enclosed the death-row exercise yard and reached the roof of a nearby building before he was stopped on his way to the death house, site of the state's electric chair. He had intended to disable the chair's generator. He came close to being killed for his efforts. But he had taken that into account, so much did he love the man who was about to die. When they learned what had happened, Bill's relatives made Mike one of their own. They might as well have opened a folding chair for him or smoothed out a special place for him on one of their quilts — so much was his presence felt among those who had been denied access even to the large waiting area adjacent to the prison's visitation rooms.

During those final days, I often sat outside with Bill's family. Sometimes I would get a look at how he was doing, for I, too, would leave the group briefly and dash in for a visit. Often when I saw him, the atmosphere in the visiting room was pretty light. There was the easy conversation of persons accustomed to each other, and Bill was enjoying it. In this atmosphere, he would listen with delight to stories of his childhood that various family members occasionally related. For example, on the last day of school one year, his mother had told him that one of his sisters would have to repeat the second grade and that Bill should not say anything to the little girl about it. But of course he had done so, blurted the words out the minute his sister had come home: "Mom said I shouldn't say anything about you being held back. . . ." Another time, when the family had been stationed in Germany, he would spend his ice-cream money on flowers for his mother. One day when the dimes had run out, however, he had brought home a bunch of flowering weeds that had smelled up the whole house. On still another occasion, he and some friends had set up a pup tent in his backyard and had been reading his comics under the canvas. Then it had started to rain, and he had insisted that a place be made in the small tent for his dog, a German shepherd. When his friends had balked at this, he had threatened to take his comics and leave. A little later, his mother had looked out into the yard and seen that the boys had reached a kind of compromise: along with the German shepherd, they had been lying in the rain with their heads tucked under the tent.

Even before the deeply emotional good-byes at mid-afternoon on Friday, the 29th, there were, of course, times when the difficulty of the occasion was clearly visible. There were moments when Bill and his guests would fall into an uncomfortable silence. There were also times when he would wince as someone on the verge of tears would ask to leave the visiting room to use the bathroom or to "freshen up." And I remember once, after I had visited him, how slowly Bill walked to the door of the room with me; one of his arms was draped limply around my shoulders. He was tired after so much visiting and so many days of waiting to die. He whispered simply, "Am I doing okay?" I eked out the words "You're doing okay," gave him a hug, and watched him walk — again slowly — back to his guests.

And I believed he was holding up okay, though I knew that the strain of the ordeal must have been almost unbearable at times. My sense of the situation — indeed, much of what I had come to believe about Bill since I had begun visiting him — would be confirmed a couple of days after his execution, when I read two letters that he had recently written.

His writing of both of these pieces may have been affected by what he had learned, in the closing weeks of his life, about someone whose significance I had tried to describe for him.

I think I had been visiting Bill for about a month when, in early April of 1987, I mentioned to him how deeply influenced I had been by Dietrich Bonhoeffer since my college days. I tried to explain how impressed I was by Bonhoeffer's faith, which was active in the world and was not confined by the trappings of piety: he had shown his faith by acts of love, not by maintaining a posture of "holiness." I also told Bill that his faith reminded me of Bonhoeffer's, for both men had discovered transcendence in their relationships to their "neighbors." I noted that Bill's helping Jerome Bowden write letters was something that Bonhoeffer would have valued a lot.

I hoped that Bonhoeffer's story might inspire Bill and help him make some sense out of, discover meaning in, his own plight. And I wondered if the way the German pastor had often expressed his beliefs during the last years of his life might be of interest and importance to Bill. Thus, at one point, I mentioned to him how Bonhoeffer had formulated many of his most important thoughts in deeply honest and probing letters that he had written to family and friends while he was in prison. Bill listened carefully, as was his manner. I do not recall that he said much in response. But when he wrote to me a day or two later, he referred to Bonhoeffer's *Letters and Papers from Prison*. So I sent him a copy of the book.

During the crisis days of April and May, with his execution near, Bill said nothing more to me about Bonhoeffer. But during this time he carried out two of the most important writing projects of his life: a kind of journal, in the form of a long letter to his family, and a letter to Georgia's Board of Pardons and Paroles. I never learned whether reading or hearing of Bonhoeffer had played a role in his deciding to write his letter-journal, which Bill sent to me to type up and pass on to his family and friends. Nor did I learn if the model of Bonhoeffer's rigorously honest letters might have made Bill's difficult letter to the Board easier for him. Bill had written many letters over the years, and he was the kind of person who could have accomplished both writing projects without the example of the martyred pastor. If not decisive, perhaps his knowledge of Bonhoeffer helped Bill write each letter.

◄ ►

In his letter-journal, Bill made clear much of what he was thinking and feeling during those difficult weeks and days when he was trying to take leave of his family and friends. Often he reflected on the positive state of his mind or soul. For instance, on the 25th of April he wrote, "I have full confidence . . . that 'all things work together for good to them that love God.'" Even in the waning moments of his life, he was astonishingly composed. In his very last journal entry, which he made on the 29th of May as he was being readied for execution, he was able to write this:

> My right leg has been shaved. As all this was going on I prayed for the souls of the men who cut my hair, shaved my leg, and who will be escorting me to the chair. . . .
> They will be coming within the hour and I am prepared. God has granted peace in these last few hours. . . . I'll close off for now so that I can have some quiet time, with what is left.
> I love you all!

If such entries revealed the entire story of Bill Tucker's final days, we would have the record of an almost superhuman life. It is significant, however, that passages such as these do not tell the full story. They do not suggest the deep process of grieving that Bill Tucker was going through and, in fact, had probably been experiencing for years in regard to some issues. They do not indicate his struggle with a sense of loss at the very heart of his life. Other passages contain compelling signs of this struggle and show an important — if at times hidden — motif that profoundly shapes the whole letter.

As a careful look at the subject reveals, our modern culture too often seems to conspire against one of our deepest needs: our need to grieve our losses. We fear that the grieving process may cause us to lose control of our lives, a perhaps unpardonable sin. Thus, we teach succeeding generations to block the feelings called up by loss — emotions such as anger, sorrow, remorse, and anxiety. Indeed, we have concocted an unending array of strategies to avoid grieving. We turn to drugs and alcohol, we sleep excessively, and we try to lose ourselves in our work, our amusements, and our idle talk. Unfortunately, in attempting to avoid the often lengthy grieving process, we shut down one of the principal ways we maintain our health and our humanity. Woodenness develops, as can lasting despair and resignation and even violence.

Bill Tucker was moving away from all of these things. He sought to face loss — past, present, and future — and he grieved. I saw something of his grief in his face, in his eyes, and I heard it in his voice as we talked from time to time about his losses in the weeks before his death. After I read his letter-journal, I felt the grief even more powerfully — both in and behind his words.

Prominent at places in this journal — as it was in some of our visits — is Bill's confrontation with what might be called his loss of innocence in regard to his capacity for destruction. As his life drew to a close, his heartache over his terrifying and — for him — unparalleled outburst of brutality a decade earlier lingered. He was still grieving because of his murder of Kathleen Perry, which he finally could recall only long after his conviction.

His journal entry for the 14th of May makes clear one way that Bill struggled with his loss of innocence. He wrote then of something that was on his mind, as it had been for years: "the need to contact" Mrs. Perry's family "and tell them of my remorse and sorrow for the pain I

75

caused them. The problem is that I have lacked the courage and words to do so. . . . I just don't know if I have it in me to write to the victim's family."

So far as I know, he was never able to write such a letter.

His journal also records his need to go before his own family and confront his loss of innocence. He put things this way on the 17th of May:

> I asked Dad [his stepfather] to gather all of you up here some time next week; there's something I have to say to you as a family and it would give me the opportunity of making the most important of statements, my apology to you. I have to apologize for the shame I put you through when I brought the name of "murderer" to the family.

He was able to summon the courage to make this difficult apology.

On May 19th, after he had learned that his attorneys wanted to open up his background to the press before presenting his case to the Board of Pardons and Paroles, Bill elaborated on the pain associated with his lost innocence:

> I quit writing last night when I felt the full impact of what opening up to the press means. All the attention will again be focused on me and the murder. I'll have to relive the pain of what I've done. Just as I had made peace with the pain and in a strange way accepted it as a constant companion and put away all the hostility and fear, this comes crashing down. I'm having a hard time dealing with it, especially as a Christian since God's Word says I'm forgiven. Yet I feel an enormous burden of guilt each time my case is mentioned. The fact is that every time I have to face this I get kicked back two steps.

Somewhat later in the entry, he went on to say this:

> I wish I could show them all [the public] how I really am: that I'm a caring and breathing human being, almost broken by remorse and shame, whose only desire is to in some way make things better since I can't "not do" what I have done. I look up at my calendar

and see eight boxes which could well represent the remainder of my life and take comfort in knowing that soon I could be at rest and no longer burdened with so much guilt and pain.

As profound and painful as it was, his loss of innocence in regard to his destructive power was not the only loss that Bill Tucker encountered and wrote about, grieved about. Because of all that he had experienced since his imprisonment, he had, for example, also lost considerable faith in the goodness of his country. Though the initial shock of this loss was long gone in the days when I knew Bill and we talked about the matter, elements of his grief remained — in his sadness and his anger. In his letter-journal, he faced the loss by writing about his native land as a place of tragic executions and monstrous prisons; both his sadness and his anger seem to inform all of these comments.

On the 14th of May, when he reflected on the coming execution of Joe Mulligan, scheduled for the very next day, he wrote, "You know, the really sad thing is that Joe may be innocent; there's been enough doubt cast to question the conviction and yet there may very well be an execution tomorrow. It's really tragic! But it's not really surprising since justice isn't the point; rather good old-fashioned revenge is in style these days." After mentioning a newspaper article that he had read concerning the many persons in Georgia who were willing to act as the state's executioners, he concluded his entry for the day with this comment about the death penalty: "Where else in the world can you find a government willing to provide the auspices of legality to out-and-out murder? South Africa, Iran, and Russia come to mind."

Bill took up the issue of execution again a little over a week later, on the 22nd of May, and showed the depth of his feelings about the subject. At this point, Joe Mulligan had been electrocuted and another man, Richard Tucker (who was not kin to Bill), was to die within hours. He wrote,

> From what I hear Richard isn't doing too well. God, I hope he can find strength and peace in his last hours. You know, the real horror of death row is watching a friend, someone you've lived with for years, being picked up and moved out to what you know is the "death watch" and being so helpless to respond. Anger, hostility, and an incredible amount of tension threaten to overcome you

and only a strong force of will can keep them from succeeding. I'm at peace with my own case but exceedingly angry over the nine previous executions. I despair so for each of them. . . .

Richard was pronounced dead at 7:23 p.m. I grieve at the waste of so much valued life!

After the execution of Richard Tucker had taken place, Bill's was to be next. On Wednesday, May 27th, he wrote of his encounter with something, he well knew, that our nation had given birth to: the monster-like prison that held him captive while he awaited his death. He had awakened early in the morning and listened to the prison wake up:

It's like a great beast slowly aroused; first one eye opens, then another. It seems to take an enormous yawn trying to shake the sleep from its fogged mind. It doesn't fool me though. I know the name of the beast; it's a predatory creature that gorges itself on the broken remains of once proud men. With the grace of God I have managed to escape being devoured for over ten years now but the beast waits patiently for Thursday evening.

As it turned out, Bill did not die then. A brief court stay delayed the end. On that Thursday, the next-to-last day of his life, he summed up his view of his looming execution: "Never would I have contemplated dying in the electric chair. It's barbaric and not in line with what would be envisioned of America."

While grieving over the loss of his innocence concerning his destructiveness and over having to surrender considerable faith in the goodness of his native land, he found the strength to grieve other losses. One of these was the loss of his family — something that his execution would bring about. His difficult struggle to face this loss is reflected in his letter-journal, which records things that I sensed in our visits.

At times his faith seemed almost to elevate him beyond thoughts of losing his family. Thus, he wrote the following on the 24th of May:

I'm sitting here about to explode from within with joy! The full revelation of my faith has struck me! I want to plead, "Now, Father, now! If this is just a sample of what awaits me, take me now!"

As selfish as this may sound, if it were not for a few extra days with you I would beg it this instant.

But such times of joy gave way to more sober moments. What he wrote on the 27th of May may well suggest his sadness at losing the persons he tried so hard to shield from grief in the visiting room by his upbeat manner:

> I don't really know what to say. I'm spending what could conceivably be my last night on earth and I'd like to be able to leave you all with a portion of the "wisdom" I've found these past few years (meager as it is) but instead all I can think about is the love I have for each of you.

As his final hours approached, his sorrow over the impending loss of his family became even more explicit. Late in the afternoon on May 28th, he "received word that the U.S. Supreme Court . . . [had] granted a twenty-four-hour stay of execution." He went on to write,

> I don't know what tomorrow will hold but I pray that I can get a favorable decision from the court, just to save us all from hurting all over again. One thing you should know: I have never before this asked to be spared but now after days of visiting with you I want to share a lifetime with all of you.

Here the note of grief is clear. By the end of his life, he faced directly the "hurting," the sorrow, that he felt over the loss of those he loved so much.

And in the days before his electrocution, he experienced still more sorrow by facing another loss: the sudden and tragic death of his birth father years earlier, when Bill was a young man. In our time together, Bill had real trouble speaking of the event and what it meant to him. Maybe he had grieved the loss for a long time; I do not know. He never discussed the death fully with me; in fact, when he began to talk about it a couple of times, he soon became quiet, overcome by his sadness. When I read his letter-journal, I thought that his failure to write directly in those pages about his father's death confirmed how hard it was for him to deal with it.

But in another context Bill was able to write about the loss with forthrightness, if with difficulty. I realized this vividly after I read a statement that he wrote for Georgia's Board of Pardons and Paroles and that his mother shared with me one day when I visited her shortly after Bill's execution. His attorneys had asked him to write such a statement, which he composed in the form of a letter; they wanted to include it along with other documents they were submitting to the Board in the hope that its members would commute Bill's sentence from death to life in prison.

Bill mentioned this statement in his letter-journal on the 14th of May: "I had to write a letter to the State Board of Pardons and Paroles the other day and that exacted a real emotional price." In this four-and-a-half-page, handwritten letter to the Board, he admitted freely that he had committed the "horrible" crime of murder. He was not writing, he said, to "excuse" his actions, for which he took full "responsibility." But he did want "to help bring to light the cause of . . . [his] behavior in August of 1977," the time of the murder. There were "extenuating circumstances" that he wanted to bring to the Board's attention.

He did so by telling about his years-long failure to experience his father's love, then about the moment when he finally saw this love expressed, and finally about the terrible time after his father's death when he had to live without the man's love. Bill knew the best way to communicate how overwhelming it was to lose this love after he had finally experienced it: as well as he could, he had to explain how much he had yearned for it for years and how his life had been tormented by its felt absence.

Bill began his story this way:

I am the sixth child in a family of seven children, five girls and two boys. My father, a career soldier, was an alcoholic who had little time for his family. All my life all I ever wanted was to be able to find approval and affection in the eyes of my father, something I never quite achieved. Looking back now, I can see that he had too many problems of his own trying to make ends meet, feeding a family of nine on a soldier's pay. He often worked a second and third job which left him little time for sleep much less time for a home life. He took to the bottle and was rarely without [it]. I resented it and became a problem child.

Perhaps because of his love for his father and also because of the pain of reliving his parent's rejection, Bill failed to mention something about his role as "problem child" that his family clarified for me in the closing days of his life and that his attorneys set forth in their petition on his behalf to the Board: his father had dealt out excruciating emotional and physical punishment to his children for years, and in this situation Bill became a scapegoat. When Bill cried out for help for himself and his siblings, he received still more abuse from his father, who would beat him, tell him what a failure he would become in life, and predict that the boy would land in prison one day.

Though his letter to the Board is silent about these abusive deeds and words, as it progresses it does make clear some of the painful consequences of the abuse. Undoubtedly dogged by such things as a lack of self-worth and an accompanying sense of shame, Bill often coped with his evolving world in destructive ways. In school, he said, he "resisted discipline of any kind." And he made this admission: "At the age of 13 while in Frankfurt, Germany, I began to use drugs on a regular basis." After that, his relationship to his parents "deteriorated," and "fighting became the only contact" he had with his father. At seventeen, Bill was sent to a school for "problem children," but he was "unwilling to accept . . . [the school's] help." Eventually he served a stint in the Army, during which time he overdosed on drugs and went through a "drug rehab. program." Honorably discharged, he entered Columbus College in Columbus, Georgia, and broke "with all chemical drugs," but still used marijuana.

Then an especially important event in his life occurred. In May of 1977, his father asked him to come over for dinner, and Bill agreed. In his letter to the Board, Bill explained what happened after dinner:

> We carried our beers outside to the back yard and sat and talked. My father talked of his life, of the many disappointments he had had. He told me that regardless of the fact that we had not gotten along he had always loved me and always would. He asked me to forgive him and refused to allow me [a] share of the blame. He said that he didn't expect me to return his love but hoped that we could become friends. I never loved him more than I did at that moment. We promised to work at establishing a solid relationship.

Tragically, they never got a chance to do so. At about four o'clock the next morning, Bill's father died of a heart attack; Bill tried in vain to save him by performing CPR.

He went on to tell the Board that he had been "devastated" by his father's heart attack:

> From that point on my life began to decline, I simply stopped caring. I went back to using drugs to help ease the pain. Things got worse when I dangerously mixed alcohol with the drugs.

His letter to the Board makes clear that he was in this state of "decline" on the day of the murder.

In a journal entry for the 24th of May, Bill offered this description of the decline, alluding to the tragic loss of his father:

> When real tragedy developed I reacted as I had been taught [in what he had called, a few lines earlier, a "pleasure-centered society"] by drowning the pain in drugs and alcohol. Sooner or later the pain had to surface; an outlet had to be provided for what was now anger. I killed.

In other words, he saw how his violence had grown out of his inability to grieve properly after his father's death: one evening when he had been drinking heavily and smoking marijuana, he had murdered Kathleen Perry. But surely his unbridled anger was not only a reaction to his father's recent death and the loss of a newly discovered love; it also must have been a response to Bill's powerful feelings of shame and inadequacy that began with the abuse he experienced as a child and that became especially prominent as a result of his self-destructive drug and alcohol binges.

◄ ►

During the three-month period between his father's death and the murder of Kathleen Perry, Bill was unable to grieve what he had lost. He learned later, in prison, how to grieve deeply and authentically. There, even as his days were running out, he faced loss in many forms. He came to grips with one of the most important truths of his life: though his faith might bring him moments of peace, he was not immune to real suffering. As he and I once discussed, it was a truth that was at odds with what he had heard over the years through his contact with the fundamentalist circles of southern culture. It was a truth that he put this way in his letter-journal on May 19th: "I'm set in a good foundation but I'm not the rock."

By the end of his life, Bill understood profoundly something that he noted in a journal entry on the 14th of May: "At the bottom of all doctrine lies the greatest mystery — the depth of God's love." While it did nurture him at some deep level, such mysterious love did not allow him anything approaching total control of his inner life. Even his moments of genuine peace that his journal records were not — he surely saw — his to call up at will. He was learning that the life of faith entails responding to both grace and heartache, loss as well as love.

During the closing days of Bill's life, the act of writing became one way in which he could, from time to time, confront loss and, in faith, share some of this confrontation with others. From the 24th of April to the 29th of May, 1987, the period during which he wrote his letter-journal and his statement to Georgia's Board of Pardons and Paroles, he allowed his grief to shape his written words because he was strengthened by a Word that promised that there was more to life than sorrow, emptiness, shame, and death. In telling of his encounter with both darkness and light, he found a task that provided him with meaning when he especially needed it.

◄ ►

After saying a final good-bye to Bill on the afternoon of Friday, the 29th of May, I left the prison grounds about four o'clock. I turned south on Georgia's Route 36 and drove toward the Columbus home of his mother and stepfather so that I could be with them at the time of the execution. Our camp had been broken: Bill's family had loaded up their blankets and quilts and stowed away their folding chairs. Some of his family remained nearby to participate in a vigil at the prison three hours later, when Bill was to be electrocuted; others headed in my direction.

Along Route 36 that afternoon, I thought of the struggle with grief and loss that Bill had been going through. I knew that especially the past few days had been extraordinarily difficult for him. Indeed, I wondered occasionally if he would hold up all right during the last hours before he was to die. But I was basically confident that he would be okay. I had such confidence even though I had not yet read his letter-journal, the final entry of which reveals his remarkable composure just before his death.

As I drove south, reasons for my confidence came to me. For one thing, I remembered the time that Bill and I had spent together a little more than a week earlier. At that time, Joe Mulligan had already been electrocuted, Richard Tucker's death was only a day away, and Bill himself had an execution date. It was clear to Bill that his time was running out. Nonetheless, he seemed more concerned about me than himself, and for an hour or so, I was in his care.

He was aware that I had known both Joe and Richard — and also Jerome Bowden, who had been executed less than a year earlier. My weariness in the face of so much death must have been obvious to Bill, because the first thing he did when he saw me was to ask me, with real earnestness, how I was doing. When I did not reply immediately, he asked, "Can you go on?" And slowly I began to answer, as well as I could. I do not know for sure whether or not Bill understood how much I needed to talk, but I suspect he did. And although I certainly was not feeling very strong at the beginning of our conversation, the more I talked, the more I realized that, through little doing of my own, I was stronger than I had thought. I realized that I was strong enough to get through such times as these. I could go on. And I knew why.

Mostly I spoke to Bill about Lewis Sinclair, with whom I recently had had lunch at the Union 76 Truck Stop across from the prison. On my death-row visitation days over the previous two years, I had spent countless hours at the truck stop during the two-hour period at midday when I was not allowed to meet with prisoners. Sometimes I would eat in the bustling dining room with attorneys, who would bring me up to date on where their death-penalty cases were in the appeals process. When I was alone, the restaurant was a place where I often sat in my booth and sorted through my conversations with the men I visited on the row. It was also a place where I met friends such as Lewis.

Though he looked twenty years younger, he was seventy-two years old in May of 1987. He had experienced much of our turbulent century. An African American man born in the little town of Pass Christian,

Mississippi, he had gone on to study at Alcorn College and later at the University of Tennessee. Subsequently he had spent years as an economist with the Tennessee Valley Authority, having worked his way up from his first job there as a clerk in the mail room. Along the way, he had married and helped raise a son. He had also played a vital role in the civil rights movement by serving on the board of directors (frequently as its chair) of the Highlander Folk School in rural Tennessee. At Highlander, blacks and whites would come together to learn from each other how best to work for genuine community. Martin Luther King Jr. had spent time there. Rosa Parks had been there, too. So had Pete Seeger.

What was so extraordinary about Lewis, I told Bill, was not just his human-rights work, which he would talk about only if pressed. What was also extraordinary was the way he handled defeat and loss. He had proved that it is possible to face such things and live without being consumed by them. He had given much of his life to trying to bridge the gap between blacks and whites and had lived long enough to see how deeply resistant to such change our society is. Moreover, he had lived long enough to experience the wrenching deaths of many of those whom he loved. So what did he do? He looked after two of his sisters, each older than he. And he continued his work with Highlander, expanding its reach into Central America — all the time remembering, as he said, how important it is to "meet people where they are, not where you think they should be." He did still other things, too. At regular intervals he would cook gumbo for his friends, using ingredients that he picked up on trips to the Mississippi coast. He would also find time to spend with someone like me, at an obscure truck stop outside of Jackson, Georgia.

Lewis grasped clearly the infinite value of creation in even the smallest humane gesture, in the raven's flight, in the lilies of the field. Though no churchgoer, he experienced the body of Christ nearly everywhere he turned. The truth that Lewis lived allowed him to defy such things as bitterness: he could be renewed and refreshed almost anywhere, even during his times of deepest grief. When I was with him, I felt in touch with such truth.

As I talked on in Bill's presence, I realized how in times of greatest need I stood at the center of a bright ring of friendship. Lewis formed part of the ring, along with others, such as Bill. All were part of a community of resistance and reconciliation to which I belonged and that helped me to go on. My strength came from all of them — and from the profound truth that Lewis saw so clearly and that the rest shared, to one significant degree or another. If I had eyes to see, it was a truth that bound the whole cosmos together.

That Bill was able to allow me to rediscover my strength during a time when I was reeling was a remarkable sign of his resiliency, I told myself as I drove toward Columbus. He would be all right. And as the minutes passed, I thought of yet another reason why I could make such an affirmation.

A lengthy conversation that Bill and I had had about two weeks earlier came to mind. At that time he was very vulnerable because of something that had happened recently. I was to learn later that he had recorded the event this way in his letter-journal on the 13th of May: "I received a visit from a preacher . . . on the eleventh and although his purpose was to bring comfort, he wound up confusing me in relation to my baptism." It seems that the preacher had a precise ritual of baptism in mind, and if the ritual was not performed in exactly the right way, the believer would be denied God's forgiving love. According to the minister, Bill's baptism did not pass muster. Bill had already talked to friends in the cellblock about the matter when he and I met, and he was doing much better than he had been on the day of the preacher's visit. But there was still considerable anxiety in his face.

So we went through the whole problem, just the two of us together in the visiting room that day, while occasionally a guard or other prison employee gazed in at us. We leaned toward each other, head to head, as we talked. In the beginning we both commented on the legalism of the preacher's position. After a while Bill spoke about the many moments of grace in his life, especially after his imprisonment. He explained that because of such grace, he had kept moving on, overcoming one hurdle after another, becoming someone he could be proud of: a person who loved his family, a friend and comforter to those on death row. Eventually he began to speak with confidence about the time ahead of him: relying on God's love, he would find the inner resources to face whatever lay before him, though he knew that he was in for the struggle of his life.

We must have spent a couple of hours together that day, with Bill doing most of the talking. At one point during our visit I thought about the absurdity of the approaching death of a man who had meant so much to so many persons. But the overwhelming impact on me of our time together was positive. When I left him, I was reassured that he was strengthened in his conviction that we are sustained in life by a grace so powerful that it defies any attempt to dam it up with a narrow formula. Indeed, I felt such grace fill the space between us that day, a space in which the power of all life, all being, seemed revealed.

As I continued to drive along the highway on the last afternoon of Bill's life, I thought of what I had seen in the countryside during the past few months. As I had made my way along Route 36 to visit Bill and others on death row, I had witnessed the rhythm of birth and death all around me. Though I felt that the horror of executions had obscured the deepest beauty of that time of year, I did believe that I had sometimes seen, if obliquely, something of how nature had revealed her loveliness as the weeks had gone by: in bright yellow forsythia, scattered between the tiny houses of Barnesville's black families; then in redbud trees, such as those at the edge of fields where cotton once grew, just before I came into Woodland; next in garlands of jasmine, draped about the thin pines rising up in an abandoned logging road not far from Waverly Hall; later in green-yellow tufts at the ends of oak branches, like the ones hanging over the lonely Salem Cemetery a couple of miles outside of the village called The Rock; and later still, in white dogwoods, such as those on the town square in Thomaston. Something was always dying so that still more beauty might be born. In trying to make some sense out of it all, I could not deny the experience of loss, of nothingness, the wound in every least particle in the universe. But I could not believe that nothingness was the controlling force in the womb of being.

I was willing to venture that the creative Love that drives the cosmos could use loss, nothingness, in fashioning not only beauty but also deeper levels of being. I felt something that I thought Lewis Sinclair would understand: negativity accompanies but is not the goal of all the processes of earth and heaven, the flux and flow moving through kingfishers and stars.

That this was true seemed especially clear to me when I thought of Bill Tucker's life. Despite the terrifying negativity and loss that he had experienced, a person of great inner beauty and depth of being had emerged. Confronting his pain directly, he had moved through it and found the source of all grace, of which his baptism was a sign. Despite much that his culture had taught him, he had discovered that the way of faith did not preclude his encountering grief.

As I drove toward Columbus that day of Bill's death and reflected on his life, I was experiencing the impact of a lesson in grieving whose importance to me has only increased through the years.

6

A Walk in Arcady

S wirling through saplings and grasses trying to gain a hold on life, the dust rose even higher than normal in the ditches as I drove past during the summer of 1987. I traveled to the state prison near Jackson to see Billy Mitchell some seven or eight times then, in the two months before his death. In the first light when I left home and later on those long afternoons when I drove back, the expanse of heat and dryness surrounding me seemed limitless.

After it was all over, I walked down into the bottomland on our family's farm. I wandered toward the Ossahatchee Creek that morning in early September, only hours after Billy's execution. Eventually I reached a place along the bank where I had sought the mountain laurel a few months earlier and had watched day by day as its blossoms had slowly filled the creek side. That late summer morning, the blossoms and their faint perfume were gone, having traded places with the dust that covered both laurel branch and leaf. But the cool, quiet creek bank was still alluring, somewhere I could try to begin to come to terms with the images inside my head. As I sat down, the crate that, according to Billy, Chris Carr had thrown at him, rose before me. The bursts of fire from Billy's pistol were visible, too. He had killed fourteen-year-old Chris; the boy's mother, Peggy Carr, had seen "a hole come in his chest." She herself had "felt a hot jolt . . . in the back . . . [of] the head" when Billy had shot her.

According to the testimonies of Peggy Carr and a seventeen-year-old youth who, along with his cousin, came on the scene right after Mrs. Carr and her son had been shot, the following events took place within the span of a few minutes at the IGA convenience store in Sylvester, Georgia, on August 11, 1974: About a quarter after seven in the morning, Billy entered the store. After walking to the cold drink machine, he came to the front counter, drew a pistol, and demanded money from Mrs. Carr, the clerk. She gave him the cash in the register. When he demanded more, she gave him her own money; he may have taken money from Chris also. Then Billy took her and Chris toward a cooler in the back of the store. Billy, who was African American, threatened at this time to rape Mrs. Carr, telling her that he "never had a white bitch before." He changed his mind when she protested. Inside the cooler he shot both her and her son, without provocation. Apparently he left the cooler for a minute or two, only to return and shoot his victims again. Shortly thereafter, the two cousins, both white males, drove up and entered the store. Billy tried to shoot one of them, too, but his gun failed to fire. Billy then led them to the cooler, where, outside the door, Mrs. Carr was using the phone to call for help. Billy hung up the phone, then took the three individuals inside the cooler and tried again to shoot one of the two cousins, but once more his gun did not fire. At this point Billy pulled out a second gun, took six dollars from one of the cousins, closed the cooler door, and fled.

Once he was apprehended, Billy confirmed part of this scenario for authorities. He confessed — initially at gunpoint, he later said — that he had robbed the store and then shot Chris and Peggy Carr. In his defense he mentioned that he had not fired his gun until the fourteen-year-old had picked up a crate in the cooler and thrown it at him. As this happened, Billy "got scarred [sic] and started shooting and . . . shot four or five times." In confessing, Billy said nothing about such things as the threat of rape, returning to the cooler to shoot his victims, or attempting to shoot either of the two persons who had come into the store after he had shot Mrs. Carr and her son.

In court Billy pled guilty to murdering Chris Carr, and a sentencing trial was held in which the State's witnesses talked about the horrible crime. A white judge listened to determine whether Billy deserved death or life imprisonment. Billy's white, court-appointed lawyer, who received one-hundred-fifty dollars for his work, neither called witnesses nor presented evidence to try to convince the judge to spare the defendant's life. After the trial, in partial explanation of his failure to conduct mitigation investigation into his client's past, the lawyer noted that Billy had "discouraged" him from doing so.

Thus, Billy Mitchell received the ultimate penalty for murder. Before being sent to death row, he escaped from the county jail where he was being held. But his attempt to evade the reach of the criminal-justice system failed. Weeks later, he was captured. Years later, he would die for killing Peggy Carr's son. The boy's death apparently was the second homicide in which Billy had been involved in as many days. The day before the convenience-store killing, he had evidently robbed and shot a man from Albany, Georgia. So, after his trial in Sylvester, Billy eventually pled guilty to and received a life sentence for the murder of this man.

⊲ ⊳

After reflecting on these things at creek side that morning in September of 1987, I found that my thoughts eventually turned to the previous evening.

On that evening, Billy's sister Jean and I sat on the open front porch of the black funeral home in Jackson, Georgia, where a hearse would bring Billy's body after he was executed. Other members of his family were inside, where they, too, waited for yet another glimpse of a man they had taken leave of a few hours earlier in the state prison, not far to the south. As Jean and I sat there in the twilight, we both looked out at the oak-lined street in front of us and several large, white wooden houses set in spacious yards. Occasionally a car would pull into the fast-food restaurant just up the road. It was a high-school hangout in this small southern town, which in many ways was not unlike Sylvester, where Billy's fate had been sealed years earlier. Every now and then, Jean and I could hear the voices of teenagers in the restaurant's parking lot. They were laughing, joking, probably unaware of the scheduled execution.

As Billy's life was ending, Jean and I spoke of some of the things that he had told me about and that I had read about over the summer in his appeals petitions. As one of the petitions reveals, he had been born in "the most poverty-stricken and crime-ridden section of Jacksonville, Florida." The place had been so bad that "cab drivers routinely refused to enter it and municipal bus service was eventually discontinued there." Amid all that poverty, Billy's family had been viewed as "especially poor." Even so, Billy had managed in important ways to do much more than simply survive. Embracing the goals of the popular culture, he had become captain of his football team in high school, and he had been the player to lead the pregame prayers. He had also participated in many other extracurricular activities: student council, both church and school choirs, the math club, the track team, and scouts. In addition, he had been a better-than-average student. His former high-school coach had tried to put things in perspective this way:

> To understand what an exceptional person Billy Mitchell was at that time, one must understand that, while a comprehensive high school, Butler . . . was a segregated school in the middle of a very impoverished area — what might be called today a ghetto. In that locale and setting, Billy Mitchell was a rarity because of the exceptional character he displayed at Butler.

At home, Billy, who had started working part-time in the eighth grade to help provide for his ten brothers and sisters, had been just as impressive as at school. In an affidavit she had submitted to Billy's appeals attorneys, his sister Jean had remembered this about him:

> Billy was the oldest boy in our family, and he took care of the other kids. Billy especially liked young children. When his brother Eric was a baby, Billy would be the one to get up and feed him at night. Billy washed him and put him to bed. He liked to take Eric for walks around the neighborhood and show him off. When Ronald was born, Billy wanted to name him, so my parents let him do that. I remember one time when Billy was about six years old, he got up early and fixed all the kids breakfast. That really surprised my mother. But Billy would do that regularly when he got older.

Tragically, Billy's promise was not to be fulfilled. While in his last year of high school, he had seen his world turned upside down. At that time his parents had argued violently, separated, and divorced. In turmoil over what had been happening at home, Billy had made some questionable friends, and soon thereafter he had been charged with attempting to rob a man. Billy had tearfully proclaimed his innocence. But his father, perhaps on advice from a court-appointed lawyer or maybe acting simply out of fear of the inscrutable proceedings of a white justice system, had urged Billy to plead guilty so that the court would be lenient. Billy had finally complied with his father's wishes. The charges against two friends implicated with Billy had eventually been dropped — but Billy had been sentenced to serve from six months to five years in prison.

Including the time he had spent in the county jail, beginning in the early spring of his senior year in high school, Billy had been incarcerated for over four years when he finally had been released from prison. A little over three months after his release, perhaps en route from Florida to a group of Black Muslims in California, he had committed murder in Georgia. For most of the time afterward, he had spent his days confined on death row.

When the hearse finally brought Billy's body to the funeral home, his story reached its final chapter. The body was placed on a simple wooden table, around which a few members of his family, one of his appeals attorneys, and I formed a circle. I thought to myself about how things had turned out for an individual who had seen what must have been powerful youthful dreams begin to die when he had still been a high-school student. At someone's request, I offered a prayer over the body. As well as I could, I spoke some words about Billy's struggle for freedom now being over.

◀ ▶

As I realized on the morning after his execution, much of what Billy and I had talked about that summer of 1987 had been connected with his quest for freedom, something that had been at the heart of his being and had brought meaning and purpose to his difficult days in prison.

On one of our first visits, he helped me to grasp how much he valued this quest. I asked him then how his many years as a prisoner had failed to break his spirit. And with a directness that I quickly learned was one of his defining qualities, he shot back, "I'm no prisoner." He was, of course, a prisoner — in an oppressive judicial system — and he understood this very well. But he gave his decisive answer, without elaboration, to alert me to the fact that there were kinds of freedom that were not beyond his reach. As I took in his self-assured physical presence, I knew what one kind of freedom was: carrying 240 pounds on his 5′ 9″ frame, he possessed the bodily strength, and thus the freedom, to avoid being bullied by anyone in the cellblock. He had earned the reputation on the row as someone you did not "mess with."

A little later that same day — as if to establish his right, along with mine, to set the topic and tone of our conversation — he asked me a question with his characteristic directness: "What do you believe . . . I mean, really believe?" And he bore down on me with a passion which showed that he was not motivated by idle curiosity. He was testing my authenticity, and he was discovering and affirming his intellectual freedom as the words passed between us. He was my equal in the struggle toward the truth. By answering his question with care, I hoped to engage his mind and encourage his quest for the freedom — beyond that of brute strength — that only the truth brings.

So that day I told him about my growing up in a culture defined especially by its failure to experience the depth of life and being. And I tried to explain that somehow I had come to sense this depth after having longed for it. There was something "more" than simply atoms and the void. There was something embracing us all. As a matter of fact, I felt it as we spoke to each other.

I tried to convey to Billy that at times I felt like Antonius Block, the knight in Ingmar Bergman's film *The Seventh Seal*. Like the knight, I had struggled with the "baffling reality" of God, and there were moments when I understood well Block's comment that "Faith is a torment. . . . It is like loving someone who is out there in the darkness but never appears, no matter how loudly you call." But Block's vision was also shaped by something else: his life had been joyously and profoundly transformed by the simplest of human encounters and the sublime gifts of nature. And I, too, had experienced such wonders. Like the knight, I had experienced, for instance, the magic of "faces in the evening light." I explained to Billy how important these kinds of experiences — meetings of "I and Thou" — were to me. For me, as for Antonius Block, they provided the substance of numinous memories, and like the knight I sought to tend them carefully. With such memories I, again like the knight, had "an adequate sign." For me, as perhaps for Block also, they were a sign of the Love at the heart of all being. Carrying these memories within, I felt intimately related to creation, alive — soulful, even. Though I could, from time to time, lose touch with their power, it reasserted itself again and again with astonishing resiliency.

I responded in this vein to Billy's question concerning my faith. I hardly tried to explain everything, but by the end of our visit, he seemed satisfied that I had given sufficient thought to what I believed. On other days he occasionally assumed the role of questioner again and pressed me about my views on a variety of subjects that were very important to him — for example, how to assure that the needs of poor persons and minorities were not neglected in our society. I tried to answer each of his questions with the same care that I had given to his query about my faith — to allow his freedom to grow.

Much of the time, however, I had a different role. I was a listener as he told of his past and present struggle with the burdens of his imprisonment. I do not know if the words Billy spoke to me about this theme led him to insights that he had not already gained. Such words were, I hoped, important as a continuation of his process of self-reflection, long underway before I met him.

Listening to Billy, I learned how arduous his struggle had been within a prison environment that had often threatened to destroy him. For instance, one time after we had gotten to know each other fairly well, he explained how he had been raped on one of the first nights he had spent in the Florida prison system. As he told the story of fighting to free himself from beneath his assailant's loins, he expressed himself with both sadness and searing anger. No longer a handsome youth but now a bulky thirty-five-year-old, he spun a gold finger ring as he mourned a portion of his life that had been ripped from him.

On other days he told me how he had struggled successfully to accomplish demanding tasks that he had set for himself at the beginning of his confinement. In his first years of imprisonment in Florida, he had gained his high-school diploma and completed college courses. I heard how proud he was that he had exercised his freedom to learn amid all the restrictions, noise, and turmoil of prison life. I also came to understand that the sexual attacks against him had continued and

95

were part of the turmoil he had had to contend with as a student in prison.

During one visit, I listened as he told me about some of the consequences of these attacks. Increasingly protective of his person and his "dignity," he had fought with prisoners and had "resisted" guards, with his words if not his fists. Such behavior, I concluded, surely contributed to a difficult burden that he occasionally talked about in regard to his Florida incarceration: the stretches of time he had spent in solitary confinement, sometimes sleeping on a concrete floor. He had lost a lot of weight at these times, he told me. Indeed, he said that seeing him in such a weakened, emaciated state had practically undone his mother. It was a state she had described in an affidavit filed with his appeals attorneys. She had remembered what she had seen after visiting Billy once just after he had emerged from the "hole": "His bones just stuck out. . . . He was so thin that knots were sticking out of his head."

Billy explained that eventually he had been sent to the especially dangerous Florida State Prison in Starke, where the violence had been intense and where he had once been stabbed with a pair of scissors. There, he had had to steel himself continuously, he said, to stay strong deep within himself, to stay free of fear. What he had to say about prison conditions there was consistent with the contents of an affidavit obtained by his appeals attorneys from one of his fellow prisoners who had known him in Starke. The man had remembered what another prisoner had once told Billy: "Mother-fucker, I [will] kill you and fuck you before you get cold." In his affidavit the man had also affirmed the following:

> Those years were very violent and turbulent years. There was day-to-day stabbing in . . . Florida State [P]rison. . . . In the morning prior to breakfast you could walk down the hall and see blood on the floor, sometimes on the wall, and it would remain there until the Third Team Squad who were responsible for cleaning the long corridor in each unit cleaned it up.
>
> There was a lot of fear among inmates which I knew. A lot of guys told me that — "man this place over here's a death house."

As Billy's fellow prisoner had pointed out in his affidavit, the "death house" had been a place where white guards had sometimes used terms like "nigger" and "black bastard" in reference to African American prisoners and had encouraged prejudice among white prisoners. Billy never talked to me in any detail about the problem of racism among the guards at Starke, but to him it was obviously worse than that which he had experienced in other penal institutions. I felt that I had perhaps a small glimpse of the problem at the Florida State Prison because he did mention to me once things about the racism among correctional officers at another prison where he had been confined before his stay in Starke. They were some of the same things that his sister Jean had remembered in the affidavit she had filed during the summer of 1987:

> The prison discriminated against blacks. The guards would taunt Billy just to get him angry, and they would shove him around. If he tried to stand up for himself, they would put him in the hole. Once, he told me they ordered him to fill a five gallon can with cigarette butts from an area. Billy told them there were not enough butts to fill the can, and so they punished him for refusing his work assignment.

Events like these lingered in Billy's memory that summer of his execution and were still sources of deep anger. Thus, when I mentioned to him once that one white guard in particular seemed sympathetic to blacks and whites alike on death row, he seethed. "They're all polices," he said in a hard tone. All guards had become consistent opponents of his freedom — so Billy viewed the world, long after those years in the Florida prisons.

Certainly, his desire to become free of the burden of racism had been a crucial reason for his interest in the Black Muslim movement while he had been imprisoned in Starke. An uncle of his had reported in an affidavit that Billy, after his release from prison in Florida, had talked to him in these terms about adherents of the sect: "They teach you good stuff. They teach you not to let anybody run over you. They teach you to hold your ground."

Significantly, however, Billy never spoke to me of Black Muslim teachings. When he did mention to me occasionally a religious insight that had sustained him and guided him daily toward an inner freedom that had helped him to deal with a variety of situations, including encounters with racism, he referred to Buddhism.

While he was on death row, one of his appeals attorneys had sent him a book by a Zen master, and Billy stressed to me the power of living in the present moment that he felt was revealed in the text. It was, Billy said, a truth that he had first experienced on the concrete floor of an isolation cell in Florida and that had become clearer to him over the years. I tried hard to understand the truth he had discovered, and I found that it apparently had more than one meaning for him.

During one visit, when I was first getting to know him, he spoke elliptically about a kind of detachment that I remembered D. T. Suzuki, among others, writing about: a state a person attains when, supremely mindful of the flow of experience in the present moment, he or she is liberated from the grasping ego. And I wondered on that day: Despite Billy's combative personality, was it possible that deep within himself he was sometimes actually in touch with a profound spirit of detachment that was the legacy of one of the world's great religious traditions? On another day a couple of weeks later, he alluded to his power of concentration in such a way that he seemed to be professing magical abilities. So great was his freedom, he apparently felt, that he could, for example, make dice "sing": he could command them to roll in certain configurations.

Especially as his death neared, there were times when he talked and acted in a way that allowed me another — and clearer — perspective on the power of the present in his life. There was the day after his execution date had been set and when he had less than two weeks to live. He was contending then with what he said was one of the greatest burdens of his imprisonment: the difficulty of seeing persons he cared about and who cared about him. Methodically, tenderly, he went over with me the names of family members and friends who might visit him in his last hours. He wanted my help in making sure that all potential visitors were contacted. His power of concentration allowed him to free himself of competing concerns and to be remarkably present to me at this point because it was so important for him to reveal to me his needs concerning visitation.

It was a power that was also vividly clear on his last visiting day, which he spent with a few members of his family and a couple of friends, and which, he told me, he was determined to make as humane as possible. On that day, such power allowed him to savor with great empathy the reality of deep relationships. He was emptied of all distractions then. I believed he was experiencing something like what the Buddhists called "no mind," and I told him so. In response, he laughed and said that I was finally catching his drift.

All in all, I felt that his living in the present in his final days did show that he had attained significant freedom, especially from his own bitterness and rage.

◀ ▶

At creek side after Billy's execution, as I reflected on his life, I recalled how my admiration of his strength and courage and humanity had grown as I had learned about his struggle. But I also remembered how I had felt an unmistakable sadness growing within me as the weeks of our visits passed. For, regrettably, even though Billy's quest for freedom had been underway during his incarceration in Florida, it had not saved him from the devastation of those years.

After he had been released from prison in Florida, he had been reeling from post-traumatic stress disorder, which a clinical psychologist working for Billy's appeals attorneys had diagnosed after she had conducted extensive research into his background. It was an illness whose origins had been visible early on during his imprisonment in Florida, where official records had noted his "incarceration trauma." It was a disorder that eventually had overpowered Billy and sent him toward his death.

Talking with me about the results of the examining psychologist's report was not important to Billy. He never brought up the subject of the disorder with me, and I never pressed him about it, even as the State was scoffing at the matter in the appeals courts, arguing that the diagnosis offered no compelling reason that he should not die. Still, in view of what he did tell me about his imprisonment in Florida, it seemed clear to me during our time together that he knew he had been deeply hurt, traumatized, by those years. It seemed equally clear to me that he knew that he continued to carry some of the pain of those years within him.

I felt that if he had chosen to talk about the diagnosis, he would have showed that he understood deep within himself the essential truth of the psychologist's argument: post-traumatic stress disorder can result when a person experiences an event "outside the range of normal human experience . . . that would be markedly distressing to al-

99

most anyone." It would have been evident that he understood that, upon his release from prison in Florida, he had displayed key symptoms of the disorder, as noted by the psychologist:

> First the traumatic event must be persistently reexperienced. Reports from Mr. Mitchell's family indicate that he frequently acted as if he were back in prison and would guard his food while he ate, for example. Second, the person must have persistent avoidance of stimuli associated with the trauma or numbing of general responsiveness that was not present before the trauma. The family clearly describes Mr. Mitchell as having returned from prison as distant and estranged. He refused to talk about his experiences to some people. His affect [emotional response] was restricted and he lost an interest in many significant activities. Third, the person must suffer persistent symptoms of increased arousal. Mr. Mitchell clearly suffered these symptoms as well, as indicated by his difficulty sleeping, his irritability, his exaggerated startle response and his hypervigilance.

As I sat with Billy and from time to time thought of the trauma he had experienced in prison beginning when he was a teenager, his actions inside the convenience store in Sylvester, Georgia, hardly seemed baffling to me, horrifying as they had been. His estrangement from other people had been blinding; his capacity for empathy had been severely limited. Indeed, I was not surprised that Billy had contended that he had seen the crate flying toward him in the cooler on the morning when he had killed Chris Carr. It did not seem impossible to me that the fourteen-year-old had actually made a threatening move — at a time, as Billy's appeals attorneys later pointed out, when Peggy Carr had briefly looked away from her son. But Billy had been tormented enough that morning to have interpreted almost any of the boy's actions as a threat. Even the most harmless move could have prompted Billy to do something that, as his examining psychologist noted, can result from post-traumatic stress disorder: to explode with aggressive behavior. And that is what Billy did — so great had been his deep-seated fear and pent-up rage.

When I listened to him tell his stories, I could not help believing that the threats he had felt in the past were occasionally menacing to him still, limiting his freedom. As he spoke and I thought I sometimes heard fear in his voice, I would ask myself if the crate he had said he had seen flying at him in the convenience store was not, now and then, tumbling perilously toward him in his mind's eye.

During my visit to the Ossahatchee Creek on the morning after Billy's death, I realized that I was, of course, still listening to his words. I continued to hear them from time to time in the days that followed.

About a week after he had been executed, I received a call from a woman who had befriended him in the last years of his life. She had fought for — and, in his final few days, regained — the right to see him after the prison had accused Billy and her of having sexual relations in the visiting room and had terminated her visiting privileges. She told me on the phone that she and Billy's sister Jean had scattered Billy's ashes at Callaway Gardens, not far from our farm. She went on to ask if my wife and I wanted to meet her at the Gardens one Saturday to pay homage to Billy. I heard his words "I'm no prisoner" as she spoke, for his relationship with her, a white person, was a product of his freedom.

I accepted her invitation, and on the appointed day Renner and I drove to the small lake in front of the chapel in the Gardens. As we waited for Billy's friend, I remembered how he had explained to me with pride that the woman had moved to Georgia to be near him; shortly after the move, he had said, she had discovered the Gardens, several thousand acres of lovely wooded land abounding in flowers, both wild and cultivated. When she met Renner and me, she told us that she had sent him photos of the landscape some months before his death and that he had been deeply moved by its beautiful flowers and trees. In fact, he had wanted to have his remains scattered there. As we stood at the lake's edge, Billy's ashes were still slightly visible in the shallow water.

At one point as Billy's friend and I chatted by the lake, we carefully passed between us brief stories about Billy: how he used to rail about the "bleeding," undercooked chicken that prisoners were served; how he could laugh about the undernourished mice that scampered through the death-row cells at night; how he had remarked one scorching day that he gained strength from the intense heat inside the cellblock in summer; how he had once commented that all his years in prison had not hardened him to the point that he could not take joy in watching small children play on the visiting room floor. In a way, I was listening to him still. His words were enduring signs of his powerful presence.

Near the end of our visit, I wondered out loud about the significance of the remains of a man who had passionately sought freedom finding their home here. In response, Billy's friend said nothing that I remember. Instead, she told us of her plans to get on with her life. She also told us how grateful she was — to life, to something — for the opportunity to know Billy Mitchell. I recalled how he had once made a similar comment about her to me.

◀ ▶

When I think of Billy now, various images of him come to me, as if they were carried by some lingering dry breeze of the summer of 1987. He was a man whom an FBI official once referred to as someone "who kills without provocation." He was a person who elicited equally harsh words from the head of Georgia's Board of Pardons and Paroles: "This is one case where there seem to be absolutely no redeemable qualities at all." He was someone who gloried in the fact that he was known on death row as the prisoner who had slapped Warden Walter Zant. He was a son and a brother and a friend who, in his last hours, departed with great tenderness from those he loved. In his last moments of consciousness on earth, as members of the KKK gathered on the prison grounds to cheer his death, he was a man who publicly instructed the head of the Pardons and Paroles Board to "kiss" his "ass," refused a prayer from the prison chaplain, and raised a clenched fist of solidarity toward his two appeals attorneys witnessing the execution.

When I think of this complex person, Billy Mitchell, I realize even more clearly than I did in 1987 how difficult a time he must have had in coping with the trauma that began with his incarceration in Florida. After more than a decade of reading and reflection, I have learned key things that help persons to deal successfully with trauma. Its victims need to find places of safety where they can recount their terrors to sympathetic listeners and mourn what they have lost, and they need to move on to forge trusting relations with still other persons. Billy had to

102

undertake such tasks within prison walls. Still, he managed to find ways to speak safely of his past and thus act on what Judith Herman has called the "fundamental premise" of the "belief in the restorative power of truth-telling." He was able to build trusting relationships with a few friends and re-establish intimate ties with several members of his family. As I knew from our time together, he could even grieve, in sadness and anger, what he had lost through the traumatic events of his imprisonment.

He discovered, as T. S. Eliot once put it, that "the use of memory" is "for liberation," for "expanding" our ability to love. By taking important steps to face his traumatic experiences, by integrating such experiences into his life, and by mourning his losses, Billy was able to avoid being consumed by the terrors of his past. I saw in him the positive regard for himself and the love for others that can result from the creative use of memory. I saw these things in the pride with which he conducted his quest for freedom and in his deep concern for his family and his passion for justice for all. Something especially instructive happened when he spoke of this last theme: his destructive rage, which had prohibited love, became moral outrage, which championed acts of love for oppressed persons.

Billy would have contended that he showed his freedom for love by entering fully the present moment, opening up to himself and others. In response to this position, I would say that his freedom to give himself over to the present grew from his coming to terms with his past — from his descending the dark stair of memory.

When I look back at Billy today, I find myself affirming that the man had "soul," difficult as the word is to define, odd though it may sound in a high-tech era. As James Hillman has pointed out, soul is best understood as "squarely in the midst of the world," not as a substance but as a perspective on life. And those persons who really knew Billy realized that in his presence they were frequently witnesses to a compelling, authentically human perspective. The perspective that revealed Billy's soul was often conveyed in his voice, shaped by his life experiences. The voice was indignant, mournful, perhaps sometimes fearful, when he spoke of how he had been treated in prison. It was determined and defiant when he talked about his quest for freedom from oppression. It was compassionate when he championed human rights for all. It was remarkably tender, even joyous, when he talked of how some of

103

his family made the long trip from Jacksonville, Florida, as often as they could to visit him. Occasionally the voice of his soul was shaped by shame, which I sensed once or twice, and which seems clear from the following scene that one of Billy's sisters described:

> When he was . . . in prison in Georgia, I was curious about something one day when I went to visit him. I said to him, "Billy, you know that boy you shot, did you directly shoot him to kill him?" I just wanted to know whether he did it intentionally. He hung his head down like he was real sad. He said to me, "No, I did not intentionally kill him." And that was that. I didn't ask him anything more about it.

Throughout this range of moods, the voice of Billy's soul found rich expression despite reason enough to remain silent, overwhelmed by trauma. The richness of his soul — truly "soul" in African American parlance, a revelation of the tension between freedom and bondage, joy and sorrow — endures within those who heard his cry for life. Today, when I speak of Billy to the death-row prisoners he left behind, his soul's voice often rises within me, and I am seized by the wonder of his being, as I often was when I visited him.

Billy's soul found important expression not only through his voice but also in moments of quiet in his cell. There, during the last months of his life, he discovered — or perhaps rediscovered — the gift of the imagination, which, as Hillman has noted, is of the very essence of soul. Defying bleak surroundings, Billy drew on this gift and found sustenance in a vision of beauty as he looked over his friend's photographs of Callaway Gardens. The perspective he attained hardly canceled out the terror of his past or present experience, but it must have offered a counterbalance to the horror. In gaining this perspective, which was shaped by the photographs, he called on a capacity to envision things that went far beyond the passive viewing of snapshots. It was a power that suggested to Billy where his true end lay: in beauty. Thus, he decided that his ashes belonged amid the west Georgia landscape. A profound expression of freedom, the imaginative power that he drew on revealed much about who he was. In keeping with the soul's worldliness, it was a power that connected him intimately to the things of the earth, to leaf and branch and flower.

By virtue of his gift of imagination, Billy would have grasped, I think, the importance of my trips in search of the mountain laurel each spring. He would have sensed the lure of the ten, tiny red spots in the white laurel blossom, each spot connected to the center of the flower, at one stage of its growth, by an arcing filament. He would have understood, too, my journey through the bottomland the morning after he died. The hot and dusty landscape, where beauty lingered even if it was partly veiled, was a balm to my soul; I was in touch with my version of Arcadia, the region of ancient Greece whose rustic loveliness had been revered in the Western tradition. He would have understood my journey because he had taken his own walk in Arcady before he died, contemplating his final resting place at Callaway Gardens.

I hope Billy's power of imagination would also have allowed him to understand that the statement that Peggy Carr made a couple of years before he was executed — "I won't be satisfied until I get revenge" — is a reason for profound sadness, lamentation, on the part of us all. Without beauty, her words embody a vision of life that diminishes all of our souls and shows that we as a people failed not just Billy but her too.

7

While the Earth Remains

Walking hand in hand, they had spread out "in a line a half-mile long," according to what I read in the newspaper. Prisoners and law officers alike had gone to the swampy area known as Banks Pond in south Georgia, a few miles from Ray City. It was February, and the cold, knee-deep water hurt as the men moved through it. Finally, word came from a prisoner who spotted him: "Cap'n, here he is." The body, shirtless, had been there, "floating face down." They had finally found Ed Giddens, the police chief of Ray City. He had been killed on what was to have been his final night on the job before he headed to Florida, where he had planned to join an uncle in the orange-grove business.

Late that night, on February 11, 1976, Giddens had stopped a car fitting the description of the one that had just been used in a convenience-store holdup. The car's occupants had been Henry Willis and two other men. They had overpowered the chief and driven him in their red Ford Fairlane to Banks Pond — as he had begged that his life be spared, offered to keep quiet about his kidnapping, and said that he would show them an escape route. Fearful that the chief would identify them, they had shot him a number of times, apparently as he had been trying to get away.

After I read the newspaper article, the gist of which I had often heard before, I wondered once again: What had life been like for Ed Giddens' three children without their father, who had seen his family's bright dreams fade in the dark waters of Banks Pond? And how had things gone for Henry's daughter, forced to grow up without her father? The article, of course, did not say.

◄ ►

A couple of hours after reading the piece in the newspaper, I found myself listening to Henry telling me, among many other things, about an important episode from his own early years. A black man, like each of the other two persons convicted for the murder of the white police chief, he spoke to me in the prison visiting room, not far from Georgia's electric chair, on what was to be the last morning of his life: May 18, 1989.

I had never met Henry before and had not been sure that he would want to visit then. We had exchanged a few letters during the previous several months, and I had offered to drive up to see him. In response, he had suggested that we might "try to begin a friendship" through the mail. But he had not wanted to visit; perhaps we would see each other later if things worked out, he had remarked. He had clearly been struggling, and visiting someone he had never met must have seemed difficult: "The [bad] situation with the courts has really affected me and at times I don't feel like doing much of anything," he had written one day. "Since my father died last year things have affected me [more] than usual and I often phase in and out," he had written at another time, reflecting on a man whom he had really gotten to know only after he, Henry, had become an adult, deeply immersed in a life of drugs and crime.

When it turned out that Henry did want companionship, on that morning of the 18th of May, his attorneys and friends were pleading for his life at the state's Board of Pardons and Paroles in Atlanta, about an hour's drive up Interstate 75. He never mentioned the proceedings during our time together. He spoke of things like the story from his youth that revealed much about his plight in a white-dominated culture. When he was fourteen, Henry was working at the farmer's market in Moultrie, Georgia, the town where he lived. One night he did not come home as soon as he should have. As he rode his bicycle through the darkness, he was accosted by a group of white men in a car. One of the men had a gun. Terribly afraid, Henry said only "Sir," and then peddled away furiously and escaped down a narrow alley. He was shaking so badly that his bicycle rattled long after he finally came to a stop.

This was the world he had had to contend with when he was growing up, he said. He told the story slowly and almost matter-of-factly, offering it not as an excuse for anything he had done but simply as a way of helping me understand who he was. His life had been filled with such acts of racial conflict, he told me. But he was now free of any racial hatred, he explained. He took people as they came, one by one.

He went on to say that he hoped he was also free of violence, which he had witnessed repeatedly — at the rate of a shooting or a stabbing each week — in the black community where he had spent his formative years. He could never do again what he had done back in 1976, when he was twenty-one, he said. He paused for a moment, his face becoming tense; both he and I knew that the specter of Ed Giddens still stalked him. I thought he might go on to talk about things that he had said at his trial: He had been acting under the influence of a co-defendant (who was much older than Henry) when he had shot the police chief. And when he had fired, he had believed (wrongly, it turned out, in the view of an expert witness for the State) that the co-defendant had already killed the chief. But he did not speak of these things. This much was clear to me, however, as he sat in front of me: He had great sorrow for what he had done that night thirteen years earlier. He was not free of such sorrow.

After a few seconds, he began to speak of something else that he was not free of: his sadness that resulted from his mother and father's abandonment of him when he was a child and from the indifference most of his family had shown him during his long imprisonment. I could hear the loneliness and shame that had begun so early in his life rise up within him as he spoke. Such feelings were surely compounded by what his grandmother had said in a recent interview, which he had read in the morning newspaper: "If he done that [participated in the murder of Ed Giddens], I think he should die because the Bible says 'He that kill, shall be killed.'" Still, he was without rancor. Indeed, he said he was thankful for whatever love he could find. With gratitude he remarked that his grandmother must care about him, for she had also said in the interview, "It's hurtin' me all over. I would just like to have the body, but I don't have the money to bury him."

And so we talked on through the morning while the case for overturning his death sentence in favor of life imprisonment was being heard by a Board who had never met him. (That afternoon I found out that the one black Board member was not present; I did not hear if she voted in the case or if Henry's fate was left to the remaining members, four white men.) I spent most of the time just listening to Henry, letting him determine the course of our conversation. I trusted that somehow deep within himself he would know how best to use our time together.

Sometimes he spoke of small things. For example, he talked of the care he had to take in writing letters. He was left-handed, and if he was not careful, the ink would smear as his hand moved across the page. He also told me that he still followed the advice of a sixth-grade teacher who had stressed how important it was not to write beyond the red line that formed the right-hand margin of a page. And he explained that he would start a letter all over again if he made a mistake.

With the topic of writing on his mind, he went on to a weightier matter. He spoke of how he had done pretty well in school until he had begun to get in trouble. He had dropped out after the tenth grade. He wished he had made more of the opportunities for education he had been given.

One time he spoke of reading his Bible, but not of a God who was going to pull him out of the fire at the last moment. If he held any such belief that morning when I visited him, he never revealed it to me. It was true, as I had learned after his death, that some three months before his execution he had entertained the hope of divine intervention on his behalf. On a day in February of 1989, when he had felt that all "legal avenues" had been "exhausted," he had written the following words in a letter to his friends Mark Bippes and Lise Greene, a white couple who had met him at his trial and corresponded with him regularly over the years: "The only thing that we can do now is to pray and ask the Lord to bring about a change in the situation." And he had continued, "We have to appeal to the Savior above because in the book of Matthew 21:22 he said that all things whatsoever ye shall ask in prayer, believing, ye shall receive." But hours before his electrocution, he was quiet about any such appeal or the possibility of its success.

He was resigned to dying, but he had hardly accepted his death with a saintly peace. I realized that when I commented on how composed he looked and joked that his nickname, "Cool Breeze," was fitting. He laughed, said that he was still "plenty nervous," and remarked that I should have seen him before he came down for our visit. For hours he had been shaking — even more than he had been that night twenty years ago when he had ridden away from the car full of white men. Still deeply affected by the difficulties of his past and facing directly his imminent execution, he struck me as a man profoundly in touch with himself, including his own vulnerability and weaknesses. While the temptation to retreat from the reality of his emotions and the desperateness of his plight must have been enormous, he was simply — remarkably — human.

Just before I left him so that he could visit with a couple of friends who had arrived from the hearing of the Pardons and Paroles Board, he smiled but said nothing when I told him that I never gave up hope and that I had made an appointment to see him the next day at one o'clock in the afternoon. After a few seconds, he reached out both of his hands toward me and clasped mine firmly. At that moment, as he had been the whole morning, he was not a person immobilized by depression — despite the struggle he had shared with me in his letters. Moreover, in spite of his sorrows and regrets and his precarious future, he was not a bitter man. At the time we parted, as during the three previous hours, he seemed grateful for whatever life he had.

◀ ▶

As Henry and I had talked, my mind had occasionally wandered — as his must have, too — to the proceedings going on at the Pardons and Paroles Board. Those persons trying to save his life were explaining to the Board the story of his early years, the murder, his trial, and his personal growth in the hope of staving off the forces of death that had pursued him for so long — forces that even skilled civil rights attorney Millard Farmer, who had represented Henry during his trial and subsequent odyssey through the courts, had not been able to defeat.

The story began with Henry's birth to a mother who was not married to his father and who did not want her son. When he was just three weeks old, she put Henry in a cab and sent him to his paternal grandmother. The infant shuttled back and forth between the two women from time to time. When he was six months old, his grandmother found him alone in a room of an elderly woman's house; he was in a hole in a bed, where he had been for four days, his skin peeling from his body because no one had turned him over. The grandmother, who lived in poverty, finally adopted him when he was twelve. As the years passed, he turned to drugs — and to crime to support his habit. Reeling from the pain of his youth, he took part in the shooting of Chief Giddens.

Working in Henry's defense in court, Millard Farmer had a number of judges who had been assigned to the case disqualified for racial prejudice. And Farmer was finally successful in getting the trial moved, but not where he wanted. The county selected, where fewer African Americans were living than in the county where the murder had taken place, was at the top of the prosecutor's list of choices. Thus, it was in middle Georgia's Bleckley County, in the town of Cochran, that "justice" was meted out in 1978. It was a town where black persons working for the defense faced enormous hostility, repeatedly hearing the word "nigger" used to refer to them.

The district attorney, who had burned one of his law books in protest when one judge on the case had been disqualified, knew what it took to win in proceedings in which race had already been made a crucial issue. In the D.A.'s tenure of over seventeen years, there had been a history of blacks being underrepresented on the criminal trial juries in his judicial circuit: from 1961 to 1978, only 3 percent of the members of such juries had been black, although African Americans composed some 25 percent of the population in the circuit. In Henry's case, the prosecutor had twenty of the thirty-one prospective black jurors excluded for "cause," contending that they were incapable of reaching an impartial verdict. He used all of his so-called peremptory jury strikes, which were subject to few restrictions, to eliminate ten other African Americans who might have sat in judgment on the defendant. In the end, an all-white jury found not only that Henry Willis was guilty of murder but also that he should die for the crime.

And then there was one final part of the story. The Henry Willis who had at first been hostile and uncommunicative to his attorneys and others trying to help him at his trial began to change, to soften. During the trial and the months and years that followed, he became a different person. Regretful of his past mistakes, he was a caring individual whom, as Lise Greene would tell the Board of Pardons and Paroles, she had come to love as a brother. She and her husband wanted Henry to come live with them if he was ever released from prison.

111

As it happened, the majority of the Board's members were not sufficiently moved by Henry's story. When I heard their decision, I wondered if they saw him much more clearly as a human being than the white men who had stopped him while he had been riding home from the farmer's market so many years earlier. "The crime was committed in cold blood and there was no doubt about the participation of Henry Willis in shooting the victim," said the Board's chair. That seemed to be the sum of the insight of the majority of those deliberating Henry's fate. And although I was not with Henry when he learned that they had turned down his plea for life, I do not think he was surprised by their decision or their lack of insight. How could he have been, considering all he had been through?

＊　＊

When I look back now over the hours and days after the Board's decision, a number of things come to mind. For example, I think of the time outside the prison on the evening of Henry's electrocution, originally set for seven o'clock but delayed for over four hours by a court stay. I was part of a small group that had come to hold a vigil against capital punishment that night. At one point, as we waited for Henry's punishment to be carried out, Millard Farmer spoke with great emotion to the press about his client's remorse — Henry would give anything to be able to turn back the clock and undo what he had done — and about the racism that permeated the state and the nation.

For much of the time afterward, before the hour of the electrocution, I was in the company of the mothers of two men in prison. One of the men sat not far away in a death cell as Henry's execution approached; the other man, previously a death-row prisoner himself, had recently received a life sentence without the possibility of seeking parole and was now incarcerated in a prison hours to the south. I sat with the two women in a car on the edge of the prison grounds. As the car's radio played softly, we waited for news that Henry might somehow avoid electrocution. Once or twice the two women spoke of their pain because of what the families of their sons' victims had gone through and because of the long ordeal they themselves had experienced. Both mothers had been facing their pain for some fifteen years. Most of the time we simply sat there, quietly, the night falling rapidly, our only light the faint green glow from the radio dial. At one point one of the women broke the silence by asking, "Do you think all this will ever end?" I had no answer, and the silence rushed in to fill the space around us.

As the time of execution neared, I looked over at a car next to ours and saw Lise Greene, who had been Henry's friend for over a decade. She was weeping. As the seconds ticked away, I thought of others caught up in the tragedy. Somewhere, spread across the state — and perhaps beyond — were the families of Henry, Ed Giddens, and the two men convicted along with Henry of murdering the chief. And then there were the three men themselves who had been convicted of the killing. As Henry was being readied for his death, one of his co-defendants in the case awaited his ultimate punishment on death row. Henry's other co-defendant had been only nineteen at the time of the crime and had been sentenced to life in prison. I could not imagine what the families of Ed Giddens, Henry, and his two accomplices felt on this evening. Nor could I fathom, at the moment, what was on the minds of the three men who had brought about the chief's death. I continued to think of them all as our group circled for its vigil and Henry was electrocuted.

When I think of the time that followed, I remember going into the prison the morning after the execution and visiting with three men who, I believed, might soon be meeting Henry's fate. I was weary and probably should have gone back home. But I had promised one man that I would see him, and thinking that he and the others might need to talk about what had happened the night before, I made my visits as scheduled. As the hours passed, none of the men seemed very talkative, and I did not have much to say, either. The first man I visited did ask how Henry had been on the last day, and when I simply answered "Okay," we never returned to the subject. When the topic of the execution came up in my visit with the second man, he remarked briefly that he would commit suicide before he would allow any such thing to happen to him. The third man, the person I had promised to see, made some comment like "I wonder who's got Henry's TV time in the cellblock?" at one point and passed quickly to another topic, so totally incapable was he of dealing then with what had happened.

Of the events following Henry's execution, I also think of his funeral and the hour or so afterward. After his death, I had great difficulty finding someone in his family who knew about arrangements for his burial. And when I finally learned that a kinswoman in Perry had decided to have a funeral and to try to raise the money for it later, I raced across central Georgia in my pickup, reaching the cemetery as the brief ceremony was ending. Arriving just ahead of me were Lise Greene and Ed Weir, a man who had befriended Henry, visited him regularly for years on death row, and helped set up a hospitality house for the families of condemned prisoners. Lise, Ed, and I went back to the funeral home and talked with a few of Henry's relatives for a while. Standing outside under some shade trees, we took an occasional photograph and swapped stories. One family member told of a time when Henry worked for a pizza restaurant; she said he would sometimes bring home a creation he called a "Humdinger," pizza dough filled with peanut butter and honey. After listening to her and others and offering some words of my own, I asked myself: As cordial as Henry's family was, was I actually *meeting* them at any real depth?

〽   〽

Shortly after raising this question, I leaned against a large oak, took in the scene in front of me, and thought of the last African American funeral I had attended, that of Richard Tucker, who had been executed on a May evening two years earlier. I recalled that I had asked, in effect, the same question after I had been with Richard's family on the day of his burial: Did we really meet?

I remembered sitting on the dais with a few other persons in the chapel of Randall's Memorial Mortuary in Macon, Georgia. In the small, low-ceilinged room, occasionally someone in the audience would capture my attention. One such person was a thin, elderly black woman, neatly attired in a print dress. She was Richard's Aunt Sally, with whom he had often lived when he was growing up. Not far from her was a woman in her early forties who was looking over the dais into spaces she alone knew. She was Richard's sister, Annie, his only sibling, who had also lived with her brother at their Aunt Sally's. Conspicuous in their whiteness, but somehow not out of place, was a handful of faculty from Macon's Mercer University. Members of the Glad River Congregation, they were sitting stiffly together in a pew. And then there was a black man in a wheelchair at the back of the chapel. The funeral home's proprietor, he had been a seminal figure in the town's civil rights heyday in the 1960s, and afterward. Motionless, looking down at the floor before him, he was caught up now in one more saga of his people's tragic history.

Hard moments for Richard's family and friends passed as the service progressed. There was sustained wailing. I rose to speak, trying to say what I had learned about a man I had visited half-a-dozen times in the last month of his life. Others spoke too. After less than an hour, we left the building for a nearby cemetery, a ragged, uneven piece of land, overgrown with weeds. Jumbled grave markers jutted into a hot Georgia sun. Someone said a brief prayer, and as the group of mourners bunched awkwardly around the grave site, we laid our brother Richard to rest.

Afterward, I spent an hour or so at his aunt's house, a short drive from the cemetery. I wandered about, speaking with those who had been at Richard's funeral. We served ourselves from a couple of tables laden with fried chicken, turnip greens, pound cake, and iced tea. When I finished visiting and eating, I said farewell. I embraced others and was embraced. I felt appreciated by Richard's family. But had we really met? I wondered. Would the gulf between black and white in our country ever really be bridged?

Two years later, as I looked at the tiny group of Henry Willis's mourners, I remembered asking myself another question after Richard Tucker's funeral. The question applied not only to Richard but also to Henry: How does one escape the harshness of one's surroundings, avoid the tragic consequences of a debilitating social environment? Neither Richard nor Henry had managed to avoid such consequences. Each man's life had been shaped by different events, of course. But I knew that the lives of both men had a basic theme in common: the difficult childhood they had experienced and the terrifying aftermath.

I recalled the outline of Richard's life (the formative years of which his court-appointed lawyers might have drawn on, but did not, to provide mitigating evidence at his capital trial for a murder committed in 1978). Born in 1942, he saw his early years shaped by the frequent drunken bouts of his parents. Even when they were small children, he and his sister, Annie, were at times left to themselves while their mother and father "dried out" in jail. Both brother and sister were so neglected that they had to miss school during one year because they had no shoes. When Richard was eight and Annie was six, the two went to live with their mother's sister Sally, who took care of them as well as she could. But the children felt that they were neither loved nor wanted, and would often cry at night on their pallets on the floor. Richard felt especially ill at ease after moving into his aunt's two-room house, where six members of her family were already living with her. He would eat his meals only after the others in the family had finished, not wanting to take food from their mouths. He became a "quiet" child, a "loner" who did not confide in people. Eventually he started hearing that he was turning into someone as "worthless" as his father.

In his early teens, Richard lived now and then with his mother, who had separated from his father. At this age, the youngster often saw her drunken boyfriend beat her and would try to intervene to help her. When Richard was fifteen — a time when he spent much of his life on the streets — he found his mother dying after she had been hit with the blasts of a neighbor's shotgun. She had quarreled with the neighbor over a bottle of whiskey. At seventeen, having already dropped out of school, Richard began serving a year in prison for shoplifting clothes. After he was released, he worked at odd jobs and "hustled." When he was in his early twenties, he pled guilty to killing Annie Mae Armstrong, one of his aunts. Intoxicated and angry, he had repeatedly stabbed her with a pair of scissors one day after he had gotten into an argument with her about borrowing her car. He spent thirteen years in prison for the murder. While he was there, a fellow prisoner once bound him to a cot with a leather strap and raped him. Richard retaliated violently.

In September of 1978, several months after his release from prison on parole, he was arrested for the murder of Edna Sandefur, a white nurse who had been kidnapped from the parking lot of a Macon hospital, robbed, and then bludgeoned to death with a metal pipe. Her nude body, too badly decomposed after it had been found for experts to determine if she had been sexually assaulted, had been left behind an abandoned warehouse. She had been abducted on a day when she had intended to visit her critically ill mother. It had been a day when Richard had been smoking marijuana and drinking. In line with a statement he had originally given police after his arrest, he testified at his trial that he had been involved only in the kidnapping and robbery of Mrs. Sandefur; an accomplice had actually murdered the woman, he said. Circumstantial evidence suggested that Richard had acted alone in carrying out the crimes. Reinforcing this view was a second statement that he had made to police and that he disputed in court. A jury of nine whites and three blacks gave him the death penalty.

On the day of Henry Willis's funeral, as I reflected again on the events of Richard Tucker's life and the murders of Annie Mae Armstrong and Edna Sandefur, I was filled with the horror of so much tragedy. There just had to be a way, I told myself, for persons such as Richard and Henry to break free from the trap of neglect and abuse in which they had been caught — and to avoid the destructive behavior that could result from such entrapment. This was a complex issue, I realized. Still, in regard to this issue, one important idea had surfaced in my mind during the last two years: that of the rescuer.

I thought, for example, of the life of Richard's sister, Annie. Someone — actually, several persons — had come to her rescue after she had left her parents. Both Richard and his Aunt Sally had tried to shield Annie from encountering the horrible reality of her mother's existence, which Richard had known only too well. Richard had never discussed with his sister their mother's life of drunkenness and violence, and Aunt Sally had discouraged Annie from visiting her mother. Moreover, when Annie had still been in her teens, she had received an invitation to come and live with an aunt in West Virginia who had needed a dependent to be accepted into public housing. I did not know how nurturing the woman had been, but at least Annie had had the opportunity to escape an environment that had been devastating to her brother. Eventually Richard's sister had become a successful businesswoman in New York.

The more I thought about it — especially the more I reflected on what I knew about the families of the men on death row — the more clearly I realized that I had heard again and again about the work of rescuers. Often, someone had been available at just the right time and had established a supportive relationship with a condemned man's brother or sister or cousin, who had experienced tremendous adversity in childhood; thus, a person in great need had found a way beyond neglect and abuse, shame and despair, and violence. Unfortunately, when they had been growing up, the men who awaited execution had found no such way. Part of the problem may have been their own reluctance in seeking or accepting assistance — hardly surprising for individuals who typically had few lessons in intimacy. Perhaps, too, help had been offered at

117

inauspicious times. But surely there had been another key factor in their plight: there had been few persons of strength — and, in some cases, none at all — available to reach out in sacrificial love to these deeply troubled individuals.

◀ ▶

As Henry's kinsfolk began the lengthy process of taking leave of one another at the funeral home that May afternoon in 1989, I thought of something else that bound the lives of Richard and Henry together: though Richard had given a statement to prison officials on the day of his execution, he, like Henry, had declined the opportunity to offer truly last words in his final moments. I went on to ask myself still another question, one that I carried within me long after I had left Henry's family: Were both men in a similar state of mind as they sat in the electric chair, silently, waiting to be executed?

I remembered thinking, after Richard's death, that I had at least begun to understand his silence. Partly in an effort to explain this silence to myself, I had made a series of notes in the days and weeks after his execution. They were notes like these:

When he had been a child and teenager, Richard's quiet demeanor had masked his deep frustration and anger, even rage. No longer completely given over to the terrifying silence of his youth, Richard discovered, as an adult, another kind of silence that afforded access to love and freedom.

One afternoon when I was visiting him, about a week before he died, he said something that has stuck with me ever since. We were talking about anger. I expressed my anger and frustration at a society that seemed too often to see death as the only way of dealing with its problems. He spoke of anger that he had felt toward his parents and toward some "enemies" he had made in the state prison in Reidsville, where he had served time on his first murder conviction. Then he stopped talking for a good while, something that was typical for him. His long fingers groped in the silence for clarity; they opened and closed and opened again. Finally, he spoke: "Sometimes, I am angry now, but deep inside my heart is still, and the anger passes quickly."

He was trying to tell me that he had found a place of inner sanctuary where he could deal with the ravages of his life without having to lash out at others and, in the process, destroy himself. It was from this quiet center that he could reach out to me and to others in gentleness and love, rather than strike out in rage. In touch with the stillness of his heart, he could write the following words (though he struggled to express his insight) in a letter to the Pardons and Paroles Board a week before he died: "But I have managed, despite the many . . . odds against me . . . to have reached a strong degree of collective and personal consciousness that . . . enables me to live in the best regard toward others' lives while regarding my own, without abusing either." Perhaps through the help of friends and family, he had discovered within himself a kind of oasis in the desert. At least in his last years, he was able with some consistency to reach this oasis and allow his soul to be refreshed, nourished. I doubt that he ever attained the strength to put to rest entirely the ghosts of his early years. At times he seemed too tormented for that. But he had made significant progress in dealing with these demons.

From his place of inner stillness, he remarked to me once, proudly, during his last days, "I'm a member of the human race now." He explained that the stillness he had attained had allowed him to deepen his concern not only for those persons he knew — his family, friends, and fellow prisoners — but for the human community as a whole. In his letter to the Pardons and Paroles Board, he wrote of his sense of interconnectedness to others this way: "Now I know, from the very depth of my soul, that my own resurrection of mind is the resurrection of the mind of the world also, and vice versa." And with striking simplicity, he expressed a related insight near the very end of his life in a statement he made before he entered the death chamber: "It has taken some time [to realize it], but I am a part of everyone and everyone is a part of me. No matter where I go or how I go, everyone goes with me."

From his place of inner sanctuary, had Richard come to grips with the murders of Annie Mae Armstrong and Edna Sandefur? When he did speak to me once of the killings, it was only to express his horror concerning them. Never did he deny that he was a murderer. Whatever happened the night Edna Sandefur was killed, I think Richard had indeed taken important strides toward coming to terms with whatever role he had played in her death — just as he had, I believe, taken important steps to come to terms with his murder of his aunt Annie Mae Armstrong.

I think his silence included important moments of self-appraisal, in which he took stock of what he had done in his life and the reasons for his actions. There was a gravity about the man that suggested this to me. Such gravity and self-appraisal found expression in his letter to the Pardons and Paroles Board. Trying to explain the frame of mind he had been in years earlier, he acknowledged to the Board the problem he had had dealing with his inner turmoil and keeping "others' best interests in focus . . . as a person in control of his faculties should be able to do." He went on to write the following about himself: "I perceived reality from a perspective that nobody else but me could perceive or occupy." He was not trying to "justify" his "past behavior." But, he suggested, by calling his troubled "mentality" to the attention of others, he might make himself "a bit more understood."

In my brief eulogy for Richard at his funeral, I ventured to set forth how far he had gone in his understanding of silence. Over the years, Richard had opened himself up to an inner place of stillness where he had confronted himself and where he had discovered his deep connection to the human family. As a person of faith, he had also discovered there a great and scandalous truth that had somehow remained valid at the very end of his life: Love will prevail. In his final moments, when he had offered no words from the state's electric chair, when he had simply sat there, quiet and surely frightened, he had dwelled in a silence that had revealed to him the presence of this Love, the very Creator of his soul.

Two years after my eulogy for Richard Tucker, I wondered if Henry Willis's final moments of silence had reflected a similar kind of spiritual power. It was possible that, in this silence, Henry was drawing strength from a life of the spirit that had been nurtured for years by friends such as Mark Bippes and Lise Greene and Ed Weir — just as Richard had been sustained by a few persons who had finally come his way. But the more I contemplated the horror of those last minutes and seconds before Henry's death, the more difficult it was for me to envision the reality of God's love and thus its presence in his life just before his electrocution. In fact, I began to ask myself if I had understood Richard's final silence correctly; maybe I had not faced directly the terror of what had happened to him.

The issue of the men's silence was still on my mind when I said good-bye to Henry's family and later when I drove home. As I made my way through central Georgia to my farm, I thought again and again of a detailed newspaper account that I had read of Richard's last moments. In many respects, Henry's final moments would have been the same.

The newspaper article described the slow, orderly process of execution. Warden Ralph Kemp took his place in the death chamber, which witnesses sitting on wooden pews were able to view through a pane of glass. Kemp announced that the execution was about to be carried out. Led by two of the six guards assigned to the death chamber, Richard entered the room. Once in the electric chair, "his lower lip quivered slightly as the guards tightened the leather bands around his biceps, wrists, calves and waist. Another strap clamped his thighs tightly together." One guard "adjusted the headrest" on the chair. Richard was given the opportunity to say some last words, in addition "to a statement he had tape-recorded earlier." He declined. Reverend Nolan Lavell (a prison chaplain), who had entered the chamber, offered up a prayer as "Tucker remained silent." Kemp read the order of execution from the court. "Three guards stepped forward to make the final preparations." These included attaching the strap across Richard's chin, placing a "leather cap over" his head, and aligning "straps from the cap's leather harness across . . . [his] forehead and eyes." Richard seemed "very nervous" as the preparations commenced. Next came the application of electrodes, one "with a wing nut [attached] to the top of the death-cap," a second fastened "to a wide leather band around Tucker's right leg, where his prison pants leg had been ripped to expose the skin of his calf." Richard's head "was dabbed with a saline solution that would help carry the electrical charge." One of the guards "placed the leather cover over Tucker's face." Then all but the warden and a single guard left the death chamber. These last two persons confirmed that Richard's bindings "were sufficiently tight" before they, too, departed the chamber. Hidden by one-way glass, three volunteer guards simultaneously pushed three buttons. Only one of the buttons was live, and it sent two thousand volts of current through Richard's body, which "suddenly snapped back against the chair. His back arched slightly. . . . His hands balled into a tight fist, with the thumbs on both hands tucked inside his slender fingers." The current was on for "about two minutes." There followed a brief "cooling down period." Finally, Warden Kemp and two doctors went into the death chamber. The first doctor "stuck a stethoscope under . . . [Richard's] T-shirt." The procedure was repeated by the second doctor, who also "reached under the leather face covering and checked for a pulse on Tucker's left carotid artery." The second doctor "nodded to the warden that Tucker was dead," and Kemp made the following announcement through a microphone: "At 7:23 on May 23, 1987, the court-ordered execution of Richard Tucker was carried out in accordance with the laws of the state of Georgia."

When I think back over those days after Henry Willis's funeral, I realize that I gained then an important insight into the limits of my actions and a deepened understanding of the role I played in the lives of death-row prisoners and their families. I also know that during those days I felt the absence of God with a keenness far greater than I had ever experienced before.

I was deeply frustrated. Not only had I entered Henry's life far too late to rescue him from his participation in a terrifying act of violence and from an execution whose brutality was equally terrifying; I also began to wonder if I had done anything at all to help him as he had awaited his death — so briefly had we known one another. And I was not even sure that I had truly "met" his family, whose sorrows reached deeper than I could imagine.

My frustration was compounded when I began to take stock of what I had done during the previous four years in regard to the death penalty. I had to admit that my response had been limited indeed. I had engaged in only sporadic political action. I had spent only a few hours each week with a few condemned men — and even less time with their families. And I had done nothing on behalf of the families whose loved ones the men on death row had been convicted of killing. Thus, the time after Henry's execution brought home to me with painful and lasting clarity something that I had occasionally glimpsed before:

when I looked at the big picture, I was doing precious little to foster healing and reconciliation in a state that seemed to clamor for vengeance and death.

I knew that the problems of the death penalty were far greater than any one person could begin to solve; indeed, they were far greater, I was learning, than I had imagined when I had been ordained in 1985. Still, I had to come to grips with my own moral lethargy. I found that I confronted myself time and again with the charge "You could be doing more, much more." Day after day since then, I have had to face the truth of the accusation. Such an accusation has sometimes goaded me on to do a bit more. I have, for example, spent a little more time with the families of death-row prisoners — both before and after executions — and I have tried now and then to reach out to family members of murder victims and to share something of their sorrow and anger. But for the most part, the accusation has remained a constant reminder of my enduring frailty — and that of all of us.

I have seen clearly that finally there is no unbridgeable chasm between "us" and "them": between me, for example, and the executioner. All persons are caught in an inescapable web of evil — if "only" through their inaction. The personality's shadow, which Jung wrote so much about, is a persistent companion of each of us. Thus, ever since those days in May of 1989, when I walk through the prison and encounter the faces of the people whose work makes possible sentences of death, I often see my own face in theirs, if sometimes only for a fraction of a second. In these prison employees, I meet myself. I had sensed long before I met Henry Willis that I was "a part of everything," as Alice Walker had put it; after his execution, I knew with a depth not present earlier that "everything" included profound evil.

After Henry Willis's funeral, something else of equal importance also began to come into focus for me, if only gradually: my role as *witness* in his life and in the lives of the other death-row prisoners and their families whom I had known and would come to know. The term points to a stance that I have taken that has remained important to me despite my brokenness, despite the pain of my moral insufficiency.

Ever since I was a young man, when I have thought of the concept of witness, I have remembered especially God's words to "Jacob" and "Israel" in Isaiah — "And you are my witnesses" (44:8) — and Jesus' words to his apostles in Acts — "and you shall be my witnesses . . . to the end of the earth" (1:8). I have understood that, among other things, for persons of the biblical faith a witness is someone who acknowledges a God of promise, One whose acts create hope in and beyond history.

In the aftermath of Henry's funeral, I realized that such an understanding of witness was radically different from my own. Instead of hearing and rejoicing in words of divine promise, I experienced the silence, the absence, of God — as, I told myself over and over, both Richard and Henry may well have experienced, too, in their final excruciating moments before two thousand volts of electricity coursed through their bodies. Indeed, in the days after Henry's burial, the witness that I was slowly beginning to understand was accompanied by my keen awareness of Nietzsche's proclamation of God's death, which seemed truer to me than ever before.

In this difficult time, what did the witness that I was beginning to comprehend really mean to me? It had important things in common with the concept of witness that Judith Herman would later describe, based on her meetings with victims of trauma: it included a commitment to "solidarity" with someone in great distress and an affirmation of the "value of life in the face of death." In explaining my own understanding of witness to myself, I kept coming back to my visit with Henry on a day when his lawyers had been working hard, trying to save his life: my witness then had been a frail presence in which I had struggled to be *with* him and to affirm the value of our time together, despite my knowledge of his cruel predicament, despite any clear signs that I had been "helping" him. In an act of solidarity, I had been taking in — witnessing — his pain and courage, as much as I could. And, broken as I was, I had been witnessing to the fundamental worth of life and being by the attentiveness of my gaze, by the ardor of my heart. I knew that this affirmation of worth had been strengthened by Henry's own bearing during our time together, for, troubled and afraid as he had been, he had made a similar affirmation. But I attributed neither his affirmation nor my own to the workings of the divine.

In the days following Henry's funeral, when the silence of God was deafening, I was overcome at times by nihilism and torn by my sense of the absurdity of existence. Still, I kept returning to the fundamental rightness of my witness during the three hours I had spent with the man whose friends had dubbed him "Cool Breeze."

As the months passed after Henry's death, I slowly began to recover my spiritual equilibrium — for reasons that finally lie beyond me. And the reach of my continuing witness grew. It remained a frail presence, characterized more by being than doing. But I gradually found that when I was with death-row prisoners and their families, I was witnessing nothing less than the image of God within each of them. Moreover, I was able to affirm in faith that the source of the creation whose worth I witnessed to in my meetings with these men and women is ultimately a Love that makes all my times of witness possible.

Even though I have struggled now and then over the years since 1989 with renewed experiences of the silence of God, I have sought to carry on my witness, knowing well how insignificant — or worse — it may seem to others in a time when the editorial writer of the *Barnesville (Ga.) Herald-Gazette* speaks for many of us, I fear, in the following words: "Criminals like Henry Willis III, the others executed before him and those currently under death sentences are human waste. Executing them should come as easily to a civilized society as flushing the toilet."

As I have continued my witness, I have sometimes wondered if the times are so dark that we as a people cannot, in the foreseeable future, come to grips with things that I have learned about as I have tried to listen in solidarity to persons like Henry Willis and Richard Tucker. To cite one example, I have wondered if we will admit the devastating role that traumatic events in childhood can play in an individual's development, a role stressed by the most sensitive writers about child abuse and neglect?

When I am most dispirited, I worry that our antipathy these days to what we call a "victim mentality" may blind us to the terrifying forces that have damaged some of those among us, wounded the very core of their being. I fear that our legalistic obsession with not "excusing" someone who commits a crime may make it impossible for us to have real understanding and compassion for persons who have been brutalized by forces beyond their control. And in my dispiritedness, I tell myself that we may never grasp an important truth: When an infant is very badly neglected — when he or she is left as Henry was, for example, lying in a hole in a bed for four days, with his skin finally peeling off — the trauma of such an event can have a long-term, deleterious effect on the development of his or her personality, causing it to be shaped by things such as great fear and shame and anger.

For my part, I have tried to point out, now and then, how during my

125

times of witness I have learned much about the debilitating effects of child abuse and neglect — and about other things as well, like the power of love to beget love, even in those persons who have been deeply hurt in their early years and whom society has judged to be beyond redemption. For I have seen not only how the terrors of youth can ravage the soul but how love empowers the will and allows an individual who has been traumatized to reach out to another person in the most genuine of moments. What I have learned about love in this regard is corroborated by the last letter that Henry wrote to Lise Greene and Mark Bippes, who had given him the gift of friendship all the time he was on death row:

> I didn't want to write this letter and hoped that I never would have to. . . . The day I dreaded and never wanted to see is now less than a week away. . . . I really don't know what to say in this position because I've never gone through it before, and I'm a nervous wreck right now, but because I love you two like family it was a must that I try to say what is going on, and the sad part for me is how . . . devastated you'll be. . . .

In sum, I stand by the frail witness that I have made among death-row prisoners and their families. I seek to sustain my times of solidarity and affirmation. I do so even if my encountering and remembering the lives of persons such as Henry Willis and my attempts to explain their significance may not amount to much by the standards of our contemporary society. I do so as a sign of the worth of those men and women I have met in my times of witness and as an act of fidelity to whatever truth I can bear.

◀ ▶

During the years since Henry's funeral, I have thought a lot about a verse in the book of Genesis (8:22) in which the Creator speaks these words: "While the earth remains, seedtime and harvest, cold and heat, summer and winter, day and night, shall not cease." The verse is clearly meant to underscore God's promise never again to cause the destruction Noah saw. But, I have told myself, the "author" of the text may well have been no stranger to hard times and may have intended more in his words than a simple, naive affirmation of promise. Driven perhaps more by my own needs than by exegetical correctness, I have ventured this interpretation to myself: The verse also acknowledges that while the earth remains, the extremes of existence will continue. In other words, along with promise, we will experience the burning heat of summer and the bone-chilling cold of winter. And we will have to endure the darkness, too. Moreover, I have told myself that the verse affirms implicitly that the extremes of existence do not invalidate the ultimate worth of creation.

When my ability to witness to such worth is challenged by a sense of absurdity and nihilism, I eventually recall how my encounter with Henry Willis that last morning before he died led me to an affirmation of life and being — without lessening his tragedy or that of Ed Giddens. My memory of that time helps me find my way through the darkness to witness once again. As I do, I invariably, if gradually, begin to discover grace at work. It is a grace that I hope both Richard Tucker and Henry Willis somehow experienced in their silence, in their last moments of consciousness on earth. It is a grace that leads us ultimately to assent to the fullness of promise: Love will prevail.

8

A World Far Away

William Hance often seemed to live in a world far away, removed from the facts of his existence. For example, during the seven months when I visited him in 1993 and 1994, as his death drew nearer and nearer, he delighted in telling me, over and over, about his essentially supernatural prowess with women. He did so in a series of rambling statements with a single underlying message: He could look at a woman, any woman, just the right way and make her fall in love with him.

Frequently he made another claim that was almost equally incredible, even to those most sympathetic to him: He had not beaten to death Gail Faison, a young black woman, in Columbus, Georgia, in early 1978. It was a murder for which he, an African American, had been convicted and received the death penalty later that year, after he had tried to represent himself with the assistance of court-appointed counsel. With passion and conviction, William proclaimed to me his innocence, repeating that there was no proof of his guilt. It was as if he had forgotten the abundant evidence to the contrary, including his detailed confession, fingerprint and handwriting samples that linked him to extortion letters in the case, his knowledge of the location of a weapon (a jack handle) used in the murder, and — at a 1984 resentencing trial — his admission of the crime. (A federal appeals court had overturned his original death sentence because of the prosecutor's "dramatic appeal to gut emotion" and the trial judge's improper exclusion of two prospective jurors for their views about capital punishment. Another jury had resentenced William to death in 1984, after he had served as co-counsel in his defense.)

Now and then, William moved beyond variations of these two often-repeated claims. When he did so, there were times when I thought that what he said was linked to reality. For instance, he told me once how he, as a small child, had found an injured bird, secured a box for it, fed the creature, and tried to nurse it back to life. At another time, he said that when he had been a little boy, he had almost drowned in a local river. He had feared the water ever since, he explained. He went on to say that the incident had come back to haunt him when he was a young man in Marine Corps basic training. Hoping to avoid a swimming test then, he had lied and said that he could swim. When he had been found out, he had been thrown into a swimming pool and had almost drowned as a drill instructor had kept pushing him under the water with a long pole. William told me that, to his great embarrassment, he had cried afterward.

He once related to me another troubling event that had also occurred in the service. In basic training, he had made some kind of mistake and had as a consequence been struck by his drill instructor. That much seemed plausible. However, as William continued his story, I think he quickly lost his grasp of reality, because he explained to me how, minutes after graduating from the training course, he had located a .45 pistol, cornered the instructor in the barracks, and given him a humiliating thrashing with the weapon.

I remember another time when William began telling a story with realistic details but moved on quickly to what clearly seemed to be fantasies. On that day, as he talked of a routine trip to a guard's office on death row, he soon was telling me how he had discovered and played with the officer's fully loaded personal pistol, which the man had brought from home. The trip had led, too, to William's discovery of a mysterious, seductive "investigator" in a micro-miniskirt, who had offered him sex to try to get him to divulge important information about his case.

On some occasions when William was briefly free from his stock themes, I simply did not know if he crossed the line between reality and fantasy. During one of our visits, for instance, he told me how he had been taken by death-row guards to a court hearing one day and had moved off the sidewalk leading to the courthouse. In spite of strict security measures, he had been permitted to walk to a nearby tree and rub his back against it, something he had not done in years. All the while, he had held his head back, allowing the first few drops of rain, which had just begun to fall, to touch his face. On another of my visits, he commented about camping out alone in a field by his grandmother's house when he was a small child of four or five, and watching the stars turn in the night sky. Apparently forgetting his near-drowning in a river, he added that he had learned at an early age that he could trust nature. I had no way to tell for sure if he had camped out by himself when he was so young. But at that moment I felt that I was at least encountering his honest and deeply felt longing for a world where he felt safe.

During our visits, I thought to myself that part of William's problem might well be his limited intellectual ability; he just could not comprehend the events of his life. But I felt that there was also something else at work: often he was in the thrall of fantasy, which simply rejected the real. Seldom was William able to exercise his imagination, the capacity to move *through* the real toward some authentic sense of possibility and meaning, however tragically shaped by the events of his life. Only in his very last days did I notice a few signs that he could grapple with the reality of his situation and look clearly at the lives of other persons as well.

◀ ▶

Reviewing William's personal history, especially the affidavits of those who knew him, one draws the conclusion that in many respects his was a life lived in isolation long before he was incarcerated on death row.

When he was growing up, he was "quiet"; one neighbor remembered him as "withdrawn." This is hardly surprising, considering the neglect and abuse William suffered as a child. Born in 1951, he was about a year old when his father abandoned him and his mother and sister. Thereafter, William's mother did domestic work in their hometown of Lexington, Virginia, to provide for herself and her children. The family of three lived in a small, drafty house heated by a wood-burning stove. There were times when William had little care or supervision. For example, his mother took her daughter, who was three years older than William, to work with her when the little girl was four or five; William stayed with three young cousins, still little boys, whose own mother was working. His mother eventually married a man who was an alcoholic; he regularly beat his wife with his fists and her children with a leather horse strap. One night when William's sister was ten and William was seven, the man came home drunk and raped the girl in the same bed in which both she and William were sleeping. William watched, helpless, as his sister stared at him through the ordeal.

William's isolation from others was exacerbated by his difficulty learning. As one of his teachers in a high-school science class for "slow and retarded students" remarked, William "was definitely a slow learner who had to have a lot of help.... [He] just couldn't grasp concepts." William's sister remembered what he did when people called him "dumb" and "picked on him a lot" because he was "slow": "[He] always just walked away and tried to keep out of people's way." Another Lexington schoolteacher described the consequences of William's learning difficulties this way: "William didn't run with a crowd. Rather, he was out on the edge.... I believe William's reluctance to join the crowd of kids around him was his way of hiding his mental retardation."

A former guidance counselor at Lexington High School suggested that William was isolated from reality, unable to distinguish fact from fantasy:

He impressed me as actually not simply depressed or anxious but out of touch with the real world around him.

... I remember him sitting at my desk and making his hand into a plane and going "ZOOOOOOOMMMMMMMM." He wanted to be a pilot, but there was no way he was ever going to do it. He simply didn't have the mental ability to attain such lofty goals. He didn't realize that the very behavior he was exhibiting was canceling out any chance he might have had. There was no congruence between what he was aspiring to do and what he could do. He was a very limited and disturbed boy who had no business being accepted in the service.

At the time William attended Lexington High School, there was very little in the way of special education, but he participated in what was provided for slow learners. Many students, including William, were passed socially [i.e., even though they were failing].... I thought of him as a mentally retarded person who additionally lived in a fantasy world.

131

Yet another sign of William's isolation during his youth was noted by his sister. "Sometimes Billy would just sit and stare for a while," she remembered, "and we never knew what was going on with him. Sometimes, you could shake him and he'd come out of it, but sometimes you just had to wait till he came back to himself." The nature and cause of such spells were apparently never investigated medically when he was growing up.

As frustrated and often isolated as he must have felt, William was nevertheless, as one high-school teacher put it, "very cooperative and extremely likable." Indeed, he managed to find ways at times to overcome some of his isolation. When he was in high school, he joined the Civil Air Patrol and proudly wore its uniform. As an adult, he attained increased — though still limited — competency in his culture. After graduating from high school when he was twenty, he struggled with books to bone up for military admissions tests and finally was able to get into the Marine Corps in 1971, under the reduced admissions standards developed during the Vietnam War era. He spent several years in the Marines; then, after a brief hiatus, he enlisted in the Army, serving for about a year before the murder of Gail Faison. The structure of the military suited him well. As is clear from the 1984 trial testimony of his former first sergeant in the Army, William progressed to the point where he could, with close supervision, perform such tasks as leading a group of five or six men who picked up ammunition on the post and delivered it to a unit there.

After he joined the Marines, he married a young woman he had met before entering the service. Though she remembered years later that he had been good to her son from a prior relationship and to the daughter born to her and William, the marriage must have been troubled from the beginning. One reason seems clear: William's wife had to contend with his inability to perform everyday tasks. In an affidavit, she made this point: "Billy never could do things like paying bills or the other things that have to be done to get along in life. He just didn't understand how to do those things. . . . I had to take care of all of that for our family." Eventually William and his wife divorced after she had become unfaithful to him.

After his marriage had failed, William, now in his mid-twenties, met a woman who became his girlfriend and gave birth to his son. Describing a time after William had left the Marines and joined the Army, this woman noted the same kind of problem that William had had in his marriage:

> He was like a little puppy, always following along behind you, and he was about as able to deal with the world as a puppy is. In the Army, he always had somebody telling him what to do and how to do it, so he could handle that all right, but outside of the Army, he was lost. He just didn't know how to do things like pay a bill or take care of himself in lots of ways. I had to do a lot of things for Willie to keep him on track.

Thus, even though he overcame some of his isolation during his years in the service, he was still removed then from important parts of the everyday world.

During these early adult years, before his arrest for murder, other signs of his isolation continued to manifest themselves. He sometimes still had staring spells, as his former girlfriend noted. She also observed that his penchant for fantasy continued: "One of my sisters is schizophrenic, and Willie always reminded us of her: one minute they're talking sense, and the next minute they're off in Disney World." His ex-wife remembered something similar: "He told stories that couldn't possibly be true but it was obvious that he really believed them. It was like he was possessed by something that made up stories in his head."

As his sister's affidavit explains, in his early years in the military, he had to cope with the rape of his invalid mother and her subsequent death. These events, which were truly traumatic for him, may well have aggravated his tendency toward isolation. He also had to face another potentially isolating event while he was in the service. As was brought out at his 1984 resentencing trial, his increasing financial difficulties led to his being barred from re-enlisting in the Army until he could overcome them.

◄ ►

Beginning with the preparation for his 1978 trial for the murder of Gail Faison and continuing through the appeals process, various psychological experts examined William. Those in the employ of the state's mental-health system, which regularly functions as an agent of Georgia's courts and prosecutors by evaluating defendants, ultimately concluded that he was in contact with reality, responsible for his actions, and competent to stand trial. Still, even some of the state system's own experts acknowledged that he had his difficulties. Thus, after examining him in 1978, two experts wrote to the trial court of his "moderate depression and anxiety which are associated with emotional difficulties characterized by long-standing feelings of inadequacy, inferiority, and insecurity." In a separate letter to the court, one of the two, a clinical psychologist, noted that persons of William's psychological type "tend not to be particularly able to think for themselves and their emotional difficulties frequently interfere with their judgement." He also stated (and thus implicitly questioned William's grasp of reality?) that "they typically have rich fantasy lives, especially about sexual matters."

These opinions of the expert seem not far from the views of a psychology professor who examined William for the defense before the 1978 trial. In a letter to William's court-appointed counsel, the psychologist explained that William's contact with reality was good enough to preclude calling him "psychotic in the usual sense," but he also wrote that the defendant was "prone to day dreaming and fantasies," did not "seem to grasp the seriousness of his situation," and displayed the behavior of "a child." He questioned William's ability to "assist in his own defense." The psychologist testified at William's 1984 resentencing trial that the defendant suffered from a personality disorder that was characterized by such things as "poor judgment," a failure to achieve empathy for others, an inability to take responsibility for his actions, and a tendency to behave irrationally. In an affidavit submitted in 1987 for an appeals court proceeding, a psychologist retained by William's appellate lawyers argued that William was depressed and suffered "from a Personality Disorder with Paranoid, Dependent, and Narcissistic features."

In 1994, near the end of his life, William's appeals attorneys retained two clinical psychologists with specialized training in neuropsychology to examine him. Taking into account his personal history, both psychologists saw their client as delusional — one specialist noting that William suffered from "an organic delusional disorder." Moreover, the two experts found evidence suggesting that he probably had a "seizure disorder." The psychologists — one of whom reported that William suffered from "organic brain damage," the second of whom noted his client's "organic brain dysfunction" — also saw as important two tests that had been part of a court-ordered evaluation of William prior to his 1984 resentencing trial: an EEG with some "suspicious" results and a brain scan showing "questionable" activity. (Physicians for the state mental-health system, which had done the testing, had suggested follow-up testing, though the doctor who had interpreted the brain scan had felt that its activity was "probably [a] normal variant." Such follow-up work had apparently never been done.) The mental-health system's experts had reported to the court that William had been competent to stand trial and never mentioned the problematic test results. This was a significant error, his attorneys contended in his final round of appeals.

Neither psychologist who examined William in 1994 was able to give him a complete battery of IQ tests and thus could not report specific IQ scores, for their client was (in the words of William's chief appeals attorney) not "fully cooperative" — a fact that was understandable to anyone familiar with the depth and range of his problems. Still, after reviewing William's personal history and evaluating him, both experts concluded that he was a person with mental retardation; one expert suggested and the other specified that William's mental retardation was mild. The two psychologists' conclusions were not all that different from the results of a battery of IQ tests that a mental-health examiner from the state system had administered to William prior to his 1984 resentencing trial, results which indicated that William's IQ was not far from the upper limit of mental retardation: the scores ranged from the mid-seventies to the high seventies. Somewhat higher were the results of testing done by the state system prior to William's 1978 trial: these scores were in the mid-eighties. The two psychologists' 1994 findings did differ more markedly from some of the results of a battery of tests given to William in 1987 by the psychologist retained then by his appeals counsel: the scores ranged from the low eighties to the high nineties. As William's appeals drew to a close, his lead attorney argued that the 1987 IQ exam was especially suspect because it contained significantly higher scores than other testing.

◅   ▻

William was surely someone with considerable personal difficulties, whatever their precise psychological description. And he was also someone with limited conceptual ability when, in late February of 1978, he evidently killed Gail Faison. Some two weeks later, the young soldier apparently also murdered another African American woman, Irene Thirkield, who was seen with William just before her death and who was beaten with a car jack that he later helped authorities to locate. He had met both women in a bar.

During this time, the city of Columbus, Georgia, was seized by terror because of the so-called stocking stranglings of six white women — by a person many residents believed to be black. After Ms. Faison's death, but before her body was located, William began writing a series of extortion letters related to the stranglings to the Columbus police department and the local newspaper: He threatened that Gail Faison would be killed — indeed, that a black woman would be killed every three months — if the police did not apprehend the strangler or pay a $10,000 ransom. After Ms. Thirkield had been murdered, but before authorities discovered her body, William also wrote letters threatening her life if the terms he set forth were not met. The letters, all but one on Army stationery, purported to be from a white organization, the "Forces of Evil," and were sometimes signed by its "Chairman."

It is possible that the range of William's violence extended beyond the killings of the two women mentioned in his extortion notes. Some months prior to the deaths of Gail Faison and Irene Thirkield, he may have committed another murder, that of Army private Karen Hickman, a white woman, whose body had been battered and left in a ditch. Eventually he confessed to investigators that he alone had committed all three murders; he had made up the idea of the "Forces of Evil" and written the letters to divert attention from himself, he said. His convictions in an Army court in 1979 for the killings of Ms. Thirkield and Ms. Hickman, both of whom had been murdered on the Fort Benning reservation while William had been stationed there, were overturned by a military review court, which ruled that he had been illegally arrested. (In its opinion, the review court also noted that a majority of court-martial members had doubts after the trial that William had actually murdered Private Hickman.) Army prosecutors chose not to retry William, who had been sentenced to life in prison for the crimes, because he had already received the death penalty for killing Gail Faison.

What could have motivated William to kill? He had been through a lot in the previous few years, beginning in 1972 with the death of his mother, followed by the failure of his marriage, which had ended in divorce in 1977, and then the financial difficulties that had jeopardized his career in the Army. His fragile psyche had been under siege. Perhaps he felt more isolated than ever; surely his competency had been challenged.

Given this context, his confessions to the murders of Gail Faison and Irene Thirkield offer a plausible — if partial — explanation of his violence. He said that he had become angry when the women had tried to prostitute themselves to him. Deeply upset over his own lack of self-worth and dignity and lacking ways to deal effectively with the problem, he may have been driven over the edge by the women's actions: for William, murder may well have been a desperate response to the disrespect shown him by the kind of person who, as he expressed it in confessing to Irene Thirkield's murder, only wanted "to take other people's money." As he attacked the women — first with karate chops, then with a heavy object to make sure each one was dead — perhaps his penchant for fantasy also was at work: he may have thought he was engaged in moral action, driving evil out of the world. If so, such a fantasy may not have lasted very long. For, according to statements he gave authorities in regard to both murders, his violent actions soon led him to weep, even as he was delivering his final blows to his victims. Perhaps his tears showed that he was aware that his own long-standing feelings of a lack of self-worth were only compounded by such blows.

Something else may have contributed to William's death-dealing behavior, something noted by the psychologist who was retained by William's appellate counsel to evaluate him in 1987: without discounting William's capacity to experience affection for women, the expert called attention to his client's significant "negative feelings" toward them. This negative attitude may have been shaped by William's abusive stepfather. For the only man William ever really knew as a father seems to have had no respect for William's mother and sister. Not only did William see this lack of respect manifested in acts of violence; he also once caught the man in bed with a prostitute. Other factors may also have influenced William's negative attitude toward women. As the psychologist pointed out, William's mother "was unable to prevent her husband from abusing the children." Furthermore, William's wife had been unfaithful to him. Viewed through the distorting lens of his fantasy, perhaps murder seemed a justifiable way for him to make up for the problems he had had with women.

Was racism yet another factor that contributed to William's violent behavior? For example, did he see in Gail Faison and Irene Thirkield the lack of worth that he as a black person had felt so keenly in the midst of a white-dominated society? Did his loathing at being an African American — an emotion that could have been intensified by the actions of the "strangler," clearly a black man in the eyes of the writer of the "Forces of Evil" letters — turn finally to a rage that destroyed "unsuccessful" individuals of his own racial heritage? And in a state of mind clouded by fantasy, did William perhaps think that by committing murder he was doing the world a service?

I know of no way to prove that racism may have played a role in William's violence. Indeed, though he trusted me to a significant degree, he never said anything of real importance to me about the barrier of racism that, because of his skin color, must have surrounded him all of his life. Perhaps he simply was not capable of articulating the difficulties caused by such a barrier. In any event, it is hardly impossible in my view that racism may have played a role in the murder or murders that William committed; it might even have been a factor in his killing of Karen Hickman, if he did that. Her whiteness could have fueled his rage. It seems axiomatic that simply because of the color of his skin, he had to endure the sad and brutal legacy of racism: things such as isolation, shame, and fear, which could drive a person to violence. Growing up, he no doubt experienced these things over and over, perhaps even at a time when the racial situation in Lexington was supposed to be improving: when the schools were being integrated. For one of the city's teachers described the time — when William was beginning high school — this way: "During those first few years of integration, the black kids were scared and mostly just sat quietly so everybody would leave them alone."

◅ ▻

Despite the many difficulties he faced in his life, William managed something remarkable in the days just before his death, when his need to escape into fantasy must have been great: he achieved brief moments of insight into the people and events of his present experience. Because he was never far away from his flights of fancy, such moments of insight were striking. My memories of the time I spent with him in his final days coalesce around his struggle for lucidity.

I remember one time of insight well. William wanted to have some Polaroid photographs made of him posing with the few members of his family who had been able to come to visit him: his sister and her son, his ex-wife and his daughter, and his former girlfriend and his son. His desire for the photos seemed clearly based on his recognition of how much his family cared for him, even though they had rarely been able to make the trip to see him.

Later in the day, he showed a related insight. At a time when his family was gone for a while, he leaned over to me and, with a hurt expression on his face, asked me why I had not taken part in the picture-making. For he had also asked me to be in the photos. "After all," he said, "you're family, too." We talked for a couple of minutes, and I apologized to him, explaining that I had not wanted to interfere in a special occasion, and he was satisfied that I had meant well. "It's okay," he said; "I understand." When I look back at that time now, I realize that he was struggling to see me clearly and succeeding in understanding that I was someone who did indeed care about him. Moreover, his capacity for love triumphed as he moved beyond his inner world of fantasies and into a world of genuine mutuality. I can still see him sitting there on the stool in the visiting room after I had apologized to him. After the initial hurt had passed, he was almost smiling. Bent slightly toward me, rubbing his hands nervously on his knees, he was battling the fear of being vulnerable and, in his own way, embracing me, discovering the source of all life between us, revealing the power of being itself. But after a short time, he began to talk on and on about the lack of proof of his guilt, presumably in the case that had brought him the death sentence and perhaps in the other two cases as well. With great conviction he scoffed at the idea that he had written the "Forces of Evil" letters, not mentioning the handwriting and fingerprint evidence that contradicted his claim.

Another brief time of insight occurred one morning when I spent about an hour visiting with him alone. It was Wednesday, the 30th of March, 1994, the day before he was executed. What there was of his family had gone to a clemency hearing at the State Board of Pardons and Paroles, a majority of whose members (three of whom were white, two of whom were black) could commute his sentence to life. I had not gone to the hearing because I was too closely linked with forces against the death penalty in the state. (As usual, appeals attorneys felt that it was best for the Board to hear from those persons not readily identifiable as being opposed, in principle, to all executions.) A few of William's friends had not yet arrived at the prison: a woman who had become acquainted with him years ago when she had taken part in a prison ministry project, as well as three other persons who had offered support to him for years. At one point during our hour alone together, he began to speak quietly of his fear of being placed on death watch, in a special holding cell. He told me that already twice that morning he had heard the approaching sounds of guards' boots and the clanking of keys. As it turned out, the officers had had business with someone else in the cell next to his. As William described the scene for me, I saw genuine signs of lucidity in him. For a few moments we talked with realism about his family and the important role he could play for them: strengthening them and allowing them to strengthen him in his final hours. I believed that he was sorting through some of his options clearheadedly then and attaining some imaginative glimpse of important tasks that life held for him at the end of his days. But soon he began to talk at length about how irresistible he was to a female prison employee who walked by the visiting-room door.

Later in the day he regained his lucidity. A little after three o'clock, I phoned the Georgia Resource Center, the publicly funded law firm that was handling his appeals, to get an update on his case. Then I went into the visiting room to break the news to him that the Pardons and Paroles Board had denied his plea for life. He was with members of his family. He had been allowed to visit with five of them at a time since they had arrived from the hearing at the Board. The mood was upbeat. They had not yet heard the words of the Board's white chairperson: "The punishment [death] fits the crime and the criminal." I went behind William's chair and knelt down, putting my hand on his shoulder. Their faces full of expectation, his visitors bent forward on their chairs and stools. His sister was smiling broadly. I stumbled through the words, hardly getting my message across, when William looked around at me and said with real insight, "Go ahead — it's okay. You can say it. I know. I'm going on death watch."

He spoke to me then during one of those moments of genuine

meeting: each of us was emptied of all distractions and filled the other's gaze. But I backed away from the power and honesty of such a moment, perhaps not believing in William's ability to handle so much reality. I tried to cushion the blow and said, "There's still hope left, especially in the Georgia Supreme Court. This is just something that William has to go through. 'Death watch' doesn't necessarily mean he's going to die." But in his case, I knew that there was little reason for optimism then. So did William. And so did his family members, whom I left alone with him for the last half-hour of the visitation period.

When three-thirty came and the family had to go, the pain of parting was overwhelming for them. It took a while, amid all their wailing and tears, for them actually to leave the prison. As they huddled together in a large area outside the visiting room and tried to compose themselves, I walked over to William. He was standing behind the steel mesh door of the visiting room, taking in the whole sad scene. "I'm gonna die, aren't I?" he asked, almost making an assertion. Perhaps again not trusting his ability to handle so much painful reality, I replied simply, "It's not over yet. I'll see you in the morning." I put my hand against the mesh, hoping that he would place his hand against mine. But he did not. I think he had left his fantasy world behind again and was living for a time in the immediacy of his pain. I turned and walked away with his family through the trap gates and the long tunnel out of the prison.

When I arrived early the next morning, I was shocked at William's appearance when I first saw him. A small man, he seemed even smaller than normal then, in contrast to two large guards who brought him down to the visiting room. His arms wrapped tightly across his chest, he looked somber and said nothing. It was clear that he was cold, so I asked one of the guards to bring him a jacket. After a couple of minutes, I told William that his family had left for their homes in Virginia and west Georgia and had sent him their love. I never told him why they had decided not to visit again: they could not bear one more day at the prison. William just stared for a while, speechless. Finally he commented that the smell of death was "all around the death watch cell," and I was struck by his lucidity. Then he quickly began to talk, once more, about the lack of proof of his guilt and asked me to call the head of Georgia's Department of Corrections to arrange for some kind of special meeting with the man. It seemed as if he expected the official to drop by for lunch. As William spoke, I thought of a couple of other fanciful ideas he had mentioned to others in the past: that he be banished from the state, instead of being executed, and that the governor provide him a "furlough" from prison.

Soon three other visitors arrived who had been with William the day before: Murphy Davis and her husband, Ed Loring, Presbyterian ministers who had spent most of their adult lives caring for persons lost in our midst, especially the homeless and prisoners; and Mary Sinclair, a paralegal from the Southern Center for Human Rights, who had taught all who knew her so much over the years about the value of human presence. The arrival of the other visitors helped to brighten William's mood, and soon we were doing the only thing we knew to do as we waited for news about his appeals: we were telling or laughing at funny stories. At one point, William related a story of his own. I remember that it showed some insight into his situation, and I recall our reaction to the story. He explained how, only hours earlier, he had responded to a prison official in charge of death row. The administrator had come to the bars of the death-watch cell on some errand and had asked, "William, do you know who I am?" William had put the official in his place, shooting back with, "Man, I've been here all these years, and you don't think I know who you are?" We all laughed, impressed by William's surprising show of acumen. Then, as if trying to broaden such insight, someone said, "You should have asked him if he knew who *he* was!" More laughter. For whatever reason, someone else chimed in and made an allusion to Billy Moore, a former death-row prisoner who had gone through death watch and had, at the last minute, been granted clemency: "You should have said, 'Man, I'm Billy Moore, and I've been waiting here for more than three years to go free. It's about time you showed up!'" Still more laughter followed.

And so it went for several hours: story after story, interspersed with sips of soft drinks from Styrofoam cups and shared bits of candy and cookies from the prison vending machines. It was Maundy Thursday, the anniversary of the Lord's Last Supper, and those of us who were William's visitors were celebrating a kind of communal meal with someone who, like the Nazarene before him, would soon be a victim of capital punishment. Much of the time our laughter was probably not a way of helping William face reality; instead, it was a way for all of us to come together in his world of fantasy, where we might deny or at least try to forget what seemed likely to come.

At one point early in the afternoon, our storytelling stopped long enough for me to remind William that it would soon be time to "sign those papers for me so that the prison won't hassle with your family anymore." He knew what I meant. It would soon be time to sign over his body to me so that I could make the funeral arrangements — based on donations, since his family had no money to bury him — that I had worked out earlier with his sister and his former wife. When I had tried to bring up the subject on the previous day, he had not been able to handle it and had switched topics immediately. But now, as his death loomed nearer, he was able to acknowledge the fact that his family needed help in caring for his body and to agree that I could assist them. Still, he was not able to utter the word "funeral."

Later in the afternoon, Tom Dunn, William's chief attorney from the Georgia Resource Center, joined our little group. After a few minutes, a phone call came for Tom. He learned that, without explaining their four-to-three decision, the Georgia Supreme Court had denied William's appeal. As Tom told us of the decision, I was looking at William, who accepted the news quietly. I was struck by the fact that he seemed, at first, aware of the gravity of the situation. But then he leaned back with a faraway look in his eyes. He seemed a long way from the reality of a lower court judge's key ruling, which the Georgia Supreme Court had not seen fit to challenge. In regard to William's claim of mental retardation, the judge had pointed to the inability of the two psychologists who had recently evaluated William for his attorneys to provide "results of IQ tests" — specific scores based on a full battery of tests. He had also noted other evaluations, which had put William's IQ above seventy. And he had dismissed other appeals claims — such as the argument that state mental-health experts had withheld evidence of William's brain damage — without even mentioning them, contending that they had been barred by previous court decisions or that they should have been raised earlier. As I thought of the judge's ruling, William remained impassive, sliding one of his feet quietly back and forth across the visiting-room floor.

After a few moments of silence, Tom went on to assure William that he had not given up and would fight on. He also said that he thought William would get a stay at some time before the scheduled execution at seven o'clock that evening. How long the stay might last, he did not specify. At three-thirty in the afternoon, one by one we took our leave of

143

William. When my time came, I could get out only a few words. I told him "I'll see you" and gave him a hug. "Yeah," he replied, hardly focused on the moment. I wondered if he was lost in his fantasies again.

◀ ▶

After I left the prison, I drove over to the African American funeral home in Jackson with Mary Sinclair to make final arrangements for the cremation of William's body. That was the least expensive way we could have his remains sent back to Virginia for burial. She and I then went to the truck-stop restaurant across the highway from the prison; we planned on waiting there until heading back to the prison for a vigil at the time of the execution. For a while, my hopes rose slightly as I talked on the telephone in our booth with George Kendall of the NAACP Legal Defense Fund in New York, who had been on the phone all day trying to convince the U.S. Justice Department to intervene in William's case because the handling of it raised important civil rights issues. A later phone call to George, at about six o'clock, brought word that the Justice Department had not seen fit to try to stop the execution. I did not learn why.

After I got the bad news from George, I looked over at Mary, who was sitting across the table from me in our booth. She knew the result of my telephone conversation without my having to tell her. Occasionally leafing through a petition that William's appeals attorneys had filed on their client's behalf, we began to talk about William's fate at his trials.

Soon we were discussing the plight of the only black person on the jury at William's 1984 resentencing trial. The woman had been enmeshed in an essentially white legal system, which had included not only eleven white jurors but a white judge, a white prosecutor, and white, court-appointed defense counsel. She had eventually acquiesced in fear to the white jurors' verdict, even though she had not agreed with it.

The juror's story came out in an affidavit that she had submitted to William's attorneys some ten days before he was executed. Throughout the jury's deliberations, she had continued to hold out against the death penalty because, as she put it in her affidavit, she "did not believe that he [William] knew what he was doing" when he had committed murder. In exasperation she had finally told her fellow jurors, "You do what you have to do, but I won't vote for a death sentence." She had "walked away from the table," not taking part in the final vote in the jury room. Then, according to her affidavit,

> the other jurors decided to go out and tell the judge that we had voted for a death sentence. . . .
> When we went out into the courtroom I was scared to death. From what the prosecutor and other jurors said, I was afraid I could get charged with perjury or something for telling the lawyers that I could not vote for a death sentence. I was afraid I would get in trouble for not participating in the vote, so I said "yes" like all the other jurors, even though it wasn't true. I did not know then that if I had not agreed during the jury poll, the judge would have issued a life sentence.

Another juror, a white woman who had held out with her for a long time before succumbing to the pressure from the other white jurors, corroborated that the black woman had indeed refused to participate in the vote for death in the jury room. The white juror also explained the following:

> There was a good deal of racial tension in the jury room, and the other jurors made repeated comments between themselves about the race of the defendant and the one black woman holding out. I specifically remember one white woman, back in the hotel room, stating "The nigger admitted he did it, he should fry." . . .
> I believe racism played a large part in Mr. Hance's death sentence.

Thinking of the lone black juror among those deliberating William's sentence, Mary and I wondered out loud what it would take for the country to understand the role that race can play in meting out the death penalty. A stay had temporarily delayed William's execution, and as the light from the large window beside us gradually dimmed, we talked on about how racial bias in jury selection had, from the beginning, characterized his trials for the murder of Ms. Faison. In the petition to which Mary and I referred from time to time, his appeals attorneys called attention to the problem:

The District Attorney systematically used his peremptory strikes on black jurors. At the first trial [in 1978], the District Attorney used nine out of ten strikes to remove blacks resulting in a jury with eleven white members. At the resentencing trial in 1984, Mr. Smith [the District Attorney] used 7 out of 8 strikes to remove black venirepersons. Once again, 11 of the 12 jurors who sentenced Mr. Hance to death were white.

After a while, I remarked with sarcasm that at least William had been fortunate enough to have had a black person on each of his two juries. After all, I continued, the four African Americans who had received sentences of death in the Chattahoochee Judicial Circuit in the two years before his 1978 trial had been tried before all-white juries; the one black man who had been given the death penalty there between William's 1978 and 1984 trials had had the same kind of jury. I added parenthetically that the murdered victims in four of these five other cases had been white.

Eventually Mary asked, "Who are we killing William for, anyway? Not for Gail Faison's family, apparently." And I knew, of course, what Mary meant, for Ms. Faison's brother was opposed to William's execution — a view he made known in an affidavit that he filed with William's appeals attorneys on March 20, 1994. The brother also affirmed that Ms. Faison's recently deceased mother had opposed the execution. None of the Faison family spoke out in favor of William's electrocution. In 1990, William Smith, who had prosecuted William and who had gone on to become a superior court judge in the Chattahoochee Circuit, had maintained that his normal practice as D.A. had been to contact the victim's family in a potential capital case to see if they wanted him to seek the death penalty. But he had added, "There was really no family to talk with in [the case of] Brenda Gail Faison. She was from Miami, was living up here with a great aunt." Significantly, Gail Faison's mother's phone number and address in Miami had been in the investigation files at his disposal, so he easily could have gotten in touch with her if he had wanted to do so.

Because Gail Faison's murder had been committed at a time when Columbus had been terrorized by the stocking strangler, thought by the city's coroner and many others in 1978 to be black, a key point suggested by William's petition seemed compelling: at William's trial during that year, the D.A. needed "to get the death penalty against a black man." Not surprisingly, especially in light of the prosecution's neglect of other families of black murder victims in the judicial circuit that William's appeals petition documented, the wishes of the Faison family had not been important. Nor were they important when the D.A. again sought the death penalty against William at his 1984 retrial, which began a few days after an African American had been arrested in connection with the stocking stranglings. (He was later convicted of three of the crimes.)

After reflecting on all of these things, neither Mary nor I was able to think of anything else to say for a long time. As the tables around us emptied and filled and emptied again, we watched the lights of the traffic on the interstate not far away and listened to country songs over the restaurant intercom. William's petition, which lay open on the table between us, seemed to have been written in vain.

◄ ►

When Mary and I joined those who would participate in a vigil for life on the prison grounds, it was nearing nine o'clock. We soon found out that the U.S. Supreme Court had lifted its temporary stay. The execution would take place. I would learn the next day that only Justice Blackmun had explained his vote, a dissenting one along with the votes of two other of the nine justices. He believed that William's death sentence should be overturned. He had felt that there was "substantial evidence" indicating that William was both "mentally retarded" and "mentally ill" and that there was "reason to believe that his trial and sentencing proceedings were infected with racial prejudice."

Those of us keeping the vigil — there were nine of us — gathered together in a circle. What must have been a security helicopter circled overhead. Traffic from nearby Route 36 droned by noisily. The lights and sounds from TV trucks, replete with satellite transmitting equipment, filled the cold night. In the context of what was happening, the powerlessness of our tiny circle was overwhelming.

As I stood in the circle, I recalled how I had begun the day, in the trailer that served as a hospitality house for family members visiting their kin on death row at the prison less than ten minutes away. I had awakened at about five o'clock in the morning. Bright moonlight highlighted the tall pines outside my window then. The sharp edges of reality stood out severely. The cold, early spring air only added to the harshness of the scene. A southern whippoorwill in the distance seemed to lash out at the day. I struggled to see the beauty that I knew *must* be present at such moments, but I was overcome by sadness and anger.

As I lay in my bed, I could not help thinking about the preparations for the execution that were underway at the prison. I thought especially about the buffet meal that corrections officials, State witnesses, and various dignitaries present for the electrocution would enjoy later in the day. I remembered how a reporter for the *Toronto Star* had written of the buffet served just before Richard Tucker had been put to death: there had been tables "laden" with meats, salads, bread, and dessert. When I had caught glimpses of such meals over the years, they had hardly seemed to be conducted in a spirit of mourning. I began to wonder if the buffet might not be a symbol of something important: the obscene joy that we as a people obtain from executions. After a while, as I thought of the men cheering the arrival of Joe Mulligan's hearse, the sadism of the death penalty seemed more than a remote possibility.

Such sadism could be a way of diverting us from the problems that William Hance faced in life. It could also be a way of avoiding all the sorrows of the loved ones of his victim or victims. As the psychologist Mary Williams had argued, the sadist tries with all of his or her might to deny the claims of death for himself or herself. Ultimately identifying with death as the "indestructible destroyer," the sadist projects his or her mortality on the victim; in killing, the sadist experiences a kind of ecstasy brought on by feelings of immortality. In our culture, perhaps the logic of the sadist had found political expression, become law. State executions might well be the height of the sadist's passion — and perversity — in the realm of politics. People like William Hance must die so that others of us can avoid death. And our actions against him reflected the laziness that seemed to be found in many variants of sadism. For in a person like William, we were not targeting the powerful. We were going after someone we thought we could dispose of easily.

From the vantage point of my small bedroom, I mulled over the possible sadistic implications of capital punishment for some time. Then, as the moonlight cut savagely through the darkness, I wondered about the significance of something that had happened on the previ-

148

ous day: the Pardons and Paroles Board had entered the name of another man on its form denying William's petition to have his sentence commuted to life in prison. Did William's real identity as a person matter in the ritual of death that was being carried out? Was the human being William Henry Hance actually invisible to us? Eventually, seemingly out of nowhere, some words from Habakkuk (3:17-18) came to me:

> Though the fig tree do not blossom,
>   nor fruit be on the vines,
> the produce of the olive fail
>   and the fields yield no food,
> the flock be cut off from the fold
>   and there be no herd in the stalls,
> yet I will rejoice in the LORD,
>   I will joy in the God of my salvation.

The words were difficult to fathom.

When I came out of this dark reverie during the vigil, I was not sure if William was dead yet. I waited, along with the others in our tiny group, for official word from the state that the electrocution had, in fact, been carried out. Soon I thought of William's final moments inside the execution chamber. I expected he would talk about his innocence. (As I would read in the paper the next day, he had done just that, enraged.) Standing in a field just inside the prison gate at the hour of his death, I wondered if his flights of fantasy might not have served him well, in a sense, in the crises of his life, shielding him, for instance, from the full awareness of terror that night when he lay beside his sister and watched her being raped. Indeed, perhaps his fantasies somehow spared him the full impact of our culture's madness during his time in the death chamber. For a moment I wondered if they might actually be the work of a grace I could not fathom. But this thought left me as quickly as it had come.

When I returned home after the execution, it was slightly past midnight. I learned that William's sister had called and had wanted me to phone her back. When I did so, she asked, "Did he feel any pain?" To her, he was not invisible.

Good Friday was just beginning.

9

On Wandering Spirits

I t was years ago that I received it. Realizing my need to try to make sense of the difficult days after an execution, Mary Sinclair of Atlanta's Southern Center for Human Rights sent me a brief quotation typed on a strip of white paper. The quotation has found a place in the back of the legal pads on which I make notes about my prison visitations. Each time when I tear off the last sheet of yellow paper in a pad, I see my friend's neatly typed words, pause for a second to think of our common struggle to get through hard times, and then place the strip at the back of a fresh pad. In one corner of the strip of paper, in Mary's small, precise handwriting, are these words: "written on wall of abandoned building in Detroit." The quotation itself is powerful every time I read it: "We remember that when people lose their lives as a consequence of injustice their spirit wanders, unable to pass over — seeking resolution."

Though the words of the quotation do not suggest the ultimate reach of my faith, they are an apt description of the way I have felt at times since the death of Jerome Bowden in 1986. For during these years, especially in the days following an execution, there have been moments when I have tried in vain to affirm that God fully embraces those who have had their lives taken by the terror of the State. I have struggled to understand how even this Love could bind up such deep wounds as the men experienced. At these times I have sensed the wandering spirits of my friends move, unresolved, before me; insofar as

150

their final fate is concerned, I have indeed seen through a glass darkly. As I have encountered these spirits, I have experienced a variety of feelings: sadness, anger, bewilderment, and love. And I have invariably asked myself, among other questions: What have the men meant to me?

This is an especially difficult question to answer, given all the mystery and profound resonances, all the moments of unknowing, that make up human relationships. Yet the question has been important. I have felt that it has been a sign the men have left behind for someone to decipher who is not forced to wander with them. Indeed, as I have encountered the spirits of the men and the issue has pressed up from deep within me, I have felt that whatever testimony I could bear to the significance of their lives would further the men's struggle for resolution. So I have undertaken to answer the question, as an act of fidelity — perhaps as a final act of friendship.

◀ ▶

One answer that I have given to my question is this: My relationships with the men who were executed on Georgia's death row have initiated me into the necessary but difficult struggle to grieve. Over the years I have watched men like Bill Tucker undergo this ordeal week after week as they faced their deaths and the loss of persons they loved. Sometimes the men struggled successfully with loss, looking into the abyss looming before them; at other times they were less successful, trying desperately to avoid grief. I have thought of all of these efforts — both successful and unsuccessful — as I have tried to come to terms with their deaths.

I have often felt that I have been simply reeling from one death to another. Though I certainly have been aware of loss, I have not been capable of experiencing its most profound significance. I have been incapable of allowing the pain of loss to overcome me. Though I have awakened the morning after an execution, remembered a face I would never see again, and felt an unsettling melancholy and the beginnings of disorientation, I have held myself in check, no doubt fearing the loss of control associated with the deepest grieving. I have never simply broken down and wept. Like a tightrope walker moving over one gaping chasm to the next, afraid to look down, I have always tried to keep my balance.

Yet there have been times when the pain of loss, coming like a thief

151

in the night, has nearly robbed me of my composure. One such occasion occurred after I had written about the life and death of one of the men whose story I tell in these pages. Surely propelled by my grief over his loss, I wandered late one evening for an hour or so around and around the perimeter of the pasture in front of our house, hoping perhaps that the fullness of the pain would find me, tear at my limbs and flesh. But it did not. Eventually I lay down by a strip of yellow daffodils, white in the moonlight, and waited in vain for the pain to bloom in my soul, for the mystery of loss to be unveiled.

I am still waiting, hoping that the grief locked inside of me does not finally undo me and make me a casualty of my own unresolved sadness or anxiety. That I have been brought face-to-face with this central human struggle — with loss and grief — is an important legacy of my friendship with the men who have died. It is a legacy that their wandering spirits have reminded me of time and again.

❦ ❦

When these spirits visit me and I begin to think of my friends' early years, I realize another important meaning that so many of the men have for me. They showed me with striking clarity how our childhood experiences can be of crucial importance for the way we live out the rest of our lives. Typically, the men grew up feeling the pressure of economic distress, often downright poverty, and had to contend with the absence or the death of at least one biological parent; the abuse of alcohol was hardly uncommon in their families, nor were outbreaks of violence. As children, most of the men were badly neglected; many were severely abused. As a rule, their families were simply too distressed, too fragmented, to provide the kind of affection and bonding that every infant needs in order to form, among other things, a basic trust of himself and others. It seems safe to say that because of their difficult childhoods, most of the men struggled for much of their lives with problems such as attaining self-esteem, achieving intimacy, and discovering a truly human identity.

Characteristically, the men were unable to attain the clearheadedness of self-reflection — of self-transcendence, as the existentialists would say. Too often they were unable to find the eye of the storm in which they were caught up. They were buffeted by powerful feelings such as depression, anxiety, fear of abandonment, a sense of helplessness, and, perhaps most importantly, shame. Struggling — with little or no safety and support — to deal with the demons that tormented them, they carried the recurring stresses of their often traumatic pasts within them for years. The results were not surprising. Men who were consistently in turmoil in a world in which self-esteem, trust, and love were frequently mere words without substance eventually responded to their lack of any real sense of genuine power and worth by becoming conduits for rage. Richard Tucker, for example, illustrated this well when he stabbed his aunt Annie Mae Armstrong — and (if he committed this crime) when he beat Edna Sandefur to death. In a number of cases, the men's rage became easier to express because it was fueled by alcohol, sometimes mixed with other drugs. In the lives of the African American men, the rage was surely exacerbated by racism. Because they were unable to develop the capacity for empathy when they were children, most of the men did not attain — in time to ward off tragedy — the sense of personal responsibility for others that is necessary for living creatively rather than destructively. Schooled in the violence that is a part of the masculine gender stereotype in our culture, they killed. In turn, they paid the ultimate price.

Even after their deaths, the condemned men still speak to me at times of their longing for the love and care of which they were so frequently deprived when they were children. Often creatures of the night, of dream and shadow, the spirits of the men call out of the darkness at a time in our history that is filled with shrill and superficial demands for increased individual responsibility. Their spirits plead for the creation of true community in which both children and adults receive the support and nurture they need for genuine responsibility to flourish. For in such community, where "I" and "Thou" meet, we discover our deepest capacity for freedom, both for ourselves and others.

During their time on death row, most of the men continued to carry their frequently oppressive burden of shame. Even someone like Joe Mulligan, who may not have experienced the ravages of shame when he was a child, came to know the depths of this emotion and showed it during his days on the row. Like the rest of us, all of the men were flawed human beings, but they had their flaws exposed to public scrutiny to a degree most of us never experience, and they had few people to tell them that despite their frailty they were worthy of love. Still, in view of the bleak and often hostile prison environment in which they were confined, most of the men managed to do something remarkable: perhaps aided by a family member or a friend, they struggled heroically with their shame, resiliently seeking life and the light of understanding rather than allowing this crippling emotion to best them. This struggle and the opportunity the prisoners gave me to play a small part in it have been of great significance to me over the years. The men's wandering spirits bring these things back to me.

My role in the men's struggle was actually very simple. I tried to provide them with a "secure base," to use John Bowlby's metaphor, from which they might venture forth in memory and imagination into the fury of their lives: in a spirit of acceptance, I encouraged the men to take the risk to tell the stories of their past and present experience. From time to time, they came to see, or see again, that among the ruins were pearls of great price, evidence of strength and goodness. They encountered, in other words, signs of meaning. I heard, for example, of Joe Mulligan's agency and competency during his boat excursions, of Richard Tucker's struggle against the destructive powers of anger and rage, of Billy Mitchell's quest for freedom, and of Jim Messer's basic skills as an auto mechanic. And I heard of gestures of love on the part of all of the men toward various members of their families. Sometimes the men did not at first put much stock in their stories of strength and meaning. But frequently the value they placed on these narratives grew. So did, I believe, their sense of worth as human beings, as people capable of responding with dignity to key tasks life set before them.

Occasionally, as the men told their stories and became more secure about their worth as persons, perhaps they were also able to look more clearly and discerningly — that is, without being torn apart by rage or abject depression — at their violent deeds. In the company of someone who would not reject them, maybe they even moved ever so slightly forward in the journey toward attaining the stillness of mind and heart necessary to understand the childhood origins (for the most part) of their debilitating shame and of much of their later behavior. To the extent that they looked at themselves and their pasts with discernment, perhaps their sense of gaining self-transcendence grew.

154

Whatever degree of transcendence, great or small, the men found, their courageous struggles with their burden of shame were signs of life and hope that have provided me with a powerful and ironic contrast to our culture's dark and often deadly obsession with this emotion. For we seem unrelenting in using enforced shame, even humiliation, as a tool of social control — something that Hawthorne, in depicting the marking of Hester Prynne with the letter "A," knew lay at the very beginnings of the American experience; something that the thirteen-year-old knows who is accused of a violent crime and is tried in full public view as an adult; something that the incarcerated man or woman knows who carries the words "STATE PRISONER" emblazoned on the back of his or her shirt day after day; something that death-row prisoners know when they view their crazed-looking "mug shots" time after time in the newspaper.

Tragically, our obsession blinds us to the notion that the stimulus of much of the violence and crime we experience today may well be the excessive shame that neglected and abused children have suffered. Our obsession also keeps us from seeing that by carrying out the ultimate act of shaming — capital punishment, which brands a person as unworthy of living — we fail to come to grips with our own shortcomings in performing our roles as mothers, fathers, teachers, clergy, and neighbors. We load our collective failures on the backs of persons on the economic margins of society and drive such individuals even further from us, into the wilderness of the death chamber. Sadly, our preoccupation with shaming actually takes us further and further away from the spirit of compassion and reconciliation that we need to bring healing to the profound sorrows of those family members who survive the victims of murder.

In an important sense, my meetings with the men who were to be executed afforded me a journey through a culture of shame. Over the years, their wandering spirits have reminded me of this — and of the courage the men finally showed in struggling to resist such an ethos.

The spirits of the seven African American men I knew who died in Georgia's electric chair have called to mind yet another journey that I have made. For as these seven men I visited told me the stories of their lives, I began to move toward a deeper, more painful understanding of racism in our culture. And I began to understand that those who have faced the curse of racism can find freedom from the hatred it engenders. My first important teachers about race, the black men have left me with an enduring legacy.

As a consequence of my relationships with the men, I have come to appreciate the power of Ralph Ellison's metaphor of the "invisible" black person in our culture. I have come to the grim realization that we as a people never knew — or cared to know — the individual black men we have executed; their rich, if often turbulent, inner lives, their hopes and fears, were not things we made an effort to understand. Raised in a segregated society, hidden away in their prison cells, occasionally the subject of brief news stories, men such as William Hance were practically invisible to us, even less visible, I believe, than the whites we have killed. Since I was over thirty-eight years old when I first really began to get to know someone — Jerome Bowden — of African American heritage, I understand only too well the reticence of the white mind to come to grips with the reality of black persons' lives. Today, I feel sharply something of the pain in the words of the protagonist of Ellison's *Invisible Man:* "You often doubt if you really exist. You wonder whether you aren't simply a phantom in other people's minds. Say, a figure in a nightmare which the sleeper tries with all his strength to destroy."

Several years ago, the law professor Derrick Bell contended that racism was a permanent feature of our national life. As the spirits of the executed black men remind me of the predicament of African Americans charged with capital murder in our state (which is 27 percent black), I realize that I have come to the point where Bell's emphasis on the "permanence" of racism has the troubling ring of truth. I think of the all-white juries that sentenced to death six of the twelve black men we have executed in Georgia since the U.S. Supreme Court's 1976 *Gregg v. Georgia* decision revived capital punishment: Jerome Bowden, Joe Mulligan, and Henry Willis, as well as three other men before them. I contemplate the plight of the sole black juror at William Hance's 1984 resentencing trial. And I remember that Warren McCleskey's appeals attorneys pointed out that, in Georgia, persons charged with murdering whites were four times more likely to be sentenced to death than those charged with killing African Americans. To be sure, in recent years, I have seen hopeful signs in the election of two black persons to the state's supreme court;

both justices have sometimes made important criticisms of our pursuit of capital punishment. However, those elected officials who select, prosecute, and try Georgia's capital cases remain overwhelmingly white: forty-seven out of forty-eight district attorneys, 161 out of 176 superior court judges. And our recently elected black attorney general, who could exercise powerful leadership to help end the death penalty in the state, is a proponent of capital punishment; he is someone who is hardly in the lineage of African American human rights advocates such as Rosa Parks, Martin Luther King Jr., and Thurgood Marshall. So I ask myself: Have we really moved far from the lynch mob's noose in Georgia? Is the life of a black person today really worth as much as that of a white person? And my questions are substantially rhetorical, for their troubling answers come quickly enough.

As I encounter the wandering spirits of the African Americans who were executed, I experience their anger over the fate of black citizens in a racist society. I can still hear the sharp words that Billy Mitchell, defending his dignity in a racially biased judicial system, spoke to me: "I'm no prisoner." But I also experience something else that I found to be characteristic of the black men as I knew them: the remarkable freedom from hatred that they could display toward me, a white man. At the beginning of our visits, I was often overwhelmed by what I felt to be the black men's ability to accept me simply as a human being, even though, as a white person, I was inevitably allied to the racist powers in our culture. And throughout our time together, I believe the men continued to accept me, despite my inability to do anything to alter their fate and despite the puzzlement and pain I must have caused them because of my failure to understand the nuances of their heritage.

Did I misread their acceptance of me? Was it ultimately an illusion I chose to cultivate because I could not face their hostile attitude toward me? Or did they hide their true feelings about me because they were unable to express their anger toward — even hatred of — a white man in his presence? I can only say that I believe the answer to these questions is no. I believe the black men's compassion toward me was real, a sign of great strength. Indeed, the depth of their acceptance of me lingers in my memory as a vivid sign of the power of forgiveness. So generous were the men to me. So generous do they continue to be. Their capacity for forgiveness defines a vital meaning their lives have for me, for without forgiveness we would all be lost. So fallible, so broken, are we all.

When the wandering spirits of my friends visit me, I realize that the men, black and white alike, have meant something else to me, too.

Unlike the knight in Bergman's *The Seventh Seal*, about whom I spoke to Billy Mitchell, I accomplished no bold deed on behalf of the condemned that would justify my life. Providing such an occasion for heroism was not one of the gifts the men gave me. I could perform no feat like that of the knight, who upset the chess pieces and diverted the attention of Death, his opponent, and who was thus able to allow three of Death's potential victims to escape. I was able to do nothing at all to save the men from electrocution; indeed, as I have come to see clearly, I am at one with their executioners in the frailty of my moral life.

Regardless of my moral frailty and despite my limited ability to help the men find healing and comfort, something of special significance to me emerged from my visits with them: an enriched understanding of the importance of witness as one expression of my humanity. In helping me gain this insight, which has become increasingly clear to me since Henry Willis's death, the men have meant a great deal to me.

As a guest in the closing circle of their lives, I was a witness to events of almost unimaginable terror. But I saw more than this.

When I think of what I witnessed in the presence of the men who were to be executed, I think of something that Elie Wiesel once said: "We know that every moment is a moment of grace, every hour an offering; not to share them would mean to betray them. Our lives no longer belong to us alone; they belong to all those who need us desperately."

Haltingly at first, then in moments of powerful self-disclosure, the men dared to share themselves with me because they glimpsed the grace incarnated in the moment when two human beings truly meet. Moreover, I have often thought that they somehow sensed that they were giving me a gift I needed badly in the great middle passage of my own life. In any case, in these middle years, as I sought direction amid the confusion of changing values and unpredictable stirrings of the soul, the men became in a sense true North for me by showing me their courageous struggles for intimacy, meaning, and dignity — struggles that were nothing less than expressions of the resiliency of their deeply felt longing for life. Consequently, I knew that it was somehow right that I was *there,* with the men. I knew that my witness was intrinsically important as an acknowledgment of their worth, and ultimately that of all life and being.

In light of what I experienced in the men's presence, I can also say that my witness was important as an acknowledgment of the profound inner dynamic of our souls to seek and give love. I saw that we are created for love and find our fulfillment in it. In this regard, I think especially of things that Nicky Ingram explained to me gradually over the last two years of his life, before his execution in the spring of 1995.

It might seem that he had every reason to have lived his life in absolute bitterness. When he was a boy, he suffered the abuse and neglect so typical of the early experiences of the men on death row. As his appeals attorney wrote after Nicky's death, his client's childhood was filled with such horrendous events as "his former stepmother bashing him over the head with a bottle, making him pile rocks in the back garden to keep him out of sight and out of mind, or feeding him alcohol to the verge of a coma from age 13 onward." Probably such experiences did, in fact, embitter Nicky. Indeed, he may well have been bitter one June day in 1983, when he was nineteen. Appearing "glassy eyed" and talking rapidly, the young white man was acting "crazy" then, as Mary Eunice Sawyer remembered. (According to his appeals attorneys, he was psychotic and delusional at the time. For one thing, he was talking about war experiences that he had never had.) According to Ms. Sawyer, on that day he tied her and her husband, J.C., to a tree in the woods near their Marietta home and shot them both, killing her husband. Nicky was so high on drugs and alcohol then that, afterward, he could not remember shooting the white couple, something he did during the act of robbery.

Years after J. C. Sawyer's death, perhaps Nicky also had his bitter moments when he learned that his appeals attorneys had discovered that he had been treated with the powerful antipsychotic drug Thorazine before and, evidently, during his 1983 trial. At the request of the Cobb County Jail and with the apparent approval of the prosecution, a psychologist had evaluated Nicky after the young prisoner, who had been awaiting trial, had attempted suicide. Recognizing his client's psychotic state of mind and possible organic brain damage, the psychologist had advised giving him psychotropic medication, and Thorazine had then been prescribed by a physician. Thinking that he had simply been given something for his "nerves," Nicky had not mentioned the Thorazine to his trial attorneys; moreover, it had not been reported to the judge or to Nicky's court-appointed trial counsel or to mental-health experts responsible for evaluating the defendant for his trial. Drawing on expert affidavits, his appeals lawyers contended that the drug had made Nicky incapable of helping his counsel in his defense at his trial and of being evaluated properly by mental-health professionals then; they also argued that the Thorazine had rendered him largely emotionless and that, in the courtroom, the district attorney had capitalized on this impassiveness by calling attention to the defendant's lack of remorse. As I say, the Thorazine episode may have provoked Nicky to bitterness.

But during our visits, I saw — witnessed — something else. As his trust in me deepened over the months, he began to speak about a series of journeys that he had recently taken. It took a while for him to get the story out, he once told me, for fear that I would think he had "gone nuts." What had happened was this. Night after night he would lie in his dark cell until the cellblock had grown quiet, and then he would "visit" persons he loved. Watching their expressions of joy and sadness, he would sit in their living-room chairs or at their bedsides; sometimes he would embrace the individuals he visited or caress their faces. Nicky thought that such journeys were in the tradition of the Native American shamans, whom he admired and about whom he had been reading for years. Love is bigger than time and space, he once told me. The shamans knew that, he explained, and as his family and a few friends began to rally around him during the years he spent in prison, he began to learn that, too. It was only logical, he figured, that no prison, nothing at all, could hold his love in check.

As I began to learn of Nicky's journeys, I was skeptical, and I told him so. Though I did not come right out and say so, I thought at first that they were only lingering symptoms of the psychotic episodes he had been diagnosed as having when he had been in the Cobb County Jail. I believed that his "travels" were merely remnants of a past that simply would not go away. But as I got to know him better and better, I found that I could not dismiss his journeys as simply an "illness." Though they may have been, in part, indications of psychological distress, there was more to them than that. And though I was not sure exactly what to make of his shamanic claims, I came to regard his nightly travels as, in

160

some sense, important signs of his struggle to express a love he showed daily to those about whom he had come to care so much.

It was a love, I believe, that came from deep within him. It was a love that led him to balk at allowing the courts to be informed about all the details of the horrors he had experienced as a child; he wanted to spare his family the embarrassment such publicity would bring. During the last difficult days of visitation, it was a love that tried to "absorb," as he explained to me, the grief of his family: he attempted to soak up the pain through his intense presence, sometimes by the gentleness of his touch. He knew, of course, that he could not manage to absorb all the pain. He understood well that his visitors left hurting for him and for themselves. But he was convinced that he was able to take some of their pain away. For when he returned to the cellblock after visitation and lay down on his bunk, he felt as if a sledgehammer were pounding inside of him, so filled was he with the hurt of others who cared about him.

The love he felt within him was also something he wanted to show to Mary Eunice Sawyer, and he tried to do so by expressing to her his sorrow for the death of her husband — a man he still could not remember shooting, even as the execution day approached, but whom he must have killed, he had come to believe, and whom he could bring himself to talk about only with great difficulty. It was a love that Nicky wanted to express quietly, without fanfare, so he wrote to Ms. Sawyer and arranged to have his letter delivered to her, after his execution, by one of his attorneys.

Three days after Nicky's death, his love for his family and friends was almost palpable to them as, in the gathering darkness, they arrived at the shores of Lake Allatoona in north Georgia. They came together there to pay him a final earthly tribute. At first they assembled on a dock and let a steady breeze blow his ashes across the water. Then, one by one, those present tossed fresh flowers out into the night onto the face of the lake. Death was simply a season, Nicky was fond of saying, hardly an end to love. It was a truth that those who were bound together that evening knew, too.

The love that Nicky Ingram discovered in prison did not preclude his being sharp-edged at times, which those who held him captive experienced. In fact, they may well deny that he had a capacity for love. When asked to put his signature on some form just days before his death, he refused to sign the sheet on a prison employee's desk; instead,

161

he took the paper and signed it on the floor. An Atlanta newspaper quoted a "prison spokesman" as saying that Nicky "entered the execution chamber an angry and defiant man." And at the very end, this defiant man spat at the warden when the official asked him if he had any last words. Where was the love at moments like these?

Without a doubt there was a spirit of defiance in Nicky Ingram; it was directed at those who would take his life. Was his defiance a justifiable expression of his great love of life and his refusal to compromise this love in the presence of those who would seek to destroy life? Was this defiance perhaps even an expression of the judgment of God on the way we as a people have often chosen to organize our society — around death instead of life? Or did Nicky's defiance signal the limits of his love by showing that his love of living interfered with his ability to love others?

For years I have seen vital signs of love in Jesus' admonition to love our enemies, in his capacity for forgiveness — even on the cross, in the face of death. It is a way of love that found renewed expression in our time in the lives of Gandhi and Martin Luther King Jr. Was Nicky's defiance consistent with such a way of love? Especially in light of his spitting at the warden, I believe that on occasion his defiance did fall short of the most exalted form of love. But I must add this immediately: his defiance challenges me not to sentimentalize either love or forgiveness and provokes me to seek fresh ways to show in my own life that, in the face of oppression, love and forgiveness are not only acts of reconciliation but also deeds of resistance against evil.

Though Nicky was capable of losing his way in regard to love, I can still affirm this with confidence: in his last years, he had become much more than simply the "angry young man" his appeals attorney described him as having been in 1983, when he was sentenced to die. If he had lived longer, I trust that the depth and range of Nicky's love would have grown. In any case, I realize the power of the love he did discover whenever I sense his wandering spirit and remember the nightly journeys he described to me.

And when I think of these journeys, I recall the profound expressions of love shown by all of the executed men I have known. Having witnessed many such expressions firsthand, often in the men's interactions with their families, I believe that I have seen a force of powerful resiliency that presents us with our highest calling and defines the ultimate destiny of our very being. Moreover, when I think of the love that the men revealed, an insight of Augustine's often comes to mind: Our task in this life is "to heal the eye of . . . [the] heart whereby God may be seen." Somehow all of the men, in their own way, if only for brief times, managed to find such healing; their love was a sign of it. In knowing them, I too have been guided by a reckoning not of my own toward the One the heart alone can see.

Thus, I can say this finally: through my friendships with the men, I have witnessed — and been able to witness to, to affirm — the love of God, which is in tension with the powers and principalities over against us. This is the ultimate meaning the men's lives have for me. This is a conclusion that I eventually draw after encountering the wandering spirits. For when the spirits visit me, I always end up realizing once again that they are condemned to wander only in my mind, in an imagination shaken and stymied by the power of human evil. At the very deepest level of reality, my friends have found resolution. They have found acceptance and forgiveness, which I hope they glimpsed in my acceptance of them.

To be sure, as my experience of the spirits seeking resolution suggests, I have also witnessed and often been almost overwhelmed by the silence of God and the bone-chilling cold of the night of the spirit. I have been frequently silent myself as I have tried to find my way theologically in a time whose secularism has found demonic expression. I have not been able to forget, for example, that I live in a land where the gap between rich and poor is of obscene proportions: where the top one percent of our families owns almost 40 percent of our wealth, the top one-fifth owns well over 80 percent, and the bottom fifth has a negative net worth. I have not been able to dispel other thoughts as well: I am the citizen of a country where millions of children are growing up poor (nearly 20 percent of all children, some 37 percent of black and Hispanic children), exactly the kind of environment in which juvenile crime and violence flourish, precisely the kind of environment in which so many of the executed men grew up and received such brutal beginnings in life. I am alive at a time in our history when the phrase "children's prison" seems to have passed into our discourse with ease and when we have been determined to spend more and more of our money on prisons of all kinds, locking up our people at the second highest rate (behind Russia) reported on earth.

Facing execution after execution in such a culture, I have, as I say, known the silence, the absence, of God. But because of what happened in the space that unfolded between the men and me — where I met Thou — I have never lost sight for long of the Love that is the source of all life and being. I have felt its pull, at times with the certainty of gravity. It is a Love which proclaims that the fate of all of us is inextricably bound to that of the least of us, so interconnected is all creation. Through this Love, each of the executed men I have known has become for me a unique word of grace in the persistent language of the heart. They are words that I wish would one day reach the often unrecognized despair of our contemporary culture. Should that day come, perhaps we could begin to move, like Dante and his guide, from the innermost reaches of darkness and walk "out once more beneath the Stars." Perhaps, too, we could feel the promise of the fullness of spring and its renewal of life in the cold earth beneath our feet.

10

Postscript: A Letter to Chris Burger

December 14, 1993

Dear Chris,

You have been gone for a week now, having traveled to lands beyond the sun. I have had to make my way these past days without the possibility of our journeying together, as we did from time to time over the last six-and-a-half years. Your loss became especially painful to me several days ago when I went to the prison for the first time since your execution, knowing that there was no longer the chance of seeing you there and engaging in one of our talks about nearly everything concerning God and the world. When I returned home, I noticed that the tea olive that had begun to bloom just before your death, in defiance of all the signs of the coming winter, no longer filled the air around our kitchen window with its thick fragrance. A bitter wind shook the tree's dark green leaves.

I have just come back from a walk in the woods and fields of the farm. It was one of those daily rounds I used to tell you about. Walking softly, I was hoping to spy out the albino deer that has been grazing at the edge of the pastures lately or perhaps even get a look at the gray fox with the red head on one of his hunting forays at sundown. But today I saw only a screaming hawk, circling high overhead in the cold, gray sky. You would have liked that, though: he displayed tremendous freedom in arcs of graceful motion.

At one point near the end of my walk, I became aware of the resil-

165

iency of the fescue grass under my boot soles. I wish you could have experienced that. Grass was a scarce commodity where you lived, and you often longed for its press of life beneath your feet. I remember your telling me that you had asked the guards for one chance to take your shoes off and walk on the grass on your way to the death house in your final minutes on earth. You were hoping mightily that they would grant your request. I never heard if they did.

Though I feel somewhat rested after my walk, I am hardly at peace. After an especially difficult couple of days, I find that I can envision again, as I did in your last hours, your soul in God's care. But I am still struggling with your loss, unsettled by my longing to see you. Thus, I am not sure if my mind is clear enough to write this letter — the last, I suppose, of our off-and-on correspondence that stretched over the years. I would like to try, however. It is important for me to write these lines whether or not you can read them from your current vantage point. Perhaps they will help me make some progress in taking leave of you as someone I will not meet again as a fellow pilgrim on this blossoming and dying earth. Maybe I can gain some practice in learning to live close to my inner image of you, in a world where no frost kills forever.

I am at that place in my struggle where I am flooded by memories of your life — and, now and then, of how I spent the final hours before your death. Some of my memories of the events of your life are mixed with an anger that I carry inside of me with the fidelity of love. I feel particularly angry when I think of how you fared in the courts. To begin with, your court-appointed trial attorney had little understanding of who you were. How could he? He conducted no thorough investigation of your background. As a result of his representation of you, no jury ever heard what really happened to you in your childhood or youth and had a chance to take these things into account in deciding whether or not you should be sentenced to death. As your appeals developed, the truth about your past finally came out, but few persons seemed to want to listen. You were, in a sense, a small and unimportant figure in the judicial landscape.

What did happen to you when you were growing up, I pieced together from our conversations. I feel anger about the events of your early years, too. But mostly I just feel sad now about the long night you experienced then. It seems that you never saw, never lived the morning.

166

I remember especially one story that you learned from your mother. When you were an infant, you fell from your crib, hit your head on the floor, and lost consciousness for fifteen or twenty minutes. Your father was incarcerated then, and your mother — who was living with her mother-in-law, you, and your sister in a two-room, cold-water apartment — had no money for a doctor. So your mother and your grandmother treated you as well as they could themselves by simply putting a cold compress on your head. For days afterward, you were lethargic.

Before you started school, your father began hitting you in the face with his fist, and your mother was telling you that you were worthless. What was happening inside of you on those occasions — or when your mother made you lock yourself in the bathroom so that she couldn't kill you?

From the time you were eight, you were shuttled back and forth between your divorced parents. You clung to the doorknobs in your mother's house when you were about to be sent back to your father. On one of these shuttle trips, you had to sell your shoes to pay for food as you hitchhiked from the Midwest to Florida. How old were you then? Thirteen, maybe? During one period of time when you were staying with your mother, she turned your supervision over to her boyfriend, who made you play the "game" of dying cockroach: a form of punishment, actually, in which you had to lie on your back with your arms and legs extended in the air for as long as you could stand the pain, until you collapsed and the boyfriend kicked you. It's hardly surprising that you took to sniffing glue and paint thinner to escape such horrors. After your mother married for the third time, her husband, a neo-Nazi, introduced you to hard drugs; he forced you and her to take them in a room filled with "black light." What did you feel then? And what was it like for you the time she gave you six Valium tablets and you washed them down with gulps of bourbon? Returning from the emergency room after that episode, you must have thought the night would have no end.

Despite all this, you forgave your mother — and perhaps your father also, though you rarely spoke of him. I remember how you talked about her a lot, no doubt sensing a common bond between the two of you that made your act of forgiveness easier. You understood that she had faced a night of her own as dark as yours. And you were deeply moved when you told her story. Your maternal grandmother had died giving birth to her, and your mother found love hard to come by from the time she was a child. During one five-year period, a caregiver bound, gagged, and beat her regularly. This person also denied your mother food, and she was diagnosed as malnourished when an aunt had her examined by a doctor. Little wonder that at age fourteen your mother ran off and married the sixteen-year-old who was to become your father. Unfortunately, the night continued. She experienced a series of miscarriages. Eventually, after giving birth to four children, she was seized by depression, and she would sit day after day in her darkened house, fearful of leaving or letting you or your sisters or brother leave, either. After her divorce from your father, her depression became so bad that she overdosed on sleeping pills and was taken to the psychiatric unit of a hospital, where she was given shock treatments and psychotropic drugs before she was released. Later, she moved across the country and struggled through a number of bad relationships.

But her story was not simply one of heartache, you explained to me with joy one day. She finally met "Pop," who loved her deeply, and she married him. He knew how much both you and your mother needed each other in your last years as your appeals began to wind down. So he agreed to move with her and their small trailer from Louisiana to Georgia, where he tried, as much as his frail health would allow, to work as an auto mechanic to help put food on the table. You understood her great courage in coming to Georgia. She was facing the reality of your life and her own. And you began to discover in her a love that you had sought so desperately as a child. As you once put it, you and she "found each other" at last.

Perhaps your deepening relationship to her helped you to seek yet another kind of love several years ago, when a young woman from a distant country began writing you in one of those curious acts of fortune. Three years ago, during your previous death watch, when you were almost executed, you once told me that the love you and the woman had for each other was so great that it was impossible for you to believe that God would allow it to end with your electrocution. You and she had written to each other daily for a year then, before she came to the United States, to Georgia, with her two small children, with the intent to marry you.

After a court stayed your execution and it seemed that you had a new lease on life, I angered you greatly, I know, when I said that you and the woman should first get to know each other in person for a while before I, as a pastor, would consider marrying you. Red tape from the immigration authorities finally stymied your marriage plans, and I felt your anger toward me ease. I still think about those days and wonder if I should have acted differently, and if I had, would things somehow have turned out better for you. Perhaps I made a mistake. I don't know.

Anyway, I can still remember what happened after that; it was a couple of years ago. The woman and her children had come to visit you around Thanksgiving, just before they left for a brief trip to their native land. And you never saw them again. After that a letter arrived in which she explained to you that she would be marrying an American she had met during the lonely vigils she kept between her weekly visits with you at the prison. Though she wrote to you a few more times after the wedding, soon her letters stopped. I didn't know if you would survive the shock, the hurt. But you did, telling me for a time that her marriage was an elaborate strategy she had devised — and couldn't explain to you, for some reason — so that she could remain in this country and one day marry you once you were free.

During that difficult time after she left you, I remember telling you a little story of my own, with the hope that you might know that I understood how hard it is to come to grips with loss, how its pain can surface again and again throughout our lives. As I spoke, I sensed that you knew that I was telling the story for my sake as well as yours. I talked about a young woman with whom I had been very close in my teenage years. She was a college sophomore in 1966 when she was killed in a car accident. I first heard about it just hours afterward, and I have thought about it many times since then over the years. I told you about driving to Birmingham, Alabama, several days before my visit with you and recalling, along the way, the details of her death. Though my knowledge of the accident had come only from sketchy, secondhand reports, it had seemed — once more — almost as if I had been there. I recall how focused you were as I told you what had happened as I neared the Coosa River Bridge at Childersburg, Alabama, at dawn. Suddenly, driving through the small-town sprawl along U.S. Route 280, I was startled by images of the wreck: the winter night in North Carolina, the quick scream of tires on blacktop, the spray of metal and glass through the air, not even a sigh escaping her.

After I ended my brief story, you didn't comment on it. You were just quiet for a few seconds. I was never sure, then or later, if you thought that I really understood your plight or not. In any event, you finally came to accept the fact that the woman you felt was the life of your very soul all those months had indeed fallen in love with someone else. And even in your last days, you never spoke of blaming her for how things turned out between the two of you. Nor did you speak of blaming her husband — or me, for that matter. You simply took on the pain of loss.

Though you had lost her, I believe you continued to love her right up to the end. In this regard, I remember the day not long ago when you quoted to me from memory some lines of poetry from Gibran, someone I had never thought much of as a writer. Your passion brought to life the poet's words as he spoke of how love "may shatter your dreams as the north wind lays waste the garden" and how it "threshes you to make you naked." You went on to explain to me that the lover must be ready to pay the greatest of prices without rancor.

In the weeks and months after you had lost the woman you loved, I noticed that you turned your attention more and more to a topic you had brought up with me from time to time: all the persons you had wronged during your life. I recall especially your talking a lot about how you had devastated the family of Roger Honeycutt, the fellow soldier and part-time cab driver you and Tom Stevens had been convicted of murdering. You spoke sparingly to me of the details of that September night in 1977 when you were seventeen — when you drove Honeycutt's cab, with him locked in the trunk, into a pond. And I remember your giving me only one brief explanation of the murder. On the day of the crime you were drinking heavily, and you let your anger get out of control as you thought about how, you suspected, Honeycutt had been interfering with the petty drug business you had had during your brief stint in the Army. But if your words about the details of his murder were few, your anguish over your participation in the killing was often visible in your face during our visits in the last couple of years of your life.

You revealed much of this anguish to the public in the brief television interview that you granted two weeks before your execution. It was an interview that I recall your having thought long and hard about before you agreed to it. Your appeals attorneys had cautioned you that any public declarations you might make could be used against you by the State. Indeed, they had warned you that such remarks could even lead to the setting of an execution date.

It has seemed fitting to me that I watched the interview, which your mother had taped, one day when I went over to sit with Pop shortly before cancer claimed his life. For both he and I had talked often about your struggle with the burden of having committed murder. I was deeply moved by how you responded to the interviewer after he asked you if you wanted to say anything to the victim's family. You were so choked up that you could hardly speak. I will never forget how, after a long silence in which you looked away from the camera, you finally managed to get a few words out, punctuated by awkward pauses: You had heard that Roger Honeycutt's mother had died of grief. . . . You had caused much pain in the world. . . . You were so frustrated because you couldn't do anything about that now.

Soon after the interview, when you learned that a death warrant had been signed and that you were to die sometime between the seventh and fourteenth of December, you debated the wisdom of talking to the reporter. Then, hoping that the public — perhaps even some of the victim's family — saw that you weren't "an animal," as you put it, you let the matter go.

In the last few days that we spent together, I often thought of something that I had been reminded of while I was watching the television interview: how young your face looked at times, younger even than a thirty-four-year-old's. Others also noticed your youthful appearance. For example, one of the guards who saw you in your final moments, when you were strapped in the electric chair, reportedly said that you resembled a frightened child. Perhaps you too sensed your boyish appearance as you struggled to maintain the composure of an adult, to remain as strong as possible for your mother.

On the day before your death, you talked a lot about the importance of such composure. We spent much of that day alone together, while your mother and a few others were at the Board of Pardons and Paroles asking that your life be spared. I remember that at one point you joked that if you felt you were about to "lose it" on the last day, you and I would huddle together at the far end of the visiting room and try to figure out what to do next. (You knew full well, of course, that I would be about as far gone as you if such a crisis came.) After a brief silence in which neither of us knew quite what to say, we nervously changed the subject and spoke wryly about the nutritional value of the meal of macaroni and cheese, wilted lettuce, and brownies that we were allowed to share that day. With a grin, you commented that you had sworn off brownies in deference to the slight bulge around your waist.

I think you were especially helped in your search for composure by your belief that the Pardons and Paroles Board would grant you a life sentence the next morning. When I came to see you that morning, just after the Board had announced its decision, and I had to tell you that it had denied your appeal, we both understood that all was lost, that you would die in a few hours. While we hugged each other, I felt how hard the Board's decision hit you: your body tensed and then went limp. But when you soon joked that I could have broken the news to you more gently, I realized that the composure you valued was yours again, and it remained with you the rest of the day, as far as I know.

I believe you understood that during the times when I wasn't with you on the last day, I was waiting just outside the visiting room as a little stream of visitors trickled in to you. Half-expecting you to call me in for a last-minute huddle, I never left the prison. I was dreading such a call, for I remembered how you had broken down and wept during your death watch three years ago, telling me then, "I've never lived. In a few years, I'll have spent half my life in prison. I only want to live." This time, no such breakdown came. And as you held up hour after hour, I thought of a dream you had had recently and had told me about a couple of days earlier. You had awakened screaming in the night after having imagined that you had been in the clutches of a great dragon-like beast with tremendous wings. The more you had struggled to be free, the tighter the dragon's grip had become. You said the dream meant that if you could find some measure of composure, the grip of death would not be so terrifying. I think you achieved what you wished for.

After your mother and I and a few other visitors said good-bye to you at three-thirty in the afternoon, I went to her trailer with her and some of her friends. Worn out from the previous several days, I stretched out on the floor in a corner of the small living room and watched how well her friends cared for her, a woman whose husband had died just days earlier. They brought her a sandwich, coffee, and cake, and they told her stories. One friend talked about the time he had stayed up all of a rainy winter night, fighting his way through bramble patch after bramble patch, rounding up his neighbor's runaway cows.

Another friend related the saga of a local family who had come from a failing south Georgia farm after the Second World War to work in one of the town's textile mills. They were stories as rich and sturdy as the lives of those persons doing the telling. As I lay there on the floor, I looked over at your mother at one point and thought of something I had said to her and Pop last summer. Even though he had been battling cancer, they had stood before me and renewed their wedding vows, and I had said to them, "Your love for each other is a sign, a reminder, of a Love that is stronger than death." As the hour of your execution approached, I told myself that surely the evidence of such Love is visible in these moments, among the people in this room.

I called Patsy Morris of the Georgia Resource Center about nine o'clock that night and learned that all of your last-minute appeals were exhausted. On hearing the news, a local Baptist pastor who had come to be with us prayed simply for grace for us all. Less than an hour later, Mary Sinclair of the Southern Center for Human Rights telephoned. The living room was completely still as I took the call and learned that the execution had been carried out. You were gone. The remarkable ministry of your mother's friends continued a long time after that — long after I had left her trailer for home.

◄ ►

This is not the end of the flood of memories washing over me now. There are more. They come when I ask the question, Who really was the Chris Burger I knew? I think of several things now in response to the question.

One thing that always impressed me about you was your capacity for wonder. Despite the terror of your boyhood, you never lost the child's gift of wonder. Even all the isolation, all the loneliness of prison couldn't take away the gift, couldn't stop you from being amazed at the richness of life. You frequently expressed your wonder in questions, often so swift and direct that they caught me off guard. You were questioning even in your last days: What is it like to make love to a woman all night long? Does God forgive *everything*? Is it all right to think that God isn't a man, that God simply *is*, beyond gender? What do hunters feel when they kill a deer? Do new cars still smell the same inside as they did years ago? Do men pass through stages of life as you had heard women do? Did I think you would ever make a good father? And there were more questions, many, many more, welling up inside you from some deep source.

You were able to draw on this capacity for wonder because you were a person who understood that vulnerability is the key to our remaining human. You knew that without such vulnerability, the capacity for surrender, there is no experience of wonder and, ultimately, of life. Sure, at times you could swagger with the best of them. You must have felt sometimes that the guise of toughness could get you through the tight spots, earn you respect, even love. The tattoos on your body and the weight lifting you did in the cellblock with stacks of books tied together were a reflection of this tough, swaggering you, who had learned hard lessons of survival on the streets. But you also learned other lessons, profoundly human ones. It was okay to cry when you found out that Phyllis, a friend for years, was expecting her first child. And when you heard of the time your mother had stood outside her trailer in the rain and held an umbrella over her and a hospice worker as the woman had explained to her what Pop's final hours would be like. And when you saw your brother again for the first time in years. By the end of your time on earth, you had learned that to let yourself feel what is going on inside of yourself — the pain, the love, the questions, the wonder — is to experience the very stuff of life itself.

Because you could feel so deeply, you were in touch with your own fear, especially in your last days. And by admitting that you were afraid, you showed how great the courage was that defined so much of your life as you faced death. Your composure was not purchased at the price of denying your fear.

When it came to matters of religion, you refused to sacrifice your humanity to the false god of certainty, who would take the fear away. Thus, in those final days, you lived as a person of faith: it was a frail and tiny vessel on deep and stormy seas, as you sought safe harbor. Typically, when we talked of faith, you didn't speak abstractly. You never asked, for instance, if it is okay for Christians to doubt. Instead, you asked if *I* ever doubted the existence or the goodness of God. And you wondered if *you* would be sent to hell for doubt. I answered as well as I could, and I think you understood: there are times in our lives when the forces of suffering are so arrayed against us that the only honest human response is bewilderment and doubt. This is the testimony of the loneliness of the cross. It is part of the mystery of whatever faith is real and true, I tried to tell you, that it takes doubt into itself. Doubt helps keep faith from turning into dogma. In fact, doubt makes faith come alive.

As the end drew near, you came to witness one of the great truths of life: though faith may come from an inexhaustible source of grace, it is received by mere human beings. You realized this truth one night about a week before your death when you saw that you had been trying to block out all of your doubts for several days and you began to vomit and shake all over in fear, your faith in crisis. You also realized this truth one day shortly afterward when you finally had to turn loose of a concept of death that you had stubbornly applied to yourself since your childhood. You had seen a dead tree fall in a forest one time when you were very young, and you had come to think that your life would end in a similar fashion: as the result of a natural process of aging. It finally became clear to you that such a death would not be yours, and at some moments the insight really shook your faith. By the time of your execution, you realized that the only faith we know is faith on earth. You had reached the point, as you once put it, where you sensed that you were "on the threshold of a great mystery," but you had also learned that there is no crossing the threshold in this life.

Your growth toward a deepened understanding of faith in those last days was very much in keeping with something extraordinary about you: you were never a person to stand still. You had too much wonder, too much courage for that. You were always in motion through the years, seeking to come to grips with who you were, struggling to accept yourself as a human being. Last Friday at the prison, one of your friends in the cellblock and I had to laugh at the lengths you had gone to in the early days of your incarceration to avoid reality, to invent an identity worthy of your imagination. We recalled the stories you had told: of Chris as a tank commander, of Chris's journey to India and the Taj Mahal, of Chris in Panama, of Chris in a prestigious art school. As I say, we laughed, and we loved you no less for your boldness. But you outgrew such stories. They became dry husks surrounding your true identity, and you discarded them, leaving them to be blown from the cellblock by the least breeze rising on a hot summer afternoon.

As you grew over the years, you came to see yourself as a person capable of great kindness and love. With pride you understood that you were no longer the traumatized teenager who had killed, striking out in rage at a threatening world. You knew that you were no longer a person constantly on edge, always on the brink of great violence. But you also grasped the fact that you were still capable of such things as pettiness, dishonesty, manipulation — and worse. You came to see that we are all that way. Despite our attempts to lead upright lives, we stumble and fall: we make mistakes, sometimes very bad ones. You came to understand that this is what it means to be human. And though it was sometimes difficult for you to accept God's forgiveness, at your best moments you saw that you could get up and go on after you had fallen because you were, after all, a creature of infinite worth, regardless of anything you might do that you were not proud of. You were sustained by grace, even as you struggled with the burden of your past actions.

Because you had grown to accept your own humanity and to affirm this sustaining grace, you could do what you did in your last hours on earth, even as you were battling fear. You could partake of the meal of unleavened bread and water that you had requested, and you could ask in your final words simply for forgiveness: "I'd like to say I'm sorry. I'd like to say I'm sorry to anybody and everybody I've ever hurt. Please forgive me."

◀ ▶

An hour or so after you had taken leave of the world this way, I said good-bye to your mother, and she asked me, "Is life worth it, worth all the pain?" I was struck deeply by the question, its directness, its honesty. It could have come from you. And in fact it did, for you and I had discussed this very same issue on many occasions. I answered her as I had answered you and as you had answered the question for yourself: "Yes."

I can't fully explain why, and neither could you, though we tried to do so many times. Finally, I suppose, speaking the word "yes" in this context is a mystery as deep and impenetrable as faith or life itself. Indeed, as you and I both agreed, to speak it is a wager. We could be wrong. Moreover, to speak it is an act of freedom that refuses to accept the events that have shaped our lives in the past as our destiny. To speak the word "yes" fully, completely, means openness to the new, to possibility, even to hope. For you, perhaps to say "yes" was to believe nothing less than that one day you would feel the grass springing up beneath your feet again. If I were a betting man, I would bet that somehow you feel the grass now.

I send you my love.

Randy

Notes

PREFACE

xi   **more than 18,000 lives:** James R. Acker, Robert M. Bohm, and Charles S. Lanier, "Introduction," in *America's Experiment with Capital Punishment: Reflections on the Past, Present, and Future of the Ultimate Penal Sanction,* ed. James R. Acker, Robert M. Bohm, and Charles S. Lanier (Durham, N.C.: Carolina Academic Press, 1998), p. 5. For information on the number of executions since 1976, see Death Penalty Information Center,* www.essential.org/orgs/dpic/dpicexec .html. The Center posts the jurisdictions (thirty-eight states plus the U.S. military and the U.S. government, as of 19 November 1999) that allow capital punishment at www.essential.org/orgs/dpic/dpic1.html. Unless otherwise noted, subsequent Internet citations in this chapter are to the Center's Web site.

    Throughout this preface, I note sources that I have found to be particularly helpful in understanding the death penalty in the United States. I make no attempt at an exhaustive current bibliography. For extensive lists of works on the subject, see www.essential.org/orgs/dpic/Materials.html; the chapter references in *America's Experiment;* and the chapter references and the bibliography

---

*While this book was going to press, I learned that the Web site of the Death Penalty Information Center had been changed to www.deathpenaltyinfo.org. I believe that as new and updated information about capital punishment becomes available from this and other sources, the momentum to abolish the death penalty will increase.

in *The Death Penalty in America: Current Controversies,* ed. Hugo Adam Bedau (New York: Oxford University Press, 1997).

xi **persons who were children:** For an in-depth treatment of juvenile executions, past and present, in this country, see Victor L. Streib's Web site at www.law.onu.edu/faculty/streib/juvdeath.htm. For a convenient summary of data concerning juveniles and the death penalty in recent years, see also www.essential.org/orgs/dpic/juvchar.htm.

As of June 1999, according to the latter Web site, the following information was accurate: "Jurisdictions with an age minimum of 18 for capital punishment: CA, CO, CT, IL, KS, MD, MT, NE, NJ, NM, NY*, OH, OR, TN, WA (by Court decision), and U.S. Other states have either no minimum age or a minimum under 18. (*NY's law only allows the death penalty for those 'more than 18.')." Since 1976 (when the U.S. Supreme Court allowed executions to proceed after approximately a decade-long moratorium), we had executed thirteen persons who were under eighteen at the time of the crimes for which they were convicted. On death rows across the country, there were seventy prisoners convicted of crimes committed when they were juveniles.

people with mental retardation or mental illnesses: Since the reinstatement of the death penalty in 1976, we had, as of 19 November 1999, executed thirty-four persons with mental retardation. "Twelve states forbid execution of the mentally retarded: AR, CO, GA, IN, KS, KY, MD, NE, NM, NY* ['*except for murder by a prisoner'], TN, WA, and U.S." See www.essential.org/orgs/dpic/dpicmr.html.

For discussions of sentencing to death individuals with mental retardation, see, for example, Robert Perske, *Unequal Justice? What Can Happen When Persons with Retardation or Other Developmental Disabilities Encounter the Criminal Justice System* (Nashville: Abingdon Press, 1991); Emily Reed, *The Penry Penalty: Capital Punishment and Offenders with Mental Retardation* (Lanham, Md.: University Press of America, 1993); and Southern Center for Human Rights, *Capital Punishment on the 25th Anniversary of* Furman v. Georgia (Atlanta: Southern Center for Human Rights, 26 June 1997), pp. 17-18.

On the execution of persons with mental illnesses, see Amnesty International, *United States of America: The Death Penalty* (London: Amnesty International Publications, 1987), pp. 76-87. For a more recent overview, see Southern Center for Human Rights, *Capital Punishment,* pp. 19-20. The Center's report (p. 19) notes the following:

No state prohibits the execution of those who suffer serious mental illnesses. Although the Supreme Court ruled that states cannot execute

179

people who are insane, "insane" has been so narrowly defined as to allow people with severe mental illnesses to be put to death. Even if a person is found incompetent to be executed, the remedy is to treat the person until he or she regains competence so that the execution can be carried out.

xi **unable to retain:** Characteristically, the persons we sentence to death are the economically marginalized. See, for instance, Amnesty International, *United States,* p. 51; and Hugo Adam Bedau, *The Case against the Death Penalty* (Washington, D.C.: American Civil Liberties Union, 1997), p. 14.

modest or downright questionable interventions: See, for example, Stephen B. Bright, "Counsel for the Poor: The Death Sentence Not for the Worst Crime but for the Worst Lawyer," *The Yale Law Journal* 103 (May 1994): 1835-83; Michael Mello and Paul J. Perkins, "Closing the Circle: The Illusion of Lawyers for People Litigating for Their Lives at the *Fin de Siècle,*" in *America's Experiment,* pp. 245-84; and David Cole, *No Equal Justice: Race and Class in the American Criminal Justice System* (New York: The New Press, 1999), pp. 76-100. In Georgia, even though we have a multi-county public defender office that specializes in capital cases, it is small and thus has a limited impact. See Southern Center for Human Rights, *A Preference for Vengeance: The Death Penalty and the Treatment of Prisoners in Georgia* (Atlanta: Southern Center for Human Rights, 1996), p. 17.

endure prolonged suffering: For important discussions of the cruelty of the death penalty, see Amnesty International, *United States,* pp. 108-19; Bedau, *Against the Death Penalty,* pp. 21-27; and Deborah W. Denno, "Execution and the Forgotten Eighth Amendment," in *America's Experiment,* pp. 547-77.

at least twenty-three such people: On the execution of the innocent, see Michael L. Radelet, Hugo Adam Bedau, and Constance E. Putnam, *In Spite of Innocence: Erroneous Convictions in Capital Cases* (Boston: Northeastern University Press, 1992); and Michael L. Radelet and Hugo Adam Bedau, "The Execution of the Innocent," in *America's Experiment,* pp. 223-42.

xii **well over half of the country's legal killings:** Approximately 60 percent. See Amnesty International, *United States,* pp. 208-9. This same work (pp. 9-13) provides a good, brief overview of the death penalty in the United States from 1900 to 1967.

Georgia led the nation: Amnesty International, *United States,* pp. 208-9.

large numbers of executions in the South: The figures in this sentence were current on 19 November 1999 according to the information posted at www.essential.org/orgs/dpic/dpicreg.html.

xii **Gregg v. Georgia:** For a brief summary of the court's decision (428 U.S. 153 [1976]), see Amnesty International, *United States,* pp. 15-16.

local lead prosecutors: In a telephone conversation on 29 April 1999, I confirmed this point about the decision-making power of lead prosecutors with Jeffrey J. Pokorak, Clinical Professor of Law at St. Mary's University School of Law, San Antonio, Texas. Part of his extensive research on lead prosecutors and the death penalty has been published as "Probing the Capital Prosecutor's Perspective: Race of the Discretionary Actors," *Cornell Law Review* 83 (September 1998): 1811-20.

shaped by political motives: See, for example, Stephen B. Bright and Patrick J. Keenan, "Judges and the Politics of Death: Deciding Between the Bill of Rights and the Next Election in Capital Cases," *Boston University Law Review* 75 (May 1995): 781-84; and Richard C. Dieter, *Killing for Votes: The Dangers of Politicizing the Death Penalty Process* (Washington, D.C.: Death Penalty Information Center, October 1996), pp. 19-22.

with few exceptions, elected: In a telephone conversation on 29 April 1999 with Professor Jeffrey J. Pokorak, I confirmed that in Connecticut, Delaware, and New Jersey, local lead prosecutors are not elected.

lack of solid proof that it deters crime: On the issue of deterrence, see, for example, Amnesty International, *United States,* pp. 162-67; Richard C. Dieter, *Twenty Years of Capital Punishment: A Re-evaluation* (Washington, D.C.: Death Penalty Information Center, June 1996), p. 7; Bedau, *Against the Death Penalty,* pp. 5-10; Ruth D. Peterson and William C. Bailey, "Is Capital Punishment an Effective Deterrent for Murder? An Examination of Social Science Research," in *America's Experiment,* pp. 157-82; and Ronald J. Tabak, "How Empirical Studies Can Affect Positively the Politics of the Death Penalty," *Cornell Law Review* 83 (September 1998): 1431-39. Consider these facts, among the many that Tabak points out in regard to the question of deterrence:

> In 1995, 386 randomly selected police chiefs and county sheriffs throughout the country ranked the death penalty *last* among seven potential ways to reduce crime. Rather, they responded by a 67% to 26% margin that they do not believe that the death penalty significantly lowers the number of killings. (pp. 1433-34)

xii **its enormous financial cost:** For summaries of studies of the costs of the death penalty, see, for example, Dieter, *Twenty Years of Capital Punishment,* pp. 7-8; Bedau, *Against the Death Penalty,* pp. 31-32; Tabak, "How Empirical Studies Can Affect Positively the Politics of the Death Penalty," pp. 1439-40; and Robert M. Bohm, "The Economic Costs of Capital Punishment: Past, Present, and Future," in *America's Experiment,* pp. 437-58. Consider, for instance, the situation in two states highlighted by Dieter:

> The death penalty costs North Carolina $2.16 million per execution, more than the cost of a non-death penalty murder case with a sentence of life imprisonment. . . . In Texas, a death penalty case costs an average of $2.3 million, about three times the cost of imprisoning someone for 40 years in a single cell at the highest security level. (pp. 7-8)

also elected officials: "Thirty-two states both elect their judges and sentence people to death." See Bright and Keenan, "Judges and the Politics of Death," p. 779.

responsive to their constituents' desire for sentences of death: As U.S. Supreme Court Justice John Paul Stevens has remarked, "Making the retention of judicial office dependent on the popularity of the judge inevitably affects the decisional process in high visibility cases, no matter how competent and how conscientious the judge may be." Our practice of electing state court judges is, he stated, "profoundly unwise." See "Supreme Court Justice Declares Election of Judges Is 'Unwise,'" *Columbus (Ga.) Ledger-Enquirer,* 4 August 1996, sec. B, p. 8.

For important discussions of death-penalty politics and the judiciary (both elected and appointed), see Bright and Keenan, "Judges and the Politics of Death," pp. 759-835; Stephen B. Bright, "Political Attacks on the Judiciary: Can Justice Be Done amid Efforts to Intimidate and Remove Judges from Office for Unpopular Decisions?" *New York University Law Review* 72 (May 1997): 308-36; and Dieter, *Killing for Votes,* pp. 1-14.

sufferings of murder victims' families: Consider this observation in Amnesty International, *United States,* p. 187:

> The death penalty does not lessen the loss to the family and friends of murder victims. Far from relieving their pain, the lengthy procedures and uncertain outcome of capital cases may prolong the anguish and suffering caused to victims' families. Indeed, executions often draw attention away from the victims and focus it on the prisoners being killed by the

state, thereby increasing the feelings of rejection that the relatives of victims often experience.

Consider also the following, in Shannon Brownlee, Dan McGraw, and Jason Vest, "The Place for Vengeance," *U.S. News and World Report,* 16 June 1997, p. 28:

> More often than not, families of murder victims do not experience the relief they expected to feel at the execution, says Lula Redmond, a Florida therapist who works with such families. "Taking a life doesn't fill that void, but it's generally not until after the execution [that the families] realize this. Not too many people will honestly [say] publicly that it didn't do much, though, because they've spent most of their lives trying to get someone to the death chamber."

For a look at the plight of victims' families — and that of condemned prisoners' families as well — see also Margaret Vandiver, "The Impact of the Death Penalty on the Families of Homicide Victims and of Condemned Prisoners," in *America's Experiment,* pp. 477-505.

xii   **two-thirds of the people executed in the South:**   For this statistic and the following quotation, see Amnesty International, *United States,* p. 10.

recent study of Philadelphia: See Richard C. Dieter, *The Death Penalty in Black and White: Who Lives, Who Dies, Who Decides* (Washington, D.C.: Death Penalty Information Center, June 1998), pp. 7-14. The study covers the years from 1983 to 1993.

Since *Gregg v. Georgia:*   On 19 November 1999, the percentages I cite in this sentence were current. See www.essential.org/orgs/dpic/dpicrace.html.

over 80 percent of the slain victims: See the Web site cited directly above for the data in this sentence.

"Virtually every study of race and the death penalty":   See Cole, *No Equal Justice,* p. 132.

xiii   **white person is only rarely executed:**   Out of a total of 566 executions since 1976, according to LDF, 298 (52.65%) were carried out against white persons whose victims were white, 11 (1.94%) against whites whose victims were black, 3 (.53%) against whites whose victims were Latino/a, and 3 (.53%) against whites whose victims were Asian. In addition, there were three whites who had

NOTES TO PAGES XIII

"multiple victims of different races." See NAACP Legal Defense and Educational Fund, *Death Row U.S.A.* (New York: NAACP Legal Defense and Educational Fund, 1 September 1999), p. 7.

xiii **hasn't happened once, for instance, since 1976 in Georgia:** See NAACP Legal Defense and Educational Fund, *Death Row U.S.A.*, pp. 9-20.

according to a study: David C. Baldus, George G. Woodworth, and Charles A. Pulaski Jr., "*McCleskey v. Kemp:* Background, Record, and Adjudications," in *Equal Justice and the Death Penalty: A Legal and Empirical Analysis* (Boston: Northeastern University Press, 1990), pp. 306-69.

both prosecutor and judge are typically white: In a telephone conversation on 1 December 1999 with Mary Sinclair, a paralegal and researcher for the Southern Center for Human Rights in Atlanta, I confirmed the following: in Georgia, only one of our forty-eight elected district attorneys is an African American, and of the state's 176 elected superior court judges, only fifteen are black. The state's population was 27 percent black, according to the 1990 census (*1998 Information Please Almanac,* ed. Borgna Brunner [Boston: Information Please LLC, 1997], p. 759).

limited and sometimes no participation: For a brief discussion of the problem of lack of fair representation of minorities on juries in capital cases in Georgia, see Southern Center for Human Rights, *A Preference for Vengeance,* pp. 3, 11-12. Among other things, the report notes that six of the twelve African American men executed in Georgia since 1976 were "sentenced to death by all-white juries" (p. 3). On the issue of racial bias and jury selection in death-penalty cases in and beyond Georgia, see also Southern Center for Human Rights, *Capital Punishment,* pp. 5-6.

nearly 98 percent: Pokorak, "Probing the Capital Prosecutor's Perspective," p. 1817.

in a highly arbitrary fashion: See Southern Center for Human Rights, *Capital Punishment,* pp. 2, 13-14. The quotations that I cite in this paragraph appear in the report on p. 14. A portion of Judge Heaney's opinion — *Singleton v. Norris,* 108 F. 3d 872, 874-75 (8th Cir. 1997) (Heaney, J., concurring) — is quoted on p. 2 of the report. Justice White's words are originally from *Furman v. Georgia,* 408 U.S. 238, 313 (1972) (White, J., concurring).

3,600 death-row prisoners: LDF reports 3,625, including 29 prisoners sentenced to death by the U.S. government and the military. See NAACP Legal Defense and Educational Fund, *Death Row U.S.A.*, pp. 1, 22-23. In a telephone conversation on 8 December 1999 with Deborah Fins, Director of Research and Student Services, Criminal Justice Project, LDF, I confirmed that all of the prisoners currently on death row in the United States were convicted of murder.

xiv   **on the books for other crimes:** For a summary of these crimes, see Michael Higgins, "Is Capital Punishment for Killers Only?" *ABA Journal,* August 1997, pp. 30-31.

military permits death sentences: See Amnesty International, *When the State Kills . . .* (London: Amnesty International Publications, 1989), p. 227. See also www.essential.org/orgs/dpic/military.html.

eight individuals on its death row: NAACP Legal Defense and Educational Fund, *Death Row U.S.A.*, p. 22.

federal government can seek: On the use of the death penalty by the U.S. government, see www.essential.org/orgs/dpic/feddp.html.

there are twenty-one: NAACP Legal Defense and Educational Fund, *Death Row U.S.A.*, p. 22.

Canada and Western Europe: For current information concerning the death penalty worldwide, see Amnesty International, www.amnesty.org/ailib/intcam/dp/current.htm.

speeded up the appeals process: For an overview of the efforts — including the speeding up of appeals — to make the reversal of death sentences more and more difficult, see, for instance, Stephen B. Bright, "Does the Bill of Rights Apply Here Any More? Evisceration of *Habeas Corpus* and Denial of Counsel to Those under Sentence of Death," *The Champion,* November 1996, pp. 25-29.

since 1973, eighty-four persons: The data in this sentence were current on 24 November 1999. See www.essential.org/orgs/dpic/Innocentlist.html. The *Chicago Tribune* has also recently conducted and published the results of a study relevant to this issue. In part, the study found the following:

> Since a 1963 U.S. Supreme Court ruling designed to curb misconduct by prosecutors, at least 381 defendants nationally have had a homicide con-

viction thrown out because prosecutors concealed evidence suggesting innocence or presented evidence they knew to be false. . . .

Of the 381 defendants, 67 had been sentenced to death. . . .

Nearly 30 of those 67 Death Row inmates — or about half of those whose cases have been resolved — were subsequently freed. But almost all first spent at least five years in prison. One served 26 years before his conviction was reversed and the charges dropped.

See Ken Armstrong and Maurice Possley, "The Verdict: Dishonor," *Chicago Tribune,* 10 January 1999, sec. 1, pp. 1, 12. No one knows, of course, how many persons remain on death row or have been executed as a result of the kind of prosecutorial misconduct that the *Tribune* researched.

xiv **closed down or slashed the funding:** In 1995, Congress stopped all federal funding for death-penalty resource centers. The centers that have survived have had to rely on state or private funding. For important information concerning the reasons for the attacks against the resource centers and the consequences of their being closed or radically downsized, see David Cole, "Too Expensive or Too Effective? The Real Reason the GOP Wants to Cut Capital-Representation Centers," *Fulton County (Ga.) Daily Report,* 8 September 1995, pp. 6-7; and Bright, "Does the Bill of Rights Apply Here Any More?" pp. 1-5.

"Perhaps one day this Court": *Callins v. Collins,* 114 Sup. Ct. 1127, 1138 (1994) (Blackmun, J., dissenting from denial of certiorari). Justice Blackmun was one among many who know our legal system intimately and who see the lack of justice in the way we implement capital punishment. In 1997 the House of Delegates of the American Bar Association passed a resolution calling for a moratorium on executions until the death penalty can be carried out with fairness. See, for example, Henry Weinstein, "ABA Calls for a Halt to Executions," *Los Angeles Times,* 4 February 1997, sec. A, pp. 1, 11. Regrettably, the ABA did not simply call for an end to the death penalty.

xv **men on Georgia's death row:** Few women have received death sentences in the state since 1976. They have not been incarcerated in the prison that holds the men on Georgia's death row. I have not visited any of the female death-row prisoners.

In a conversation on 19 November 1999 with Thomas Dunn, Executive Director of the Georgia Resource Center in Atlanta, I confirmed that there was at that time one woman under sentence of death in Georgia. Nationwide, as of 1 September 1999, only 1.38 percent of all prisoners on death rows were women; three women (none in Georgia) have been executed in the United

States since 1976. See NAACP Legal Defense and Educational Fund, *Death Row U.S.A.*, pp. 1, 9-20.

xvi **Georgia's electric chair:** As a result of legislation passed by the 2000 Georgia General Assembly and signed into law by the governor, the state is making the transition from the electric chair to lethal injection in its executions. Persons receiving the death penalty for "capital crimes committed on or after May 1, 2000" will be executed by lethal injection. Should the courts rule that the electric chair is unconstitutional, those individuals "sentenced to death for crimes committed prior to" that date will also be executed by lethal injection. See the final version of House Bill 1284 (from Section 1 of which I quote).

1. INTRODUCTION: A DISTANT SPRING

2 **He couldn't make a skateboard:** My notes were based on conversations that I had with Jerome; his half sisters, Shirley Thomas and Josephine Henderson; and his niece Linda Jenkins. I also reviewed Jerome's school records and statements submitted by neighbors and teachers. My information about his prior prison record and the crimes committed at Ms. Stryker's house came from Mary Sinclair, then a researcher for the Clearinghouse on Georgia Prisons and Jails, Atlanta. I present a shortened, edited version of my notes here.

The notes I originally made were incorporated into Jerome's clemency petition, filed before Georgia's State Board of Pardons and Paroles. The gist of the petition has been presented in Robert Perske, *Unequal Justice? What Can Happen When Persons with Retardation or Other Developmental Disabilities Encounter the Criminal Justice System* (Nashville: Abingdon Press, 1991), pp. 29-32.

3 **At Jerome's trial:** In writing about Jerome's trial and the question of his guilt or innocence, I follow the lead of Perske, *Unequal Justice?* pp. 28-29. I have also consulted the following: Trial Transcript, *State v. Bowden*, Criminal Action No. 37693 (Superior Court of Muscogee County, 7-9 December 1976).

4 **A written confession:** Jerome's clemency attorney made the following comment about the confession: "The only evidence of his participation in the crime was his purported 'confession,' which was drafted and typed by police and which Mr. Bowden could neither have read nor understood if it had been read to him" (Perske, *Unequal Justice?*, p. 29). The confession "sounded strangely, impossibly articulate to those who knew him" ("Spare Mentally Retarded Convicts," *Atlanta Constitution*, 7 July 1987, sec. A, p. 8).

The confession itself begins as follows:

My name is Jerome Bowden, I am a black male and I am 24 years of age. At the present time I live at 1604 12th Avenue.

I am now in the detective office of the Columbus Police Department. I have been talking to Detectives Sergeants C. E. Hillhouse, A. L. Hardaway, and W. W. Myles, and I am about to give the following statement.

I have been advised by the detectives of my legal rights under the Constitution of the United States and the State of Georgia to remain absolutely silent and make no statement whatsoever. I have been advised of my rights to consult a lawyer prior to making this statement and of my right to have a lawyer present at this time while I am making this statement.

For the complete text of the confession, which does at places contain grammatical errors that are characteristic of Jerome's speech, see Trial Transcript, *State v. Bowden*, pp. 191-98.

4   **an all-white jury:** See Death Penalty Information Center, *Chattahoochee Judicial District: The Buckle of the Death Belt* (Washington, D.C.: Death Penalty Information Center, 1991), fig. 6, following p. 3.

results of the psychologist's test: See Perske, *Unequal Justice?* p. 32.

four whites and one black: In a telephone conversation on 1 June 1999, I confirmed the composition of the Board with Mary Sinclair, paralegal and researcher for the Southern Center for Human Rights, Atlanta. The Board did not disclose which, if any, of its members voted to spare Jerome's life.

6   **"I would like to thank":** Perske, *Unequal Justice?*, p. 34.

Georgia legislature barred: See "Bowden's Legacy," in Perske, *Unequal Justice?* pp. 34-38.

Georgia Supreme Court protected: *Fleming v. Zant*, 259 Ga. 687; 386 S.E. 2d 339 (1989).

Tom Stevens: For information on Tom Stevens and William Hance, see pp. 17-19 and pp. 128-49 respectively of this work.

7   **All told, sixteen:** For a list of persons executed in the United States since the

reinstatement of capital punishment in 1976, see NAACP Legal Defense and Educational Fund, *Death Row U.S.A.* (New York: NAACP Legal Defense and Educational Fund, 1 September 1999), pp. 9-20.

7 **over 130 men and one woman:** My statement about the number of persons on Georgia's death row was accurate as of the fall of 1999 according to the Georgia Resource Center's director, Thomas Dunn (in conversation with the author, 19 November 1999). The number is in flux because of decisions of trial and appellate courts.

7-8 **mob-instigated lynchings:** See, for example, Stewart E. Tolnay and E. M. Beck, *A Festival of Violence: An Analysis of Southern Lynchings, 1882-1930* (Urbana: University of Illinois Press, 1995).

8 **what Jürgen Moltmann has suggested:** See his essay "Open Friendship: Aristotelian and Christian Concepts of Friendship," in *The Changing Face of Friendship,* ed. Leroy S. Rouner (Notre Dame: University of Notre Dame Press, 1994), p. 30.

10 **the story of his life:** I have checked the accuracy of the story Jim told me against research compiled by his appeals attorney and presented in the following documents: Application of James E. Messer for a 90-Day Stay of Execution and for Commutation of His Sentence of Death, before the Board of Pardons and Paroles, State of Georgia, July 1988; Petition for Writ of Habeas Corpus, *Messer v. Kemp,* Civil Action No. 86-V-670 (Superior Court of Butts County). In checking details of the crime, I have also consulted the following: Trial Transcript, *State v. Messer,* Case No. 2090 (Superior Court of Polk County, 4-8 February 1980).

I have on file applications for clemency — made available to me by appeals attorneys — that I have consulted in preparing this work.

12 **Judge Frank Johnson:** For his views, see *Messer v. Kemp,* 760 F. 2d 1080, 1093-97 (11th Cir. 1985) (Johnson, J., dissenting).

It is exceedingly difficult for a convicted person to show, in post-conviction proceedings, that his or her trial attorney was "ineffective" and thus that the case should be retried. See, for instance, David Cole, *No Equal Justice: Race and Class in the American Criminal Justice System* (New York: The New Press, 1999), pp. 76-81.

2. THE TIES

17   **events of his life:** The details of Tom's life — including his role in the murder for which he received the death sentence — that I mention in the text are consistent with the information put together by his appeals attorneys in these documents: Application of Thomas Dean Stevens for a 90-Day Stay of Execution and for a Commutation of His Sentence of Death, before the Board of Pardons and Paroles, State of Georgia, June 1993; Petition for Writ of Habeas Corpus, *Stevens v. Zant*, Civil Action No. 93-V-329 (Superior Court of Butts County); and Amendment to Petition for Writ of Habeas Corpus, *Stevens v. Zant*, Civil Action No. 93-V-329 (Superior Court of Butts County).

psychologist's evaluation: Tom's clemency petition (see Application of Thomas Dean Stevens, pp. 8-10) points out the following: The psychologist, Jethro Toomer, Ph.D., who evaluated Tom just days before his execution, concluded that Tom's intellectual and emotional development had been impaired by organic and social factors. The psychologist believed that Tom's IQ, below 60, was likely affected by his client's depression in the face of his pending electrocution. Still, Dr. Toomer believed that even in normal circumstances Tom would be considered as someone with mental retardation. The clemency petition also notes a 1988 state-administered IQ test given by a "behavioral specialist." According to this test, Tom's full-scale IQ was 78. The clemency petition argues that this score was within the range of mental retardation, allowing for a possible error in measurement.

The issue of Tom's mental retardation was also a part of his appeals in the courts. For a detailed defense of the claim, see Amendment to Petition for Habeas Corpus. For the State's response, see, for instance, Transcript of Proceedings, *Stevens v. Zant*, Civil Action No. 93-V-329 (Superior Court of Butts County, 24 June 1993), pp. 53-61. As part of its response, the State pointed to Tom's "correctional file": "It shows his IQ test in August of 1981 as being 116" (Transcript of Proceedings, p. 59). No other information about the test is mentioned.

In his brief state habeas corpus ruling, the judge wrote that Tom's "claims [including that of mental retardation] could have reasonably been raised in previous petitions, and nothing offered herein [i.e., in Tom's petition] provides relief under the Georgia or Federal Constitutions." See Order, *Stevens v. Zant*, Civil Action No. 93-V-329 (Superior Court of Butts County, 24 June 1993). In a 4-3 vote, the justices of the Georgia Supreme Court rejected Tom's mental retardation claim, along with other of his claims, without explanation. See Order, *Stevens v. Zant*, Civil Action No. 93-V-329 (Supreme Court of Georgia, 28 June 1993).

17 **such things as holding and acceptance:** For classic discussions of the importance of holding in human development, see D. W. Winnicott, *The Maturational Processes and the Facilitating Environment: Studies in the Theory of Emotional Development* (Madison, Conn.: International Universities Press, 1965). For explorations of the vital role of acceptance in the therapeutic relationship and, by implication, in each human relationship, see, for example, Carl R. Rogers, *On Becoming a Person: A Therapist's View of Psychotherapy* (Boston: Houghton Mifflin, 1961).

19 **With the State arguing:** On the importance of the testimony and recantation of Robert Botsford, who alleged at both the original trial and a resentencing trial that Tom had spoken in advance about killing the victim, see Petition for Writ of Habeas Corpus, pp. 14-28. ("Exhibit A" of the petition is Botsford's sworn affidavit of 17 June 1993 containing his recantation.) For the State's reply, downplaying the importance of the recantation, see Motion to Dismiss as Successive, *Stevens v. Zant,* Civil Action No. 93-V-329 (Superior Court of Butts County), pp. 13-14.

21 **"the green fields of the mind":** The words are from former baseball commissioner A. Bartlett Giamatti. See his essay "The Green Fields of the Mind," *Yale Alumni Magazine and Journal,* November 1977, p. 9.

25 **"shame-based":** For Gershen Kaufman's remarks on the "scripts" of a "shame-based culture," see his *Shame: The Power of Caring,* 3d ed. (Rochester, Vt.: Schenkman Books, 1992), pp. 31-33.

the gaze of others and ourselves: The experience of being exposed lies at the heart of shame, as Erik Erikson points out in his book *Identity: Youth and Crisis* (New York: W. W. Norton, 1968), p. 110: "Shame supposes that one is completely exposed and conscious of being looked at — in a word, self-conscious." In *Shame* (pp. 8-9), Kaufman expresses the point this way:

> To feel shame is to feel *seen* in a painfully diminished sense. The self feels exposed both to itself and to anyone else present. It is this sudden, unexpected feeling of exposure and accompanying self-consciousness that characterize the essential nature of the affect of shame. Contained in the experience of shame is the piercing awareness of ourselves as fundamentally deficient in some vital way as a human being.

Kaufman suggests — rightly, I believe — that the relationship between shame and guilt is as follows: "Guilt refers to shame which is about clearly moral matters, a poignant disappointment in self owing to a sudden break with one's own most cherished values in living" (p. 127).

25 **effects of the penetrating gaze:** See Kaufman, *Shame*, p. 9.

26 **Born of impotence:** A book that has especially helped me to understand the connection between powerlessness and rage is William H. Grier and Price M. Cobbs, *Black Rage* (New York: Basic Books, 1992).

30 **beating deaths of an elderly white couple:** For a brief summary of the crime and the evidence presented against Leonard, see *Frazier v. State*, 257 Ga. 690, 690-91; 362 S.E. 2d 351, 354 (1987).

3. VOICES

33 **"I seek God!":** In this and the following paragraph, my citations of Friedrich Nietzsche are from *The Gay Science*, in *The Portable Nietzsche*, ed. and trans. Walter Kaufmann (New York: Viking Press, 1968), pp. 95-96.

"fate of our times": My quotations from Weber are from "Science as a Vocation," in *From Max Weber: Essays in Sociology*, ed. H. H. Gerth and C. Wright Mills (London: Routledge and Kegan Paul, 1970), p. 155, cited in Barry Smart, *Postmodernity* (London and New York: Routledge, 1993), p. 85.

35 **his difficult days:** What I write about Warren's youth, young manhood, and trial, as well as the trials of his co-defendants, is consistent with the information presented in his clemency petition, prepared by his attorneys: Application of Warren McCleskey for a 90-Day Stay of Execution and Commutation of His Sentence of Death, before the Board of Pardons and Paroles, State of Georgia, September 1991. Important insights into Warren's life are contained in the following interview with him: "I Deeply Regret a Life Was Taken," *Atlanta Journal-Constitution*, 21 September 1991, sec. A, p. 12. For other insights into his life, see Mark Curriden, "Ready to Die, But Insisting He's Innocent," *Atlanta Journal-Constitution*, 21 September 1991, sec. A, p. 1; Joyce Hollyday, "A Gift of Dignity: The Story of Warren McCleskey," *Sojourners*, January 1992, pp. 24-26; and Murphy Davis, "Warren McCleskey: A Faith Refined," *Hospitality*, January 1992, p. 3.

36 **U.S. Supreme Court ruling:** See *McCleskey v. Kemp*, 481 U.S. 279 (1987). For a careful, detailed discussion of the decision, see David Cole, *No Equal Justice:*

Race and Class in the American Criminal Justice System (New York: New Press, 1999), pp. 134-41. Cole says this of the decision, "*McCleskey* may be the single most important decision the Court has ever issued on the subject of race and crime" (p. 137).

36 **Camus's term "absurd":** The concept of the absurd is the focal point of Camus's essay "The Myth of Sisyphus." See Albert Camus, *The Myth of Sisyphus and Other Essays,* trans. Justin O'Brien (New York: Vintage Books, 1955), pp. 1-102. The lines and phrases quoted here and on the following page are from this same source.

37 **Board of Pardons and Paroles:** In a telephone conversation on 1 June 1999 with Mary Sinclair, paralegal and researcher at the Southern Center for Human Rights in Atlanta, I confirmed that there were three whites and two blacks on the Board at the time of Warren's execution.

explained to its members: On the jurors' meeting with the Board, see "Warren McCleskey Is Dead," *New York Times,* 29 September 1991, sec. 4, p. 16. The jurors' reactions to learning that a key trial witness was a police plant are a part of Warren's clemency petition (Application of Warren McCleskey), which also argues for the possibility that Warren was not the trigger man, notes the lesser sentences of his co-defendants, and shows how he eventually overcame his difficult childhood and became a positive influence on those around him.

a key trial witness: The issue of the informant was also litigated on appeal. For two very different views of the issue, see *McCleskey v. Zant,* 499 U.S. 467, 470-503 (1991); and *McCleskey,* 499 U.S. 467, 506-29 (Marshall, J., dissenting).

38 **stays that will delay his death:** For an account of the last hours and minutes of Warren's life, see Mark Curriden, "McCleskey Put to Death after Hours of Delays, Final Apology," *Atlanta Constitution,* 26 September 1991, sec. D, p. 3.

"I pray that": "Warren McCleskey, 1948-1991," *Hospitality,* January 1992, p. 1.

murdering three other white people: For a brief account of the crime and the evidence presented against Larry, see *Lonchar v. State,* 258 Ga. 447, 447-48; 369 S.E. 2d 749, 750-51 (1988).

39 **"Woe to him who saw":** Viktor E. Frankl, *Man's Search for Meaning: An Introduction to Logotherapy,* trans. Ilse Lasch (New York: Pocket Books, 1963), p. 121.

39   **as his siblings have made clear:** See the affidavits (of Paul Lonchar and Christina Lonchar Kellogg, 20 March 1990) that are a part of the appendix to Petition for Writ of Habeas Corpus, *Kellogg v. Zant,* Civil Action No. 90-V-2735 (Superior Court of Butts County).

40   **first burst of electricity:** Larry's "botched execution" is recorded in Deborah W. Denno, "Execution and the Forgotten Eighth Amendment," in *America's Experiment with Capital Punishment: Reflections on the Past, Present, and Future of the Ultimate Penal Sanction,* ed. James R. Acker, Robert M. Bohm, and Charles S. Lanier (Durham, N.C.: Carolina Academic Press, 1998), p. 573.

41   **from reading D. T. Suzuki:** See, for example, Suzuki's *The Zen Doctrine of No-Mind* (London: Rider and Company, 1958).

42   **voice of Martin Heidegger:** I find Heidegger's sense of the wonder of being throughout his works. See, for example, Martin Heidegger, *What Is Philosophy?* trans. W. Kluback and J. T. Wilde (New York: Twayne Publishers, 1958). A very helpful treatment of Heidegger that grasps clearly his "astonishment" in the presence of being is George Steiner, *Martin Heidegger* (New York: Penguin Books, 1980).

43   **Martin Buber proclaimed:** I have been especially influenced by two of Buber's works: *I and Thou,* 2d ed., trans. Ronald Gregor Smith (New York: Charles Scribner's Sons, 1958); and *Between Man and Man,* 2d ed., trans. Ronald Gregor Smith (New York: Macmillan, 1965).

44   **"I feel a resistance to everything 'religious' growing in me":** Dietrich Bonhoeffer, *Gesammelte Schriften,* ed. Eberhard Bethge (Munich: Christian Kaiser Verlag, 1959), 2:420ff., quoted in Heinz Zahrnt, *The Question of God: Protestant Theology in the Twentieth Century,* trans. R. A. Wilson (New York: Harcourt Brace Jovanovich, 1969), p. 159.

45   **"How do we speak of God":** Bonhoeffer to Eberhard Bethge, 30 April 1944, in Dietrich Bonhoeffer, *Letters and Papers from Prison,* enl. ed., ed. Eberhard Bethge, trans. Reginald Fuller et al. (New York: Macmillan, 1972), pp. 280-81.

"It is not the religious act": Bonhoeffer to Eberhard Bethge, 18 July 1944, in *Letters and Papers from Prison,* p. 361.

"Jesus calls us": Bonhoeffer to Eberhard Bethge, 18 July 1944, in Dietrich Bonhoeffer, *Widerstand und Ergebung: Briefe und Aufzeichnungen aus der Haft,* ed.

Eberhard Bethge (Gütersloh: Gütersloher Verlagshaus, 1985), p. 181. The translation is mine. I use "us" where the Fuller et al. translation (*Letters and Papers from Prison*, p. 362) uses "men." Bonhoeffer's sentence reads as follows: "Jesus ruft nicht zu einer neuen Religion, sondern zum Leben."

46 **"God is beyond in the midst":** Bonhoeffer to Eberhard Bethge, 30 April 1944, in *Letters and Papers from Prison*, p. 282.

47 **"But one day when I was sitting":** Alice Walker, *The Color Purple* (New York: Pocket Books, 1983), p. 178.

she was beaten savagely: The details that I cite from the lives of Darrell and his mother, including the murder he committed, are consistent with his clemency petition, filed by his appeals attorneys: Application of Darrell G. Devier, Sr., for a 90-Day Stay of Execution and for a Commutation of His Sentence of Death, before the Board of Pardons and Paroles, State of Georgia, 10 May 1995. For an example of press coverage of Darrell's life (including the crime) and the arguments made at his clemency hearing, see "Murderer's Family Asks Panel to Spare His Life," *Columbus (Ga.) Ledger-Enquirer*, 13 May 1995, sec. B, p. 2.

49 **"One day while a handful of us":** Tony B. Amadeo, letter to author, June 1994. I have edited lightly — for such things as mechanics and spelling — the letters from prisoners that I cite in this work.

50 **trying to explain what had gone wrong:** The comments of Wes's father can be found in the following: Trial Transcript, *State v. McCorquodale*, Indictment No. A-20205 (Superior Court of Fulton County, 10-12 April 1974), p. 761.

he was drinking heavily: See the testimony of witnesses Bonnie Mae Johnson and Linda Deering (Wes's girlfriend and her roommate), Trial Transcript, pp. 746-47, 752-53.

took the life of a seventeen-year-old: For detailed presentations concerning the murder, see, of course, the trial transcript. For a brief description of the facts of the case, see *McCorquodale v. State*, 233 Ga. 369, 369-72; 211 S.E. 2d 577, 579-80 (1974).

51 **as Jung reminded us:** For a brief discussion of the shadow, see Carl Jung's *Aion: Researches into the Phenomenology of the Self*, 2d ed., vol. 9, pt. II of *The Collected Works of C. G. Jung*, ed. Herbert Read et al., trans. R. F. C. Hull et al. (Prince-

ton: Princeton University Press, 1968), pp. 8-10. For an excellent overview of Jung's concept of the shadow, see Mary Ann Mattoon, *Jungian Psychology in Perspective* (New York: Free Press, 1981), pp. 25-28.

4. A DREAM OF THE TATTERED MAN

54 **Pardons and Paroles Board petition:** Application of Joseph Holcombe Mulligan for a 90-Day Stay of Execution and for Commutation of His Sentence of Death, before the Board of Pardons and Paroles, State of Georgia, May 1987. Two key points of the petition are Joe's consistent claim that he was innocent (p. 2) and his refusal to accept a plea bargain (p. 11).

The question of Joe's guilt or innocence is especially complex. I cannot hope to do complete justice to it in the brief compass of this chapter. Readers interested in pursuing the question further should consult the complete judicial record and Joe's Pardons and Paroles Board petition.

55 **arrested months before:** "Timothy Helms was arrested in South Carolina soon after the incident [i.e., the murders, which occurred on 14 April 1974], but Joseph Mulligan was not arrested until March 20, 1975 in New York City. He was extradited and returned to Columbus, Georgia on March 6, 1976." See Petition for Writ of Habeas Corpus, *Mulligan v. Kemp*, Civil Action No. 87-V-990 (Superior Court of Butts County), p. 4.

immunity from prosecution: Trial Transcript, *State v. Mulligan*, Indictment Nos. 34590 and 34591 (Superior Court of Muscogee County, 2-4 November 1976), p. 75.

twenty-year-old Marine: Trial Transcript, p. 154.

He testified that: His testimony appears in Trial Transcript, pp. 127-63.

Joe, who was twenty-two: I refer to research ("Georgia: Age of Defendants on Date of Offense of Murder") compiled in 1984 by the late Harriet Pratt Morris. At the time, she was the ACLU state death-row monitor in Georgia.

in the first hour of Easter: The murders apparently happened between twelve-thirty and one o'clock — perhaps very near one o'clock — on Easter Sunday morning. See the testimony of witnesses Sheila Hutchinson, John Churchwell, Melvie Bell, and Brenda Riley in Trial Transcript, pp. 82-85, 89, 92-93, 95.

55   **The State alleged:** On Joe's alleged motives, see Trial Transcript, pp. 75-76.

he had been in Beaufort: See Deposition of Jay W. Fitt, *Mulligan v. Zant,* Civil Action No. 82-6-COL (United States District Court for the Middle District of Georgia, Columbus Division, 9 June 1982), pp. 14-15. Fitt was Joe's trial attorney.

When an expert testified: In his 1982 deposition (Deposition of Jay W. Fitt, pp. 31-32), Joe's trial attorney recounted the fingerprint testimony and what Joe had said to him immediately afterward. According to the attorney, Joe had made the following remarks: "I didn't tell you the truth. What really happened is they [Doe, Miller, and Helms] took me — shortly after we washed the car [which belonged to Doe], they took me to Atlanta and I caught the bus to Atlanta to go back home."

Based on the testimony of two men (Robert Teter and Leroy Moultrie) who were fellow Army officers of Captain Doe, the car-washing took place between four and five o'clock on the afternoon of 13 April 1974 (Trial Transcript, pp. 105, 116). According to another witness (Army officer Eric Barrett), Joe was at Fort Benning as late as eight o'clock that evening (Trial Transcript, pp. 121-22). Joe's comment — as remembered by his attorney — that he was taken to Atlanta "shortly after" the car-washing may or may not be inconsistent with the third officer's testimony, which Joe had heard *before* he made the comment. Perhaps to Joe, "shortly after" the car-washing meant three or four hours afterward. Perhaps Joe's or the attorney's language was not precise. Perhaps Joe or the attorney did not remember correctly the time when Joe supposedly left for Atlanta. Perhaps Joe was lying. I do not know. According to Joe's version of events, as presented in his Pardons and Paroles Board petition, some significant period of time — a couple of hours or more? — passed between the car-washing and his departure for Atlanta on April 13. The Petition does not give a precise time of departure. See Application of Joseph Holcombe Mulligan, pp. 15-16.

At one point, the lawyer's words quoting Joe obviously do not make good sense: "They took me to Atlanta and I caught the bus to Atlanta to go back home." Joe's Pardons and Paroles Board petition maintains that once Joe was taken to Atlanta, he caught a bus to Savannah, which is not far from his hometown: Beaufort, South Carolina (Application of Joseph Holcombe Mulligan, p. 16). It seems likely to me that the trial attorney simply misspoke, or that there is an error in the transcription of the deposition.

Joe's petition to the State's Board of Pardons and Paroles does not contest the point that, before the expert's fingerprint testimony, Joe had not been truthful with his trial attorney about his presence at Fort Benning before the murders.

56   **"sunk in the water":** Deposition of Jay W. Fitt, p. 32.

the lawyer had failed: His failure to interview the State's witnesses or even to request a list of them figured prominently in Joe's appeals. See, for example, *Mulligan v. Kemp*, 771 F. 2d 1436 (11th Cir. 1985).

working on a shoestring budget: For the defense attorney's account of the financial restraints he faced, see Deposition of Jay W. Fitt, pp. 6-10, and Affidavit of Jay Fitt, *Mulligan v. Kemp*, Civil Action No. 87-V-990 (Superior Court of Butts County, 5 May 1987).

In the lawyer's judgment: For the defense attorney's view of the witnesses, see Deposition of Jay W. Fitt, p. 32. He clearly felt that the witnesses were lying.

which argues that the witnesses: Application of Joseph Holcombe Mulligan, p. 12.
    According to Joe's trial attorney (Deposition of Jay W. Fitt, pp. 29-30), the gist of the witnesses' testimony was to be that Joe was home on "Easter morning" of 1974 — and, indeed, the rest of the day. The attorney's opening statement (Trial Transcript, p. 77) includes the following remarks:

> He [Joe] was not in Columbus, Georgia at the time that Mr. Whisnant [the prosecutor] or Mr. Helms, who will be the witness, claims he was, that he was in the breast of his own family back in Beaufort, that at the time that this event occurred, on or about Easter Sunday, 1974, which is a date that's significant, it's not just like any day of the week or any Sunday or any weekend, it was a special day, that members of his family will testify to you that Joseph Holcombe Mulligan was indeed home.

According to Helms's testimony, both Helms and Joe apparently did not arrive home until late in the afternoon on Easter Sunday (Trial Transcript, p. 158).
    Of course, even if the family witnesses could have been used to buttress Joe's revised alibi in court, they still could have been lying to protect him.

had not done any real preparation: In his 1982 deposition, Joe's trial attorney was asked the following question: "But as far as the penalty phase, there was no real preparation for the penalty phase trial in Mr. Mulligan's case?" The attorney answered the question as follows: "No, there wasn't." See Deposition of Jay W. Fitt, pp. 22-23.

no witnesses or evidence: In the words of Joe's appeals attorneys in their client's petition to the state's Pardons and Paroles Board, Joe's trial attorney "offered *no* evidence or witnesses at *either* phase of the trial" (Application of Joseph Holcombe Mulligan, p. 12).

56 **Joe's appeals attorneys documented:** See Affidavits in Support of Petition for Writ of Habeas Corpus, *Mulligan v. Zant,* Civil Action No. 4911 (Superior Court of Butts County). See also Exhibit A, in Application of Joseph Holcombe Mulligan.

trial lawyer did do some things: To read about his efforts that I describe in this paragraph, see Trial Transcript, pp. 154-63, 254-56, 294-304.

by his own admission: Trial Transcript, pp. 143-60.

57 **"human being":** Trial Transcript, p. 298.

the Georgia Supreme Court: See *Mulligan v. State,* 245 Ga. 266; 264 S.E. 2d 204 (1980).

petition before the Board acknowledged: Joe's lack of a prior criminal record is noted in Application of Joseph Holcombe Mulligan, p. 2; his alibi story appears on pp. 13-16 of the document.

Timothy Helms and Patrick Doe in drug dealing: Joe's Pardons and Paroles Board petition offers in an appendix (Exhibit C) a "Brief of Evidence" summarizing a hearing (30 January 1978) in regard to Extraordinary Motion for a New Trial, *State v. Mulligan,* Indictment Nos. 34590 and 34591 (Superior Court of Muscogee County). The brief contains the gist of the testimony of a man, James Reginald Everett, who said he had dealt in drugs with Timothy Helms and Patrick Doe in Columbus and had seen the two argue with one another. Unfortunately, the credibility of Everett's testimony is questionable — and not only because he had participated in drug dealings and was a prisoner "serving a sentence of life for murder and twenty years for armed robbery." Perhaps most importantly, while he and Joe had been in the county jail, they had talked together — and thus could have fabricated his claims — about Helms and Doe.

Board denied his request: At the time, four of the five Board members were white. I confirmed this fact in a telephone conversation, on 1 June 1999, with Mary Sinclair, paralegal and researcher for the Southern Center for Human Rights, Atlanta.

57 **"I'm innocent":** See Bill Davis and Ken Elkins, "Mulligan Dies Denying Guilt," *Columbus (Ga.) Saturday Ledger-Enquirer,* 16 May 1987, sec. A, p. 1.

58 **testimony of an Army officer:** See the testimony of Robert Teter in Trial Transcript, pp. 105-7.

a woman's testimony: See the testimony of Sheila Hutchinson in Trial Transcript, pp. 82-85.

they found a signed note: See Trial Transcript, pp. 150-51. Joe's handwriting is very distinctive and does indeed seem clearly to match that of the note ("State's Exhibit No. 9," Trial Transcript, p. 163).

taken a bus toward home: In regard to Joe's story of having been taken to Atlanta, from where he allegedly left on a bus for Savannah, consider also these points: He was last seen at Fort Benning at about eight o'clock in the evening. The murders happened no later than about one o'clock the next morning. Thus, Doe, Miller, and Helms would have had no more than about five hours to make a trip to Atlanta, let Joe out, pick up drugs, and then return to Columbus — a round-trip journey in excess of two hundred miles. In my view, to have made such a trip in five hours would have been difficult, though possible.

strong military ethos: The prosecutor understood that fact well. For example, in his closing argument at the sentencing phase of the trial, he called attention to the fact that Joe had cut short the career of a man (Doe) who might have gone on to become a general (Trial Transcript, p. 283). Moreover, the prosecutor called attention to his own military service (Trial Transcript, p. 287).

composed of all whites: See Death Penalty Information Center, *Chattahoochee Judicial District: The Buckle of the Death Belt* (Washington, D.C.: Death Penalty Information Center, 1991), fig. 6, following p. 3.

live with a deal: The disparity between Joe's death sentence and the immunity granted to Timothy Helms is one of the most important points made by Joe's petition before Georgia's Board of Pardons and Paroles (Application of Joseph Holcombe Mulligan, pp. 4, 20-21).

59 **"those I love":** Joseph H. Mulligan, letter to author, 15 May 1987. Subsequent references to Joe's correspondence with me are to this letter.

59 **things clinically associated with depression:** See, for instance, American Psychiatric Association, *Diagnostic and Statistical Manual of Mental Disorders*, 4th ed. (Washington, D.C.: American Psychiatric Association, 1994), pp. 320-23.

61 **"For I am sure":** Romans 8:38-39, RSV. All of my own subsequent quotations from the Bible are from this translation.

62 **as Carl Jung detailed:** See, for example, Carl Jung's *Aion: Researches into the Phenomenology of the Self,* 2d ed., vol. 9, pt. II of *The Collected Works of C. G. Jung,* ed. Herbert Read et al., trans. R. F. C. Hull et al. (Princeton: Princeton University Press, 1968), pp. 8-10; and Mary Ann Mattoon, *Jungian Psychology in Perspective* (New York: Free Press, 1981), pp. 25-28.

65 **Viktor Frankl:** Viktor E. Frankl, *Man's Search for Meaning: An Introduction to Logotherapy,* trans. Ilse Lasch (New York: Pocket Books, 1963), p. 122.

he was regaining knowledge: My understanding of the importance of Joe's storytelling became especially clear to me several years after his death, when I read Michael White and David Epston's treatment of the transformative power of narratives, *Narrative Means to Therapeutic Ends* (New York: W. W. Norton, 1990).

66 **"subjugated knowledges":** Michel Foucault, *Power/Knowledge: Selected Interviews and Other Writings* (New York: Pantheon Books, 1980), quoted in White and Epston, *Narrative Means to Therapeutic Ends,* p. 25.

68 **substantial (over 30 percent) black population:** Joe was tried in November of 1976. In 1980 the black population of Columbus-Muscogee County (the community has a consolidated government) was 34 percent. See, for instance, *Atlas of Demographics: U.S. by County from the 1980 Census* (Boulder, Colo.: Infomap, Inc., 1982), p. 29.

men sitting inside a pickup truck: I thought that the men were white, though I could not be certain.

5. A LESSON IN GRIEVING

70 **supposed to have died:** For an account of the delays and the execution of William Boyd Tucker, see Bill Davis and Ken Elkins, "Murderer Tucker Executed," *Columbus (Ga.) Saturday Ledger-Enquirer,* 30 May 1987, sec. A, pp. 1, 16.

70   **Deeply despondent:** In seeking to understand Bill Tucker's background, the crime, the trial, and the role that the "stocking strangler" murders played in his fate, I have been especially helped by his clemency petition, prepared by his appeals attorneys: Petition of William Boyd Tucker for Commutation of His Sentence of Death, before the State Board of Pardons and Paroles, State of Georgia, May 1987.

For basic information about the crime and the trial, I have also consulted the following: Trial Transcript, *State v. Tucker*, Indictment No. 77-C1804 (Superior Court of Muscogee County, 6-9 March 1978); and "Tucker's End: Hard Road to Peace," *Columbus (Ga.) Enquirer*, 14 August 1987, sec. A, p. 1.

I have gained important insight into the public defender's heavy caseload and its consequences for Bill's trial from the following expert testimony of an experienced Georgia attorney: Affidavit of Austin E. Catts, *Tucker v. Zant*, Civil Action No. 4766 (Superior Court of Butts County, 14 November 1980).

For the views of the coroner and law enforcement authorities on the race of the "stocking strangler," I have read, for example, Jay Barrow, "Task Force Adds 6 GBI Agents," *Columbus (Ga.) Enquirer*, 17 February 1978, sec. B, p. 1; and David Everett and Jay Barrow, "Klan to Patrol Wynnton," *Columbus (Ga.) Enquirer*, 23 February 1978, sec. B, p. 1.

In 1986, Carlton Gary, a black man, was convicted and sentenced to death for three of the strangling murders. For an overview of the case, see Richard Hyatt, "When the City Lost Its Innocence," *Columbus (Ga.) Ledger-Enquirer*, 28 July 1996, sec. A, pp. 1, 6.

pregnant woman: At the time of her murder, she was "one month pregnant" ("Tucker's End," p. 1).

This was the climate: In regard to the climate at the time of the trial and its possible effect on the jury, the Georgia Supreme Court explained the following in *Tucker v. State*, 244 Ga. 721, 730-31; 261 S.E. 2d 635, 642 (1979):

> A review of the voir dire examination reveals that those jurors who had been exposed to pre-trial publicity regarding the crime with which appellant was charged or the strangulation murders stated that they could lay aside any impression or opinion which they might have formed and render an opinion based upon the evidence.

Though the court noted that not all prospective jurors had been "questioned about pre-trial publicity or about possible bias stemming from the crime situation in Columbus," it pointed out that only three prospective jurors "were excused for prejudice from the panel (approximately five percent), and only one of these three was excused for prejudice regarding the unsolved strangulation murders." The court concluded, "The low percentage of veniremen [prospective jurors] excused is clearly insufficient to establish that appellant faced a biased jury."

William Cain and Richard O. Smith, Bill's trial attorneys, who had sought a change of venue in the case, obviously disagreed with this conclusion. Looking back on the turmoil in the community caused by the "stocking stranglings," Cain offered this observation in a statement of 15 May 1987: "I ... have reached the honest conclusion that Mr. Tucker would not have received the death penalty if it had not been for the feelings existing in the community." In a statement of 19 May 1987, Smith wrote the following about the stranglings:

> Never in my life before or since have I been involved in a city where so much of the population was affected by a single event as were the people of Muscogee County. Many people were living in terror and fear, not only for themselves, but for their loved ones as well. People were afraid to go out at night or to stay alone at home. Many of the feelings still linger today from that time. There was also a very strong feeling of anger throughout the population along with the frustration that occurs when there is nothing you can do about something. There was no doubt in my mind at the time of the trial that there was virtually no way this man could get a fair and impartial jury panel.

Both attorneys' statements were written to support — and were included as exhibits (N and O) appended to — Petition of William Boyd Tucker.

On the lack of effectiveness of the defense's attempt at a change of trial venue, see, for example, Affidavit of Austin E. Catts, p. 9:

> Trial counsel made a motion for a change of venue based on the climate of fear in the community and extensive pretrial publicity. However, counsel failed to have this motion ruled upon prior to trial. In addition, the motion was supported only by the affidavits of local attorneys. The proper presentation of such a motion, including preserving the record for appeal, demanded a greater evidentiary basis. Counsel could have introduced newspaper clippings and/or testimony of journalists regarding the climate of fear in the community. Expert witnesses, such as sociologists and psychologists, should have been consulted regarding the effect the wave of killings and the pretrial publicity would have on the ability of jurors to render an impartial and unbiased decision on sentencing.

70 **mental-health professional:** "Mr. Tucker's defense counsel failed to have him examined by a psychiatrist for possible use at the sentencing phase of the trial notwithstanding Mr. Tucker's history of adolescent problems, the recent

death of his father, his heavy drug and alcohol use, and the lack of any history of prior criminal activity" (Petition of William Boyd Tucker, p. 15).

71 **the Board, faced with the decision:** Its chairman, Wayne Snow Jr., maintained (in the words of a newspaper reporter) "that the board was not under pressure to send Tucker, who is white, to the electric chair because two blacks were denied commutation and executed within the past two weeks. The subject of Tucker's race was not discussed, he said." See Tracy Thompson, "U.S. High Court Issues 24-hour Stay for Tucker," *Atlanta Constitution*, 29 May 1987, sec. A, p. 18.

Rob Remar, Bill's appeals attorney for years, expressed this view about the Board's decision: "There's no doubt in my mind that it [race] was a factor. I have no doubt in my mind that if Bill had been black, they [the Pardons and Paroles Board] would have granted him clemency." See Jana Salmon-Heyneman, "Born Again, Lost Forever," *Macon (Ga.) Telegraph and News*, 9 August 1987, sec. A, p. 12.

On 1 June 1999, I confirmed the following in a telephone conversation with Mary Sinclair, paralegal and researcher at the Southern Center for Human Rights in Atlanta: at the time of Bill's execution, there were four whites and one black on the Board.

74 **"I have full confidence":** The quotation is from William Boyd Tucker, letter to his family, 24 April 1987 to 29 May 1987. All subsequent quotations from Bill's letter-journal are taken from this document. I am grateful to Bill's mother, Nancy Horan, for allowing me to quote from this letter. Lengthy excerpts from the letter appeared previously in the following: "Death Row Diary," *Macon (Ga.) Telegraph and News*, 9 August 1987, sec. A, pp. 1, 13; "Tucker's End," pp. 1, 8.

75 **a careful look at the subject:** My arguments in this paragraph are shaped largely by Jorgos Canacakis, *Ich sehe deine Tränen: Trauern, klagen, leben können* (Stuttgart: Kreuz Verlag, 1989). I have also profited from Howard Clinebell, "Bereavement Care and Counseling," in *Basic Types of Pastoral Care and Counseling: Resources for the Ministry of Healing and Growth*, rev. and enl. ed. (Nashville: Abingdon Press, 1984), pp. 218-42; and Verena Kast, *Trauern: Phasen und Chancen des psychischen Prozesses* (Stuttgart: Kreuz Verlag, 1993).

murder of Kathleen Perry: Bill was convicted "of murder, robbery by intimidation and kidnapping with bodily injury" in the case; he had also been indicted for "aggravated sodomy" against Ms. Perry, but the trial judge "directed a verdict of not guilty" on this count (*Tucker v. State*, 244 Ga. 721, 721; 261 S.E.

2d 635, 637 [1979]). The judge did so because there was "insufficient evidence to legally sustain a conviction" (Trial Transcript, p. 821).

80   **four-and-a-half-page, handwritten letter:**   The undated letter, from which I quote in this and subsequent paragraphs, is a part of Bill's clemency petition: Petition of William Boyd Tucker, Exhibit A.

81   **emotional and physical punishment:**   Such punishment and Bill's role as scapegoat are noted in Petition of William Boyd Tucker, especially Exhibit E, a letter from one of Bill's siblings. In a newspaper interview, Bill's mother acknowledged that her alcoholic husband had unleashed physical and verbal abuse on the family. See Salmon-Heyneman, "Born Again, Lost Forever," p. 12.

82   **"From that point on":**   According to the newspaper reporter who interviewed Bill's mother, Mrs. Horan expressed "remorse for not recognizing her son's problems before it was too late." In regard to the time after her husband's (Bill's father's) death, Mrs. Horan explained the following: "I was so wrapped [up] with my grief . . . that I was not paying that much attention to Buddy [Bill] and not realizing that he needed help also." See Salmon-Heyneman, "Born Again, Lost Forever," p. 12.

     "pleasure-centered society":   The phrase occurs a few lines earlier in his letter-journal entry for 24 May 1987.

     But surely his unbridled anger: The newspaper interviewer summarized Bill's mother's view of his act of violence this way: "Nancy believes those problems — emotional dishevel, drug abuse, low self-esteem and guilt over his father's death — led to the violent fury that ended the life of Kathleen Parry [sic]." See Salmon-Heyneman, "Born Again, Lost Forever," p. 12.

83   **the act of writing:**   For Bill, writing became an important ritual in the grieving process. For a discussion of rituals and grieving, see Canacakis, *Ich sehe deine Tränen,* pp. 86ff.

85   **deeply resistant to such change:**   For an important look at the persistence of racism in America, see Derrick Bell, *Faces at the Bottom of the Well: The Permanence of Racism* (New York: Basic Books, 1992).

6. A WALK IN ARCADY

89   **to see Billy Mitchell:** For a view of Billy that is based on many of the sources I use but that was written by someone who did not know him, see Peter Canellos, "Southern Justice? A Cursed Life, a Curse of Death," *Boston Phoenix,* 20 November 1987, sec. 1, pp. 1, 6, 7, 25, 27, 30, 32. Factual errors occur in the article. For example, according to Canellos, Billy and two companions confronted and demanded money from Mrs. Peggy Carr and her son in the IGA store in Sylvester, Georgia, on 11 August 1974. According to Mrs. Carr's testimony, she saw only Billy take part in the robbery, shooting, and murder. See Trial Transcript, *State v. Mitchell,* Case No. 8694 (Superior Court of Worth County, 5 November 1974), pp. 11-15, 19-30, 32-35, 68-73. See also my note under 90: **closed the cooler door, and fled.**

   the crate that, according to Billy: In regard to the throwing of the crate and the shooting, I refer to statements that Billy gave to police and sheriff's department deputies on August 11, 1974, and that were introduced as State's evidence (Exhibits 1 and 2) at his sentencing trial. See Trial Transcript, pp. 48-49, 60. The quoted material in this paragraph is from Peggy Carr's testimony at Billy's sentencing trial: Trial Transcript, p. 25.

90   **According to the testimonies:** For the testimony of William Monroe (one of the two cousins), see Trial Transcript, pp. 61-66. For Ms. Carr's testimony, see my note under 89: **to see Billy Mitchell**.

   along with his cousin: I do not know the age of the cousin who was present in the convenience store just after the shootings but who did not testify. In his notes, Billy's trial attorney seems to refer to each of the cousins as a "young man." See Brief in Support of Motion to Dismiss, *Mitchell v. Kemp,* Civil Action No. 87-V-1112 (Superior Court of Butts County), Respondent's Exhibit 14. In one of Billy's statements to sheriff's department deputies (State's trial Exhibit 2), he refers to the cousins as "white boys."

   closed the cooler door, and fled: When one combines Billy's statements to law enforcement authorities (State's trial Exhibits 1 and 2), this picture emerges: Two of his acquaintances — one of them asleep — were in his car outside the store while he was inside. The two had driven off by the time he made his exit. According to a newspaper account, police speculated that Billy's companions left after hearing shots from the "lone gunman" inside the IGA. The two acquaintances were later captured by police and charged with armed robbery. See "Robbers Kill Worth Youth, Shoot Mother Four Times," *Albany (Ga.)*

Herald, 12 August 1974, pp. 1, 5. (The article is erroneously titled, since only Billy shot Chris Carr and his mother.)

Billy's two companions eventually received life sentences for participating in the robbery. In their defense, Billy testified that they had no part in the robbery and did not know what was happening inside the convenience store. See "Mitchell Draws Life in Jail on Second Murder Charge," *Albany (Ga.) Sunday Herald,* 18 May 1975, sec. A, p. 14.

90   **He confessed:**   See the State's Exhibits 1 and 2 at Billy's sentencing trial.

initially at gunpoint: See, for example, Petition for Writ of Certiorari to the United States Court of Appeals for the Eleventh Circuit, *Mitchell v. Kemp,* No. 85-5534 (Supreme Court of the United States, October Term 1985), p. 27.

In court: See Trial Transcript.

white judge: The judge was J. Bowie Gray. Because Billy pled guilty, the trial judge could, without the deliberations of a jury, sentence him to death or life in prison. See Official Code of Georgia Annotated §17-10-32.

91   **white, court-appointed lawyer, who received one-hundred-fifty dollars:** Billy's lawyer was Clarence A. Miller. On the attorney's remuneration, see, for example, Petition for Writ of Certiorari, p. 2. On his ineffectiveness — including his failure to call witnesses or present mitigating evidence on his client's behalf — as an advocate in the case, see, for instance, pp. 2-10, 13-26 of the petition.

Billy had "discouraged" him: See Transcript of Hearing, *Mitchell v. Hopper,* Civil Action No. 478-132 (United States District Court for the Southern District of Georgia, Savannah Division, 17 April 1982), p. 33. For a summary of the attorney's defense of his actions in regard to mitigation, see, for instance, *Mitchell v. Kemp,* 762 F. 2d 886, 889 (1985).

he escaped from the county jail: For a brief — and accurate, to the best of my knowledge — account of the escape, see Canellos, "Southern Justice?" p. 30.

pled guilty to and received a life sentence: See Judgment of Conviction and Sentencing Order, *State v. Mitchell,* Indictment No. 36205 (Superior Court of Dougherty County, 16 May 1975). I did not talk to Billy about the Albany murder of Williard Williams, so I do not know Billy's version of the circumstances surrounding it. If Billy did, in fact, kill Mr. Williams on 10 August 1974, I assume that Billy was in the same traumatized state of mind that he was in when he murdered Chris Carr a day later. The information I have about the murder of Mr. Williams is too sketchy for me to comment further on his death or Billy's role in it. According to the arrest warrant of 14 August 1974 in the case, Billy Mitchell "did make the deceased lay face down on the ground between 211 N. Jefferson and 219 N. Jefferson Street, Albany, Dougherty County, Georgia and shot deceased in the back of the head (right side) with a .32 Cal., 7 Shot Guardian Pistol, Serial Number G 19289, after robbing victim of $4.00."

92 **"the most poverty-stricken":**   The quotations and other information in this paragraph, unless otherwise indicated, are from Petition for Writ of Certiorari, pp. 5-7.

ten brothers and sisters: See Affidavit of Dr. Craig Haney, May 1982, paragraph 9, in appendix to Petition for Writ of Certiorari. The petition summarizes Dr. Haney's qualifications this way: he was "a psychologist, attorney, criminologist and a former consultant to the United States Department of Justice" (p. 7).

"Billy was the oldest boy":   Petition for Writ of Habeas Corpus, *Mitchell v. Kemp,* Civil Action No. 87-V-1112 (Superior Court of Butts County), Appendix, Affidavit of Glenda Jean Mitchell, 4 August 1987, p. 2. Unless I have noted otherwise previously, all affidavits subsequently cited in this chapter are appendices to this petition.

in his last year of high school: On the time of events that I describe in this paragraph, see Affidavit of Dr. Craig Haney, paragraphs 24-26. Dr. Haney's understanding of the events is consistent with what I learned from talking with Billy's family during the final days of his life. In this paragraph I also draw on the following sources: Report of Joyce Lynn Carbonell, Ph.D., 18 August 1987, p. 4 (appended to Petition for Writ of Habeas Corpus, *Mitchell v. Kemp,* Civil Action No. 87-V-1112 [Superior Court of Butts County]); Affidavit of Josephine Mitchell, 19 August 1987, pp. 2-3; and Judgment of Conviction and Sentencing Order, *Florida v. Mitchell,* Case No. 70-1260 (Criminal Court of Record of Duval County, Fla., in and for the Fourth Judicial Circuit, 8 June 1970). At the time of her report, Dr. Carbonell was a clinical psychologist and university professor. Josephine Mitchell is Billy's mother.

93 **over four years:**   Billy was confined for some two months in the Duval County Jail, beginning 27 March 1970. After spending time in jail, he was sentenced to prison on 8 June 1970. See Judgment of Conviction and Sentencing

Order, *Florida v. Mitchell.* He was released from prison on 1 May 1974. See Petition for Writ of Habeas Corpus, *Mitchell v. Kemp,* Civil Action No. 87-V-1112 (Superior Court of Butts County), p. 22n. 10.

93   **to a group of Black Muslims:**   Affidavit of Josephine Mitchell, p. 4.

94   **"baffling reality":**   See the screenplay of *The Seventh Seal* (trans. Lars Malstrom and David Kushner) in *Literature: The Human Experience,* ed. Richard Abcarian and Marvin Klotz, 2d ed. (New York: St. Martin's Press, 1978), p. 1046. The other quotations from the knight in this paragraph appear on p. 1063 of this anthology.

95   **gained his high-school diploma and completed college courses:**   In a telephone conversation with me on 30 August 1998, Josephine Mitchell confirmed with pride Billy's academic accomplishments in prison. She still has the certificates attesting to these accomplishments.

96   **"His bones just stuck out":**   Affidavit of Josephine Mitchell, p. 3.

     especially dangerous Florida State Prison: Dr. Craig Haney referred to this prison as "widely regarded among correctional experts as one of the most brutal and intense institutions in the South" (Affidavit of Dr. Craig Haney, paragraph 37).

     one of his fellow prisoners: For the fellow prisoner's comments that I quote in this and the subsequent paragraph, see Affidavit of Horace Leroy Maddox, 20 August 1987, pp. 2-3, 5.

97   **"The prison discriminated against blacks":**   Affidavit of Glenda Jean Mitchell, p. 3.
     In his article entitled "Guards," which appeared in the *St. Petersburg (Fla.) Times* on 16 January 1971 (sec. A, pp. 1, 9), Martin Dyckman notes the following about Florida's correctional officers at the time of Billy's imprisonment in that state:

> The guard forces remain a conspicuously weak part of what everyone agrees should be a rehabilitative system.
>   "In most cases," says James Ball, personnel director for the division of corrections, "we have to take the first guy, rather than be selective and accept only the man who understands human beings. You take people who can pass the physical examination and have a high school education."

Paradoxically, prospective guards are given no psychological tests.

Their backgrounds are investigated, to be sure. But there is no professional attempt to screen out the lurking sadist.

Many guards are racially prejudiced.

There are hardly any black guards — though blacks are the majority of prisoners.

97   **"They teach you good stuff"**:   Affidavit of William C. Whitfield, 19 August 1987, p. 2.

99   **a clinical psychologist:**   For the psychologist's diagnosis, see Report of Joyce Lynn Carbonell. With access to Billy's official prison records, she notes (p. 4) the "incarceration trauma" he experienced in prison in Florida. She summarizes (pp. 4-5) some of the difficulties of his incarceration that contributed to his post-traumatic stress disorder: serving time in isolation, facing sexual assaults, enduring racism from guards, being stabbed.

the State was scoffing: The State argued that the trauma claim was not essentially different from psychological findings that Billy's attorneys had presented at an earlier stage of appeals. For a look at the State's argument, see Brief in Support of Motion to Dismiss, p. 12.

Billy did not seek clemency from Georgia's Board of Pardons and Paroles. On his behalf, Billy's appeals attorneys informed the Board of their client's remorse in the case but also his belief that the clemency process was a "charade" (letter of Richard H. Burr III and George H. Kendall to State Board of Pardons and Paroles, 1 September 1987). A portion of the letter, which the attorneys made available to me, appeared in Lee Smith, "Does Clemency Exist in Georgia?" *Fulton County (Ga.) Daily Report,* 8 September 1987, p. 1.

At the time of Billy's execution, there were four whites and one black on the Board; on 1 June 1999, I confirmed this in a telephone conversation with Mary Sinclair, paralegal and researcher for the Southern Center for Human Rights, Atlanta.

deeply hurt, traumatized: Billy presumably read his appeals petitions, knew of the diagnosis of post-traumatic stress disorder, and believed the diagnosis to be true. See, for example, his signed "verification" of the truth and accuracy of Petition for Writ of Habeas Corpus, *Mitchell v. Kemp,* Civil Action No. 870233-7 (United States District Court for the Middle District of Georgia, Albany Division), p. 39.

"outside the range of normal human experience":   The quotation, which appears in Report of Joyce Lynn Carbonell (p. 7), is originally from the following: American Psychiatric Association, *Diagnostic and Statistical Manual of Mental Disorders,* 3d ed., revised (Washington, D.C.: American Psychiatric Association, 1987), p. 250. (This source uses the word "usual" instead of "normal.") My subsequent quotation of the psychologist in this paragraph is also from Carbonell's report, pp. 7-8.

100 **Billy's appeals attorneys later pointed out:** See Petition for Writ of Habeas Corpus, *Mitchell v. Kemp,* Civil Action No. 87-V-1112 (Superior Court of Butts County), pp. 14-15.

his examining psychologist noted: Report of Joyce Lynn Carbonell, p. 8.

102 **"who kills without provocation":** For accounts — which include the quotations in this paragraph — of Billy's execution, see David Beasley and Amy Wallace, "Convicted Killer Mitchell Dies in Electric Chair," *Atlanta Journal,* 2 September 1987, sec. C, pp. 1, 4; and Joseph B. Frazier, "Murderer Dies in Electric Chair," *Columbus (Ga.) Ledger,* 2 September 1987, sec. A, pp. 1, 7.

victims need to find places of safety: My discussion of trauma in this paragraph is indebted to Judith Lewis Herman, *Trauma and Recovery* (New York: Basic Books, 1992). The quoted material appears on p. 181 of her book.

103 **"the use of memory":** The quoted material in this sentence is from Eliot's "Little Gidding," in his *Four Quartets* (New York: Harcourt, Brace & World, 1971), p. 55.

"squarely in the midst of the world": The quotation is from Hillman's *Archetypal Psychology: A Brief Account* (Dallas: Spring Publications, 1990), p. 26. See p. 16 of his work for the notion of soul as perspective.

104 **"When he was . . . in prison":** Affidavit of Lucinda Mebane, 4 August 1987, p. 4.

"soul" in African American parlance: See Preston N. Williams, "The Ethics of Black Power," in *Quest for a Black Theology,* ed. James J. Gardiner and J. Deotis Roberts (Philadelphia: Pilgrim Press, 1971), p. 84.

as Hillman has noted: On the link between soul and "the imaginative possibility in our natures," see Hillman, *Archetypal Psychology,* pp. 16-17.

105 **"I won't be satisfied until I get revenge":** She is quoted in "Robber Who Killed 14-Year-Old Dies in Electric Chair in Georgia," *New York Times,* 2 September 1987, sec. A, p. 12.

7. WHILE THE EARTH REMAINS

106 **according to what I read:** In this and the following paragraph, I draw on Jeanne Cummings, "13 Years Later, Officer's Killer Facing Execution," *Atlanta Constitution,* 18 May 1989, sec. B, pp. 1, 6.

two other men: Along with Henry were Son Fleming and his nephew Larry Fleming. It is not clear if all three men were involved in the holdup. Perhaps one of the three, Son Fleming, was not involved. See, for instance, *Fleming v. State,* 240 Ga. 142, 142-44; 240 S.E. 2d 37, 38-39 (1977).

107 **Henry's daughter:** I knew of Henry's daughter from his friends on and off the row. Only after his execution did I learn from his longtime friend Lise Greene that he also had a son who was born while Henry was in prison and who never saw his father.

"try to begin a friendship": Henry Willis, letter to author, 20 March 1989.

he had not wanted to visit: Henry Willis, letter to author, 5 April 1989.

"The [bad] situation with the courts": Henry Willis, letter to author, 5 April 1989.

"Since my father died": Henry Willis, letter to author, 20 March 1989.

gotten to know only after he, Henry, had become an adult: Henry mentioned this in passing during our three hours together.

108 **he had said at his trial:** See Trial Transcript, *State v. Willis,* Case No. 77-181 (Superior Court of Bleckley County, 9-28 January 1978), pp. 598-99.

view of an expert witness: For the not unproblematic view of James Dawson, who was assistant director of the Georgia Crime Laboratory, see his testimony in Trial Transcript, especially pp. 385-86, 393.

108 **"If he done that":** My quotations from the interview are from Cummings, "13 Years Later, Officer's Killer Facing Execution," p. 6.

109 **black Board member was not present:** For this and other information concerning the hearing before the Board, I am grateful to Henry's friend Lise Greene, who testified on his behalf. At the time, she was executive assistant to the president of Montclair State College in New Jersey.

I do not know if the black member of the Board participated in the vote in Henry's case. On 4 December 1997, Mary Sinclair, paralegal and researcher for Atlanta's Southern Center for Human Rights, wrote to the Board on my behalf to try to ascertain, among other things, if all of its members had voted each time in clemency deliberations in the cases of the men ultimately put to death by Georgia after the reinstatement of capital punishment in 1976. Ms. Sinclair received no reply to her letter.

"legal avenues": The quoted material in this paragraph is from Henry Willis, letter to Mark Bippes and Lise Greene, 28 February 1989. I am grateful to the recipients of the letter for permitting me to quote from it and another letter that Henry wrote to them which I cite later in the chapter.

110 **Millard Farmer:** According to the Report of the Trial Judge *(State v. Willis),* Farmer "was retained by defendant without cost to defendant."

111 **Millard Farmer had a number of judges:** The racial bias that affected Henry's trial is also described, for example, in Petition for Writ of Habeas Corpus, *Willis v. Zant,* Civil Action No. 89-V-2187 (Superior Court of Butts County), Part II, pp. 1-5.

twenty of the thirty-one prospective black jurors excluded for "cause": The prosecutor "sought to have only 4 of 98 white jurors excused for cause (3 for moral scruples concerning the death penalty)." See p. 3 of the Petition for Writ of Habeas Corpus cited directly above.

112 **"The crime was committed":** The Board's chair is quoted in Jeanne Cummings, "Henry Willis Put to Death for Murder," *Atlanta Constitution,* 19 May 1989, sec. A, p. 15.

113 **one of his co-defendants:** After Henry's execution, I would learn that Son Fleming was convicted of murder and received a death sentence "in Lanier County, whose county seat is only seven miles from Ray City," where Ed Giddens had been police chief. See Petition for Writ of Habeas Corpus, *Fleming*

v. Zant, Civil Action No. 86-V-662 (Superior Court of Butts County), p. 5. The petition (Exhibit F, Affidavit of Michael Russell, 19 June 1986), which records the race of the jurors in the Lanier County trial, points out that the "prosecutor used his peremptory challenges to strike *eight* out of the *ten* blacks [who were potential jurors] from the jury." The jury was eventually composed of eleven whites and one black. The petition (Exhibit F) also points out that about "30% of the residents of Lanier County were black at the time of the trial of Son Fleming." The petition (p. 5) notes that the Georgia Supreme Court (see *Fleming v. State,* 240 Ga. 142; 240 S.E. 2d 37 [1977]) granted Son Fleming a new sentencing trial because of errors by the prosecutor and judge, a trial that took place in "Cook County, whose county seat is only 12 miles from Ray City." At this resentencing trial, Son Fleming again received a death sentence. This time there were three blacks on the jury. In a telephone conversation with Mary Sinclair on 2 October 1997, I confirmed the racial composition of the Cook County jury; she had researched the issue.

113 **Henry's other co-defendant:** I would learn one day that Larry Fleming had three blacks on his jury in a town a couple of counties south of Ray City. My information on Larry (whose last name is sometimes spelled "Flemming") can be found in these sources: "Flemming Jury Being Selected," *Valdosta (Ga.) Daily Times,* 2 March 1981, sec. A, p. 1; "Prosecution Charges Police Chief's Slaying an 'Execution,'" *Albany (Ga.) Herald,* 5 March 1981, sec. A, p. 6; Lee Freeman, "Flemming Trial Gets Underway," *Valdosta (Ga.) Daily Times,* 5 March 1981, sec. A, p. 1; "3rd Man Convicted in Killing of Police Chief Gets Life," *Atlanta Journal-Constitution,* 8 March 1981, sec. B, p. 2.

115 **the outline of Richard's life:** A fuller account of the events that I relate here concerning Richard's life is contained in his clemency petition, prepared by his appeals attorneys: Application of Richard Tucker for a 90-Day Stay of Execution and for Commutation of His Sentence of Death, before the Board of Pardons and Paroles, State of Georgia, May 1987. Some of the major events of Richard's life, including those of his difficult childhood, were reported in the news media. See, for example, Jim King and Eric Velasco, "Nurse-Killer Put to Death in the Chair," *Macon (Ga.) Telegraph and News,* 23 May 1987, sec. A, pp. 1, 11; David Beasley and Scott Thurston, "Tucker Is 2nd Executed in State in 7 Days," *Atlanta Journal-Constitution,* 23 May 1987, sec. A, pp. 1, 18. The murder for which Richard received the death penalty is also briefly described in both of these articles. For detailed information concerning this murder and Richard's conviction for the killing, see Trial Transcript, *State v. Tucker,* Case No. 19668 (Superior Court of Bibb County, 8-11 January 1979). Richard's testimony, which includes his view of the murder and of statements he gave to police in the case, appears

on pp. 800-851 of the transcript. For the prosecution's summary of the evidence against Richard, see pp. 735-49 of the record. On the court-appointed status of trial counsel, see the report of the trial judge in the case.

116   **killing Annie Mae Armstrong, one of his aunts:**   In 1979, at his trial for the murder of Edna Sandefur, Richard explained that he had pled guilty to the murder of his aunt. For this and other of his comments about his aunt's murder, see Trial Transcript, *State v. Tucker,* pp. 837-43, 850-51.

    prisoner once bound him to a cot: The event, which Richard once told me about, is not mentioned in his clemency petition.

117   **jury of nine whites and three blacks gave him the death penalty:**   In a telephone conversation on 12 March 2000, I confirmed the composition of the jury with Mary Sinclair, who had researched the matter.

    that of the rescuer: I find important confirmation of my observations about the rescuer in Gina O'Connell Higgins, *Resilient Adults: Overcoming a Cruel Past* (San Francisco: Jossey-Bass, 1994).

    several persons — had come to her rescue: When I met Annie Tucker in 1987, I found her to be a person with considerable insight into the reasons why her life had turned out differently from that of her brother. I believe she understood that she had been rescued. Some of her insights into her life and that of her brother are incorporated into the text of Richard's clemency petition and into a letter that she wrote in support of it.

    had become a successful businesswoman: In talking with Annie Tucker in 1987, I learned that she had her own upholstery shop.

118   **he, like Henry, had declined the opportunity:**   Richard's silence while he was sitting in the electric chair is reported in Eric Velasco, "Leather Masks Grim Reality of 'Surreal' Electrocution," *Macon (Ga.) Telegraph and News,* 24 May 1987, sec. A, p. 14. Henry's failure to give a last statement is noted in Bill Montgomery, "Infamous Last Words," *Atlanta Journal-Constitution,* 2 April 1995, sec. D, p. 4.

    notes like these: What follows is an edited version of copious notes that I made.

119   **"But I have managed":**   The full letter appears in Application of Richard

Tucker, Appendix A. This passage from Richard's letter was printed in Beasley and Thurston, "Tucker Is 2nd Executed in State in 7 Days," p. 18. Richard's case was decided by a Board composed of four whites and one black; I confirmed this in a telephone conversation on 1 June 1999 with Mary Sinclair.

119 **the strength to put to rest entirely the ghosts:** His chief appeals attorney, Millard Farmer, argued that Richard "suffers from a serious mental disorder that should be looked into." See Beasley and Thurston, "Tucker Is 2nd Executed in State in 7 Days," p. 18. Farmer's argument was part of Richard's appeals. See, for example, Petition for Writ of Habeas Corpus, *Tucker v. Kemp,* Civil Action No. 87-V-1009 (Superior Court of Butts County), pp. 4-7. In an affidavit (of 14 May 1987) attached to the petition, clinical psychologist Howard E. Albrecht, Ph.D., made the following observation:

> It is my professional opinion that Richard Tucker was at the time of the crime, and is now, suffering from a mental disorder which likely affected his ability to control his behavior at the time of the crime. Further psychological and medical testing would be necessary to fully diagnose and evaluate Richard Tucker's psychological disorder.

In his Order, 15 May 1987, that dismissed Richard's petition, Judge Hal Craig of the Flint Judicial Circuit noted that Richard had had two psychological exams prior to his trial and concluded that "neither evaluation revealed any basis for a sanity defense." Richard's petition had argued that the prior mental-health examinations were inadequate.

"It has taken some time": Montgomery, "Infamous Last Words," p. 4.

120 **"I perceived reality from a perspective":** This sentence and a subsequent portion of Richard's letter were printed in King and Velasco, "Nurse-Killer Put to Death in the Chair," p. 11.

121 **The newspaper article described:** The details of the execution are found in Velasco, "Leather Masks Grim Reality of 'Surreal' Electrocution," pp. 1, 14.

"a statement he had tape-recorded earlier": Apparently, this is the source of Richard's words ("It has taken some time [to realize it] . . .") that I quoted above (p. 148) and that were printed in Montgomery, "Infamous Last Words," p. 4.

Reverend Nolan Lavell (a prison chaplain): In "Leather Masks Grim Reality of 'Surreal' Electrocution," Velasco identifies the person who prayed with

Richard at this point only as "an Atlanta Baptist minister, Nolan Lavell" (p. 14). Reverend Lavell was also a chaplain on the prison staff. Ministers who are not affiliated with the prison are not permitted to pray with the condemned in the death chamber.

122 **"on May 23, 1987":** Either the warden or the newspaper writer was in error. Richard was executed on May 22, 1987.

124 **One whose acts create hope:** My thinking about the Judeo-Christian God as a God of hope has been deeply influenced by Jürgen Moltmann, *Theology of Hope: On the Ground and the Implications of a Christian Eschatology*, trans. James W. Leitch (New York: Harper & Row, 1975).

the concept of witness that Judith Herman would later describe: See, for example, Judith Lewis Herman, *Trauma and Recovery* (New York: Basic Books, 1992), pp. 135-36, 140-47, 153-54.

125 **"Criminals like Henry Willis III":** "Opinion," *Barnesville (Ga.) Herald-Gazette*, 24 May 1989, p. 4.

the most sensitive writers about child abuse and neglect: See, for example, John Bowlby, *A Secure Base: Parent-Child Attachment and Healthy Human Development* (New York: Basic Books, 1988); Leonard Shengold, *Soul Murder: The Effects of Childhood Abuse and Deprivation* (New York: Fawcett Columbine, 1991); John N. Briere, *Child Abuse Trauma: Theory and Treatment of the Lasting Effects* (Newbury Park, Calif.: Sage Publications, 1992); Herman, *Trauma and Recovery;* James Gilligan, *Violence: Our Deadly Epidemic and Its Causes* (New York: G. P. Putnam's Sons, 1996); and James Garbarino, *Lost Boys: Why Our Sons Turn Violent and How We Can Save Them* (New York: Free Press, 1999).

"victim mentality": For a good example of great antipathy toward the "victim mentality," see the view of U.S. Supreme Court Justice Clarence Thomas as reported in Neil A. Lewis, "Justice Thomas Assails Victim Mentality," *New York Times*, 17 May 1994, sec. A, p. 14.

126 **"I didn't want to write this letter":** Henry Willis, letter to Mark Bippes and Lise Greene, May 1989.

8. A WORLD FAR AWAY

128 **over and over:** His ex-wife, Wanda Hance Johnson, also noted his repetitive behavior. See her Affidavit of 22 March 1994, p. 3. It is appended to Amendment to Petitioner's Pro Se Petition for Writ of Habeas Corpus, *Hance v. Zant,* Civil Action No. 93-V-172 (Superior Court of Butts County). Unless otherwise noted, all affidavits that I draw on in this chapter are contained in the appendix to this amended petition.

his essentially supernatural prowess with women: A clinical psychologist who examined William before his 1978 trial also noted the defendant's exaggerated claims of romantic prowess. See Affidavit of Lewis R. Lieberman, 21 March 1994, p. 3.

had been convicted and received the death penalty: See Trial Transcript, *State v. Hance,* Indictment No. 40353 (Superior Court of Muscogee County, 11-16 December 1978).

the abundant evidence to the contrary: For the evidence that I cite here, I rely on testimony at William's 1984 resentencing trial for the murder of Gail Faison: Trial Transcript, *State v. Hance,* Indictment No. 40353 (Superior Court of Muscogee County, 7-12 May 1984). For the testimony of persons who interviewed William for the Army (Richard Fox) and Columbus police (Charles Rowe) after his arrest and to whom he eventually confessed that he alone had committed the murder, see especially pp. 977-96, 1015-20. See pp. 1040-51 for the expert testimony of S. D. Wright (Columbus Police Department, retired) concerning William's fingerprint on one of the extortion letters (the only identifiable print on all the letters); pp. 1028-31 and pp. 1033-35 for the expert testimony of Karen Miles (Georgia State Crime Lab), who was able to link William's handwriting to a writing sample from the letters; pp. 1069-70 for the testimony of John Burrows, who was the Army investigator who found the murder weapon where William had said it was; and pp. 1190, 1196 for William's admission, in court, of murder.

At his original trial, he said that he had been coerced, at gunpoint, to confess. See Trial Transcript, 1978, pp. 932-34.

federal appeals court had overturned: See *Hance v. Zant,* 696 F. 2d 940 (11th Cir. 1983).

129 **resentenced William to death:** See Trial Transcript, 1984.

130 **the capacity to move *through* the real:** My thinking at this point has been influenced by William F. Lynch, *Christ and Apollo: The Dimensions of the Literary Imagination* (Notre Dame: University of Notre Dame Press, 1975).

When he was growing up: The information contained in this paragraph is based primarily on memories of William's sister, Yvonne Hance Boyd (Affidavit of 21 March 1994, pp. 1-4), and those of two other persons who knew William when he was growing up: June Mays (Affidavit of 22 March 1994, p. 1) and Michelle Poindexter (Affidavit of 22 March 1994, p. 1). For the date of his birth, I have drawn on a copy of William's birth certificate, appended to Amendment to Petitioner's Pro Se Petition. According to the affidavits of Boyd (p. 4), Mays (p. 1), and Poindexter (p. 1), William was "quiet"; Ms. Poindexter also describes him as "withdrawn" (p. 1).

131 **difficulty learning:** In the final round of appeals, when William's IQ became a key issue, neither the State nor his attorneys cited IQ scores from his school years, as far as I can tell.

"slow and retarded students": The quoted material in this sentence comes from Affidavit of Harold Morrison, 21 March 1994, pp. 1-2.

"dumb" and "picked on him a lot": The quoted material in the sentence is from Affidavit of Yvonne Hance Boyd, p. 4.

"William didn't run": Affidavit of George Warren, 22 March 1994, p. 1.

"He impressed me": Affidavit of Delores Bausum, 21 March 1994, pp. 1-2.

132 **"Sometimes Billy would just sit and stare":** Affidavit of Yvonne Hance Boyd, p. 5.

"very cooperative and extremely likable": Affidavit of Christine Warren, 22 March 1994, p. 1.

joined the Civil Air Patrol and proudly wore its uniform: Affidavit of Christine Warren, p. 2.

graduating from high school when he was twenty: Affidavit of David R. Price, Ph.D., 26 March 1994, p. 2. Retained by William's appeals counsel, Dr. Price was a clinical psychologist at the time of his affidavit.

132 **struggled with books to bone up:** William's successful struggle to get into the Marine Corps in 1971 (under reduced standards), his service in the Corps, and his time in the Army are noted in Application of William Henry Hance for a 90-Day Stay of Execution and for a Commutation of His Sentence of Death, before the Board of Pardons and Paroles, State of Georgia, March 1994, pp. 23, 25. The Amendment to Petitioner's Pro Se Petition, p. 18n. 4, points out the military's recognition of the usefulness of persons with marginal intelligence and in this regard cites a December 1965 report by the Department of the Army, *Marginal Man and Military Service.*

the 1984 trial testimony: See the testimony of Ronald Nelson, Trial Transcript, 1984, pp. 1131-32.

she remembered years later: For her memories, including the quoted material that I use, see Affidavit of Wanda Hance Johnson, pp. 1-2.

divorced after she had become unfaithful: See p. 12 of Affidavit of Dr. Ralph Allsopp, *Hance v. Kemp,* Civil Action No. 86-V-665 (Superior Court of Butts County, 31 December 1987). Retained by William's appeals attorneys, Dr. Allsopp was a clinical psychologist when he submitted his affidavit.

132 **a woman who became his girlfriend:** For information on her relationship to William, see Affidavit of Linda Nieves, 22 March 1994. The quoted material from her in this paragraph appears on p. 2 of the affidavit.

133 **still had staring spells:** Affidavit of Linda Nieves, p. 2.

"One of my sisters": Affidavit of Linda Nieves, p. 2.

"He told stories": Affidavit of Wanda Hance Johnson, p. 2.

As his sister's affidavit explains: Affidavit of Yvonne Hance Boyd, p. 7. She emphasizes how difficult the rape and death of their mother were for him. See also William's trial testimony: Trial Transcript, 1984, pp. 169-70.

brought out at his 1984 resentencing trial: See the testimony of Ronald Nelson, Trial Transcript, 1984, pp. 1139-40.

134 **ultimately concluded:** See the following letters: Robert W. Wildman, II, Ph.D., Clinical Psychologist II, Forensic Services Division, and Carl L. Smith, M.D., Physician II, Forensic Services Division, Central State Hospital,

Milledgeville, Georgia, to Honorable John H. Land, Judge, Superior Courts, Chattahoochee Judicial Circuit, Columbus, Georgia, 23 May 1978; Wallace Davis, M.S.C.J., Donald P. Grigsby, Ph.D., James B. Craig, M.D., West Central Georgia Regional Hospital, Columbus, Georgia, to Honorable Kenneth B. Followill, Judge of Superior Court, Columbus, Georgia, 29 March 1984; Jerold S. Lower, Ph.D., J.D., Chief Psychologist, Forensic Evaluation Team, Central State Hospital, Milledgeville, Georgia, to Honorable Kenneth B. Followill, 6 April 1984. I read a copy of the 1978 letter that is appended (Exhibit 3) to Deposition of Thomas Flournoy Jr., *Hance v. Kemp,* Civil Action No. 86-V-665 (Superior Court of Butts County, 12 November 1987). (Mr. Flournoy served as court-appointed counsel at William's 1984 resentencing trial.) Copies of the 1984 letters are included in the appendix to Amendment to Petitioner's Pro Se Petition.

134 **"moderate depression and anxiety":** Letter of Wildman and Smith to Land.

"tend not to be particularly able": Letter of Robert W. Wildman to John H. Land, 30 August 1978. I read a copy of the letter that is appended (Exhibit 3) to the Flournoy deposition.

a letter to William's court-appointed counsel: Lewis R. Lieberman, Ph.D., Clinical Psychologist, Columbus, Georgia, to Richard O. Smith, Columbus, Georgia, 19 November 1978. A copy of the letter is in the appendix to Amendment to Petitioner's Pro Se Petition.

The psychologist testified: See Trial Transcript, 1984, pp. 1103-4.

an affidavit submitted in 1987: See Affidavit of Dr. Ralph Allsopp, p. 10.

saw their client as delusional: Affidavit of Barry M. Crown, Ph.D., 26 March 1994, p. 3; Affidavit of David R. Price, pp. 3, 6-7.

"an organic delusional disorder": Affidavit of David R. Price, p. 7.

a "seizure disorder": Affidavit of Barry M. Crown, p. 3, and Affidavit of David R. Price, p. 7.

"organic brain damage": Affidavit of Barry M. Crown, p. 4.

"organic brain dysfunction": Affidavit of David R. Price, p. 3.

134 **saw as important two tests:** Affidavit of Barry M. Crown, pp. 2-3, and Affidavit of David R. Price, p. 3. For the test results, including the state doctors' interpretations, see, for example, the appendix to Amendment to Petitioner's Pro Se Petition.

135 **experts had reported to the court:** For what these experts reported, see the letter of Davis, Grigsby, and Craig to Followill; and the letter of Lower to Followill. The second letter was written after the brain scan and EEG evaluations by physicians working for the state mental-health system.

a significant error, his attorneys contended: Amendment to Petitioner's Pro Se Petition, pp. 30ff.

Neither psychologist who examined William: The information in this sentence is from Transcript of Proceedings, *Hance v. Zant*, Civil Action No. 93-V-172 (Superior Court of Butts County, 28 March 1994), pp. 72-73.

concluded that he was a person with mental retardation: Affidavit of Barry M. Crown, pp. 3-4, and Affidavit of David R. Price, p. 7.

a battery of IQ tests that a mental-health examiner from the state system had administered: Letter of Davis, Grigsby, and Craig to Followill. The scores were as follows: verbal IQ, 79; performance IQ, 75; full-scale IQ, 76.

testing done by the state system prior to William's 1978 trial: Letter of Wildman to Land. The scores were as follows: verbal IQ, 84; performance IQ, 85; full-scale IQ, 84.

a battery of tests given to William in 1987: See Affidavit of Dr. Ralph Allsopp, p. 4. The scores were as follows: verbal IQ, 99; performance IQ, 83; full-scale IQ, 91.

his lead attorney argued: See Transcript of Proceedings, *Hance v. Zant*, p. 72.

136 **seen with William:** See the testimony of Wilma Allen, Trial Transcript, 1984, pp. 928-30. See also the testimony of Johnny King, which seems to corroborate what Ms. Allen said: Trial Transcript, 1984, pp. 931-35.

a car jack that he later helped authorities to locate: See the testimony of John Burroughs, Trial Transcript, 1984, p. 1076.

136 **met both women in a bar:** See, for example, the testimony of Richard Fox, Trial Transcript, 1984, pp. 988, 990.

stocking stranglings of six white women: For more information concerning the stranglings, see, for example, the articles cited in my note under 70: **Deeply despondent.**

a series of extortion letters: The letters were State's Exhibits 1-6 at William's 1984 resentencing trial: See Trial Transcript, 1984, p. 804.

body had been battered: Timothy Martin, "Hance Outcry Stuns Court," *Columbus (Ga.) Enquirer,* 5 June 1979, sec. D, p. 1.

left in a ditch: Timothy Martin, "Hance Confession Recalled in Trial," *Columbus (Ga.) Enquirer,* 1 June 1979, sec. C, p. 12.

Eventually he confessed: For information concerning William's confession that he had murdered Irene Thirkield, I have consulted the relevant testimony of Richard Fox, who interrogated William at Fort Benning in 1978 and to whom William also confessed that he had killed Gail Faison (Trial Transcript, 1984, pp. 977-96). While William confessed to this investigator, he also admitted that he had made up the "Forces of Evil" and had acted alone in the killings. When William testified at his 1984 resentencing trial that he had murdered Gail Faison, he also admitted that he had killed Irene Thirkield (Trial Transcript, 1984, pp. 1190, 1198). For information concerning William's confession that he had murdered Private Hickman, I have consulted the following: *United States v. Hance,* 10 M.J. 622, 623, 626 (ACMR 1980); and Martin, "Hance Confession Recalled in Trial," p. 12.

At his 1979 military trial for the murders of Irene Thirkield and Karen Hickman, William claimed that coercion had been used in the process of his confession. See, for example, Martin, "Hance Confession Recalled in Trial," p. 12.

overturned by a military review court: The reviewing court ruled that the Government did not show probable cause — sufficient evidence — to arrest William. His illegal arrest thus tainted the confessions he gave and other evidence derived from them. For details of the court's opinion, see *Hance,* 10 M.J. 622 (ACMR 1980).

In its opinion, the military reviewing court also pointed out the following:

After trial, the defense counsel petitioned the convening authority to disapprove the Hickman charge and to reduce the Thirkield charge to unpremeditated murder. In support of his petition, he offered statements from several court-martial members. Five of the nine members sitting on the court signed unsworn statements in which they stated that the evidence presented at trial "was insufficient to convince me beyond a reasonable doubt that SP4 Hance killed PVT Karen Hickman." Four of these members also signed unsworn statements in which they stated that the evidence "was insufficient to convince me that SP4 Hance was mentally competent to premeditate murder." (pp. 623-24)

This information, not generally known, is significant: "Under military rules, at least six votes are required to convict a defendant. The vote in the Hance case was not announced" ("Hance Guilty in 'Forces of Evil' Slayings," *Atlanta Constitution*, 8 June 1979, sec. C, p. 1).

136 **Army prosecutors chose not to retry William:** On the reason he was not retried, see Harry Franklin, "Hance Is Put to Death in Electric Chair," *Columbus (Ga.) Ledger-Enquirer*, 1 April 1994, sec. A, p. 12. William's life sentence is noted in *Hance*, 10 M.J. 622, 623 (ACMR 1980).

137 **beginning in 1972 with the death of his mother:** For the date of her death (November 1972), see William's testimony, Trial Transcript, 1984, p. 1163.

ended in divorce in 1977: Affidavit of Wanda Hance Johnson, p. 2.

his confessions to the murders: In this paragraph I draw on descriptions of the killings that William gave to investigators when he confessed to them in 1978. See the testimonies of Richard Fox and Charles Rowe in Trial Transcript, 1984, pp. 977-96, 1015-20. The quotation is from William's confession, read by Richard Fox: Trial Transcript, 1984, p. 991.

At his 1984 resentencing trial, William testified that when he had murdered Gail Faison, his "mind had flipped" and he "had lost all sense of control": Trial Transcript, 1984, p. 1196. He said essentially the same things when he testified that he had murdered Irene Thirkield: Trial Transcript, 1984, p. 1198.

noted by the psychologist: In this paragraph I draw on the Affidavit of Dr. Ralph Allsopp, pp. 5-6, 12-13, as well as the Affidavit of Yvonne Hance Boyd, pp. 2-3.

138 **clearly a black man in the eyes of the writer:** See the letter of 1 March 1978, State's Exhibit 1 at William's 1984 resentencing trial.

138 **turn finally to a rage:** For a classic study of how racism leads its victims to rage, see William H. Grier and Price M. Cobbs, *Black Rage* (New York: Basic Books, 1992).

the sad and brutal legacy of racism: For a discussion of this legacy, see Grier and Cobbs, *Black Rage*.

"During those first few years of integration": Affidavit of Christine Warren, p. 2.

139 **three of whom were white:** I confirmed this in a telephone conversation on 1 June 1999 with Mary Sinclair, paralegal and researcher for the Southern Center for Human Rights, Atlanta.

140 **"The punishment [death] fits the crime":** The words of the Board's chairperson, James T. Morris, are quoted in "State Board Won't Grant Clemency," *Columbus (Ga.) Ledger-Enquirer,* 31 March 1994, sec. B, p. 1.

142 **banished from the state:** See the testimony of Thomas Flournoy Jr., William's 1984 court-appointed counsel: Transcript of Proceedings, *Hance v. Kemp,* Civil Action No. 86-V-665 (Superior Court of Butts County, 22 July 1987), p. 321.

the governor provide him a "furlough": The Affidavit of Lewis R. Lieberman, p. 3, attributes this idea to William. I do not know to whom William originally expressed the idea.

143 **the Georgia Supreme Court had denied William's appeal:** Order Denying Application for Certificate of Probable Cause and Motion for Stay of Execution, *Hance v. Zant,* Civil Action No. 93-V-172 (Supreme Court of Georgia, 31 March 1994).

a lower court judge's key ruling: See Order Dismissing Petition and Denying Stay of Execution, *Hance v. Zant,* Civil Action No. 93-V-172 (Superior Court of Butts County, 28 March 1994). For the claims that William's attorneys raised, see Amendment to Petitioner's Pro Se Petition.

144 **essentially white legal system:** For the composition of the jury, see Death Penalty Information Center, *Chattahoochee Judicial District: The Buckle of the Death Belt* (Washington, D.C.: Death Penalty Information Center, 1991), fig. 6, following p. 3. This document is part of the appendix to Amendment to Peti-

tioner's Pro Se Petition. The judge was Kenneth B. Followill, the D.A. was William Smith, and William's appointed co-counsel was Thomas Flournoy — all white.

144 **The juror's story came out:** The woman's story is set forth in Affidavit of Gayle Lewis Daniels, 21 March 1994; the quoted material is from pp. 1-3 of the affidavit. For important commentary on the racism and other factors that influenced William Hance's fate in the judicial system, see the following articles by Bob Herbert: "In America: Mr. Hance's 'Perfect Punishment,'" *New York Times,* 27 March 1994, sec. 4, p. 17; "In America: Jury Room Injustice," *New York Times,* 30 March 1994, sec. A, p. 15; "In America: Judicial Coin Toss," *New York Times,* 3 April 1994, sec. 4, p. 11.

145 **Another juror, a white woman:** For her corroborating statement and the quoted material in this paragraph, see Affidavit of Patricia LeMay, 25 March 1994, pp. 1-2.

146 **"the District Attorney systematically used":** Amendment to Petitioner's Pro Se Petition, pp. 65-66.

I continued: For the racial composition of the juries in these five cases, see Death Penalty Information Center, *Chattahoochee Judicial District,* fig. 6, following p. 3.

the murdered victims in four of these five other cases: For a summary of this and other information about the Chattahoochee Judicial Circuit — things I had learned by the time of William's execution — see David Baldus, "Materials for Litigating to Lessen the Effects of Racial Discrimination as Denial of Its Continuing Influence Grows" (paper presented at NAACP Legal Defense Fund Capital Punishment Training Conference, Washington, D.C., 27 July 1996), pp. 58-59.

Ms. Faison's brother was opposed: For the statement of Gail Faison's brother, who expressed his view and that of his deceased mother, see Affidavit of Robert Terry Faison, 20 March 1994. Irene Thirkield's brother, another of her relatives, and a close friend of hers also asked that William's life be spared. See Affidavits of Aaron King, 22 March 1994; Gwendolyn Lowe, 22 March 1994; and Shelia Miles, 22 March 1994.

his normal practice as D.A.: Amendment to Petitioner's Pro Se Petition, p.

63, quotes testimony of Mr. Smith concerning his contacting murder victims' families to see if they wanted him to seek the death penalty:

> I talked with, in most cases, the families of the victims. I say most cases, I'm sure that I talked with them in all of them really, except, for instance Hance. There was really no family to talk with in Brenda Gail Faison. She was from Miami, was living up here with a great aunt. . . . I don't think we talked with anyone in that case. But in most cases we talked with the family of the victim.

The testimony is taken from Transcript of Hearing, *State v. Brooks*, Indictment Nos. 38888 and 54606 (Superior Court of Muscogee County, 12 September 1990), pp. 147-48.

146 **had been in the investigation files:** Amendment to Petitioner's Pro Se Petition, pp. 63-64.

147 **"to get the death penalty against a black man":** Amendment to Petitioner's Pro Se Petition, p. 69.

in light of the prosecution's neglect: For information on specific cases, see Death Penalty Information Center, *Chattahoochee Judicial District*, pp. 10-13. Consider also these statistics, which the Center's study (p. 3) includes: the vast majority of death penalty trials (85 percent, from 1973 to 1990) in the circuit were for murder of white victims, even though 65 percent of the jurisdiction's homicides involved black victims.

a few days after an African American: According to Trial Transcript, 1984, William's retrial began on 7 May 1984. Carlton Gary was arrested on 3 May 1984 as a suspect in the stranglings. See Kathy Trimarco, "Grand Jury to Hear Case of Stranglings Suspect," *Columbus (Ga.) Ledger*, 4 May 1984, sec. A, pp. 1, 2. Mr. Gary was later convicted of three of the murders. See Richard Hyatt, "When the City Lost Its Innocence," *Columbus (Ga.) Ledger-Enquirer*, 28 July 1996, sec. A, pp. 1, 6.

Justice Blackmun had explained his vote: *Hance v. Zant*, 511 U.S. 1013 (1994) (Blackmun, J., dissenting from denial of certiorari). The justice ended his dissent this way: "Accordingly, I would grant the application for a stay, grant the petition for writ of certiorari, and vacate the death sentence in this case." Justices Stevens and Ginsberg voted to stay William's execution.

148 **tables "laden" with:** Heather Bird, "2,000 Volts, a Spasm — And Killer's Life

Ended," *Toronto Star*, 24 May 1987, sec. A, p. 14. For more information on such meals before executions in Georgia, see Michael Mears, "Celebrating the Death Penalty and the Cost of Criminal Justice," *Hospitality*, June 1998, pp. 6-7.

148 **Mary Williams had argued:** Here I draw on the arguments set forth in an article by Mary Williams ("The Fear of Death," *Journal of Analytic Psychology* 3 [1958]: 157-65), as discussed by Verena Kast in her book titled *Trauern: Phasen und Chancen des psychischen Prozesses* (Stuttgart: Kreuz Verlag, 1993), pp. 158-59.

we were not targeting the powerful: Robert Moore and Douglas Gillette argue that the sadist has "a hatred of the 'weak,' of the helpless and vulnerable (really the Sadist's own hidden Masochist)." See Moore and Gillette, *King, Warrior, Magician, Lover: Rediscovering the Archetypes of the Mature Masculine* (New York: HarperCollins, 1991), p. 90.

149 **had entered the name of another man:** See Herbert, "In America: Judicial Coin Toss," p. 11.

(As I would read in the paper): See Franklin, "Hance Is Put to Death in Electric Chair," p. 1.

9. ON WANDERING SPIRITS

152 **the kind of affection and bonding that every infant needs:** See especially John Bowlby, *A Secure Base: Parent-Child Attachment and Healthy Human Development* (New York: Basic Books, 1988).

problems such as attaining self-esteem: For these and other consequences of child abuse and neglect, see, for instance, the works that I cite in a note under 125: **the most sensitive writers about child abuse and neglect**.

self-transcendence: See, for example, Rollo May, "Transcending the Immediate Situation," in *The Discovery of Being: Writings in Existential Psychology* (New York: W. W. Norton, 1983), pp. 143-50.

153 **conduits for rage:** The connection between child abuse and murderous rage has been made forcefully by the Bernese psychotherapist J. Konrad Stettbacher, who argues that as a consequence of such abuse, "Murderers are 'made' and turned loose on humanity" (translation mine). See his book entitled *Wenn*

Leiden einen Sinn haben soll: Die heilende Begegnung mit der eigenen Geschichte (Hamburg: Hoffmann and Campe Verlag, 1993), pp. 140-41.

For other explorations of the themes of abuse and rage, see, for example, Leonard Shengold, *Soul Murder: The Effects of Childhood Abuse and Deprivation* (New York: Fawcett Columbine, 1991); Judith Lewis Herman, *Trauma and Recovery* (New York: Basic Books, 1992); and James Gilligan, *Violence: Our Deadly Epidemic and Its Causes* (New York: G. P. Putnam's Sons, 1996).

153 **Schooled in the violence:** In *Trauma and Recovery,* Judith Herman notes the following: "Trauma appears to amplify the common gender stereotypes: men with histories of childhood abuse are more likely to take out their aggressions on others, while women are more likely to be victimized by others or to injure themselves" (p. 113).

154 **"secure base":** See Bowlby, *Secure Base.*

155 **something that Hawthorne:** Nathaniel Hawthorne, *The Scarlet Letter,* vol. 1 of the *Centenary Edition of the Works of Nathaniel Hawthorne,* ed. William Charvat et al. (Columbus: Ohio State University Press, 1962).

tried in full public view as an adult: Georgia's children who are thirteen or older and who are charged with violent crimes are, with few exceptions, tried as adults. See Official Code of Georgia Annotated §15-11-5 (2)(A). Many states have no minimum age for the prosecution of children as adults for some crimes: see, for example, Arlene Levinson, "States Steadily Lower Age When Child Becomes Adult in Eyes of Law," *Dothan (Ala.) Eagle,* 27 August 1998, sec. A, p. 7.

may well be the excessive shame: For an important study of the link between shame and violence, see Gilligan, *Violence.*

156 **Ralph Ellison's metaphor:** Ralph Ellison, *Invisible Man* (New York: Vintage Books, 1972).

"You often doubt": Ellison, *Invisible Man,* pp. 3-4.

Derrick Bell contended: Derrick Bell, *Faces at the Bottom of the Well: The Permanence of Racism* (New York: Basic Books, 1992).

(which is 27 percent black): This is according to the 1990 census (*1998 Infor-*

mation Please Almanac, ed. Borgna Brunner [Boston: Information Please LLC, 1997], p. 759).

156   **the all-white juries:**   In a telephone conversation in November 1999, I confirmed the information in this sentence with Mary Sinclair, paralegal and researcher for the Southern Center for Human Rights in Atlanta.

157   **sometimes made important criticisms:**   See, for example, *Livingston v. State,* 264 Ga. 402, 413-20; 444 S.E. 2d 748, 757-61 (1994) (Benham, J., dissenting); *Gibson v. Turpin,* 270 Ga. 855, 873; 513 S.E. 2d 186,199 (1999) (Sears, J., dissenting).

remain overwhelmingly white: See my note under xiii: **both prosecutor and judge are typically white**.

recently elected black attorney general: For the view on capital punishment of Georgia's first black attorney general, Thurbert Baker, who was appointed and later elected to the post, see, for example, Kathey Alexander, "Miller Names Democrat Thurbert Baker to Replace Bowers as Attorney General," *Atlanta Journal,* 2 May 1997, sec. E, p. 3. In another article, Ms. Alexander points out the following about Mr. Baker as state legislator: "As [Gov. Zell] Miller's liaison, he sponsored legislation to curb death penalty appeals and implement the state's 'two strikes' law, which imprisons criminals for life without parole after their second conviction for violent crimes" ("Baker Now Must Earn His Own Place in the Sun," *Atlanta Journal-Constitution,* 3 May 1997, sec. D, p. 1). In his successful election campaign for the office of attorney general, Mr. Baker emphasized his tough stance on crime; one campaign ad cited his (in the words of a press report) "role in a June execution of a convicted double murderer, saying he ordered it." See Jonathan Ringel, "Candidates Duel with Shots at Crime Votes, Legal Errors," *Fulton County (Ga.) Daily Report,* 28 October 1998, p. 1.

the lynch mob's noose: I wonder how many of Stewart E. Tolnay and E. M. Beck's observations on lynching might be applied to our current practice of capital punishment. In *A Festival of Violence: An Analysis of Southern Lynchings, 1882-1932* (Urbana: University of Illinois Press, 1995), Tolnay and Beck argue the following:

> In addition to the punishment of specific criminal offenders, lynching in the American South had three entwined functions: first, to maintain social control over the black population through terrorism; second, to sup-

press or eliminate black competitors for economic, political, or social rewards; and third, to stabilize the white class structure and preserve the privileged status of the white aristocracy. (pp. 18-19)

157 **without forgiveness:** For an eloquent contemporary treatment of the necessary role of forgiveness in our lives, see Desmond Mpilo Tutu, *No Future without Forgiveness* (New York: Doubleday, 1999).

158 *The Seventh Seal:* See the screenplay (trans. Lars Malstrom and David Kushner) in *Literature: The Human Experience,* ed. Richard Abcarian and Marvin Klotz, 2d ed. (New York: St. Martin's Press, 1978), pp. 1038-79.

"We know that every moment": The quotation is from Wiesel's Nobel Peace Prize address given in Oslo, Norway, on 10 December 1986. For the text of the address, see, for example, "Wiesel's Speech at Nobel Ceremony," *New York Times,* 11 December 1986, sec. A, p. 12.

159 **"his former stepmother bashing him over the head":** Clive Stafford Smith, "Witness to Execution: 'I Watched My Friend Die,'" *Atlanta Journal-Constitution,* 16 April 1995, sec. B, p. 1.

"glassy eyed" and talking rapidly: Ms. Sawyer's remarks (part of statements she gave to police) that I cite here are included in Emergency Petition for Writ of Habeas Corpus and Consolidated Motion for Stay of Execution, *Ingram v. Thomas,* Civil Action No. 95-V-160 (Superior Court of Butts County), pp. 29-30.

According to his appeals attorneys: See Emergency Petition cited above, pp. 30-31, for this information concerning Nicky's state of mind.

According to Ms. Sawyer: For her detailed account of the crimes, I have consulted Statement of Mary Eunice Sawyer, 3 June 1983, and Statement of Mary Eunice Sawyer, 4 June 1983. Both statements, which Ms. Sawyer gave to police, are in the appendix of the Emergency Petition cited above.

Nicky was so high: The information on Nicky's lack of memory and his drug and alcohol use is from Emergency Petition cited above, pp. 27, 34.

his appeals attorneys had discovered: My information in this paragraph is based on the Emergency Petition cited above, pp. 4-37, and appended affidavits (of Dennis C. O'Brien, 3 April 1985, and Allen R. Hirons, 2 April 1995) from Nicky's trial attorneys. The petition argues, among other things, that the

State failed to disclose the evidence concerning the Thorazine treatment. For the State's position that the petition's claims should have been raised earlier, see Motion to Dismiss Petition as Successive and Response in Opposition to Petitioner's Motion for Stay of Execution, *Ingram v. Thomas,* Civil Action No. 95-V-160 (Superior Court of Butts County).

161 **to balk at allowing the courts to be informed:** Smith, "Witness to Execution," p. 1.

he wrote to Ms. Sawyer: Smith, "Witness to Execution," p. 2.

162 **quoted a "prison spokesman":** See Don Plummer and Rhonda Cook, "Ingram Dies in Georgia Electric Chair," *Atlanta Journal-Constitution,* 8 April 1995, sec. A, p. 1.

"angry young man": Smith, "Witness to Execution," p. 1.

163 **Our task in this life:** See Augustine's sermon XXXVIII from his "Sermons on Selected Lessons of the New Testament," in *A Select Library of the Nicene and Post-Nicene Fathers of the Christian Church,* ed. Philip Schaff (Buffalo: Christian Literature Company, 1888), 6: 380.

the gap between rich and poor: This information on the disparity of wealth (based on estimates for the year 1997) is from Lawrence Mishel, Jared Bernstein, and John Schmitt, *The State of Working America, 1998-1999* (Ithaca, N.Y.: Cornell University Press, 1999), p. 262.

millions of children are growing up poor: The percentages in this sentence are from the year 1997, in which over 14 million children were living in poverty in the United States. See *The State of America's Children Yearbook, 1999,* ed. Bruce Kozarsky (Washington, D.C.: Children's Defense Fund, 1999), p. 5.

the kind of environment in which juvenile crime and violence flourish: The *KIDS COUNT Data Book: State Profiles of Child Well-Being, 1996* (Baltimore: Annie E. Casey Foundation, 1996) puts the link between poverty and juvenile crime this way:

> Although many factors put children at risk, nothing predicts bad outcomes for a kid more powerfully than growing up poor. Study after disheartening study confirm the links between living in poverty and suffering a host of lousy developmental, educational, and adult outcomes.

Poor children . . . face far greater odds of being either a victim or a perpetrator of crime. (p. 5)

A recent annual report of the Children's Defense Fund — *The State of America's Children Yearbook, 1996,* ed. Belva Finley (Washington, D.C.: Children's Defense Fund, 1996) — summarizes the connection between poverty and juvenile violence: "Poverty also puts children at particular risk for violent behavior, by reducing the quality of their community supports (housing, neighborhoods, and schools), limiting their opportunities for education and employment, and dimming their sense of hope about the future" (p. 58).

163 **the phrase "children's prison":** See, for example, Ken Edelstein, "Youth Prison Back on Track," *Columbus (Ga.) Ledger-Enquirer,* 30 January 1996, sec. A, pp. 1, 6. The phrase "children's prison" occurs four times in this article.

more and more of our money on prisons: For one indication of the problem in Georgia, consider these facts from early 1998: "Since 1979, Georgia's prison population has grown by 200 per cent. During the same period, the budget for the Corrections Department has grown sixfold." See Rhonda Cook, "Time *and* Punishment," *Atlanta Constitution,* 16 January 1998, sec. D, p. 6. (The budget increases cited in this note are not, to the best of my knowledge, based on calculations in constant dollars. Even allowing for inflation, such budget growth is deeply disturbing. For example, during the period from 1979 to 1998, prices increased 125 percent due to inflation. To calculate inflation for this and other periods, see Federal Reserve Bank of Minneapolis, woodrow .mpls.frb.fed.us/economy/calc/cpihome.html.)

More recently, the same writer could make the following report:

State spending for prisons has increased almost one-third in five years, from more than $682.2 million in 1996 to the $893 million the Department of Corrections wants the governor to include in the 2001 budget request he will present to the legislature in January. . . .

Most of the overall budget increase [for the fiscal year] is needed to open additional prisons and to lease another 1,500 beds at three private prisons operated in Georgia.

See Rhonda Cook, "Jail Ailments Help Drive up State's Costs," *Atlanta Constitution,* 3 September 1999, sec. E, p. 1. (In its 2000 session, the Georgia General Assembly passed legislation, which the governor signed into law, that provides for a budget of $893 million for the state's Department of Corrections for the fiscal year 2001. See the final version of House Bill 1160.)

Nationwide, the problem of prison growth is also distressing. For example, consider these facts (Sentencing Project, www.sentencingproject.org/brief/ 1035.htm): "The number of inmates in state and federal prisons has increased more than five-fold from less than 200,000 in 1970 to 1,232,900 by 1998. An additional 592,000 are held in local jails." And consider this information reported by ABC News (more.abcnews.go.com/sections/us/DailyNews/prison-education980707.html): From 1977 to 1995, "spending on state prison systems increased by an average of 823 percent, according to census bureau data, while budgets for higher education increased by 374 percent."

163 **the second highest rate (behind Russia) reported:** See the Sentencing Project's Web site, cited in the previous note.

164 **"out once more beneath the Stars":** Dante Alighieri, *The Inferno*, trans. John Ciardi (New York: New American Library, 1964), p. 287.

10. POSTSCRIPT: A LETTER TO CHRIS BURGER

166 **He conducted no thorough investigation:** I base this judgment on my reading of the following: Brief for Petitioner on Writ of Certiorari to the United States Court of Appeals for the Eleventh Circuit, *Burger v. Kemp*, No. 86-5357 (Supreme Court of the United States, October Term, 1986), pp. 24-35; the State's Brief for the Respondent, pp. 13-14, 24-34; Reply Brief for Petitioner, pp. 7-16; and *Burger v. Kemp*, 483 U.S. 776 (1987). In this regard, I find especially compelling the opinions of U.S. Supreme Court Justices Blackmun (pp. 811-17) and Powell (pp. 817-24), dissenting from denial of certiorari in *Burger v. Kemp* (1987).

the truth about your past finally came out: See, for instance, Reply Brief for Petitioner, p. 12.

I pieced together: I have checked the following document, prepared by Chris's appeals attorneys, for the accuracy of the details that I cite concerning his life and that of his mother: Application of Christopher Burger for a 90-Day Stay of Execution and for Commutation of His Sentence of Death, before the Board of Pardons and Paroles, State of Georgia, December, 1990. With exemplary honesty, Chris's mother, Mrs. Betty Foster, has also spoken to me about the forces that shaped her and her son.

Many of the details of both persons' lives were reported in the news media, especially when Chris's case was presented to Georgia's Board of Pardons and Paroles. See, for example, the following: "To Spare an Unfortunate Life," *At-*

lanta Constitution, 17 December 1990, sec. A, p. 10; Tom Teepen, "Horrid Histories, Horrid Results," *Atlanta Journal-Constitution,* 23 December 1990, sec. D, p. 11; R. Robin McDonald, "Age, Abuse Cited in Death Appeal," *Atlanta Journal-Constitution,* 4 December 1993, sec. B, pp. 1, 6.

170 **"may shatter your dreams":** The quoted material in this sentence is from Kahlil Gibran, *The Prophet* (New York: Alfred A. Knopf, 1969), pp. 11, 12.

the brief television interview: The interview, with reporter Mark Winne, was broadcast as part of the local evening news on station WSB in Atlanta, 22 November 1993.

175 **it takes doubt into itself:** My understanding of doubt in the life of faith has been deepened by my reading of Paul Tillich, *Dynamics of Faith* (New York: Harper & Row, 1957).

176 **"I'd like to say I'm sorry":** Bill Montgomery, "Infamous Last Words," *Atlanta Journal-Constitution,* 2 April 1995, sec. D, p. 4.